COLOMBIA: THE POLITICS OF REFORMING THE STATE

Victor Bulmer-Thomas (*editor*)
THE NEW ECONOMIC MODEL IN LATIN AMERICA AND ITS
IMPACT ON INCOME DISTRIBUTION AND POVERTY

Victor Bulmer-Thomas, Nikki Craske and Mónica Serrano (*editors*)
MEXICO AND THE NORTH AMERICAN FREE TRADE
AGREEMENT: WHO WILL BENEFIT?

Elizabeth Joyce and Carlos Malamud (*editors*)
LATIN AMERICA AND THE MULTINATIONAL DRUG TRADE

Walter Little and Eduardo Posada-Carbó (*editors*)
POLITICAL CORRUPTION IN EUROPE AND LATIN AMERICA

Eduardo Posada-Carbó (*editor*)
COLOMBIA: THE POLITICS OF REFORMING THE STATE
ELECTIONS BEFORE DEMOCRACY: THE HISTORY OF
ELECTIONS IN EUROPE AND LATIN AMERICA

Rachel Sieder (*editor*)
CENTRAL AMERICA: FRAGILE TRANSITION

John Weeks (*editor*)
STRUCTURAL ADJUSTMENT AND THE AGRICULTURAL
SECTOR IN LATIN AMERICA AND THE CARIBBEAN

Colombia

The Politics of Reforming the State

Edited by

Eduardo Posada-Carbó
Senior Lecturer in Latin American History
Institute of Latin American Studies
University of London

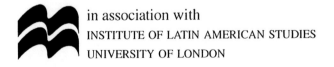

in association with
INSTITUTE OF LATIN AMERICAN STUDIES
UNIVERSITY OF LONDON

First published in Great Britain 1998 by
MACMILLAN PRESS LTD
Houndmills, Basingstoke, Hampshire RG21 6XS and London
Companies and representatives throughout the world

A catalogue record for this book is available from the British Library.

ISBN 0–333–71553–5

 First published in the United States of America 1998 by
ST. MARTIN'S PRESS, INC.,
Scholarly and Reference Division,
175 Fifth Avenue, New York, N.Y. 10010

ISBN 0–312–17618–X

Library of Congress Cataloging-in-Publication Data
Colombia : the politics of reforming the state / edited by Eduardo
Posada-Carbó.
p.   cm. — (Institute of Latin American Studies series)
Includes bibliographical references and index.
ISBN 0–312–17618–X
1. Colombia—Politics and government—1974–   I. Posada Carbó,
Eduardo.   II. Series.
JL2831.C664 1997
320.9861'09'045—dc21   97–19441
                                                                            CIP

This book is printed on paper suitable for recycling and made from fully managed and
sustained forest sources.

10   9   8   7   6   5   4   3   2   1
07   06   05   04   03   02   01   00   99   98

Printed and bound in Great Britain by
Antony Rowe Ltd, Chippenham, Wiltshire

CONTENTS

ACKNOWLEDGEMENTS

This book is the first of a series of publications resulting from the Colombia Programme that the Institute of Latin American Studies launched in 1995. The chapters in this volume were first discussed during the conference 'The Colombian Process of Reform: A New Role for the State?', which took place in London on 24–25 April 1995.

I would like to thank the following institutions for the support given to this event: the Banco de la República, the Baring Foundation, the British Council, British Petroleum, Canning House, the Colombian Embassy in London, and the Foreign and Commonwealth Office. Thanks to the support of the Isobel Thornley Bequest Fund we were able to translate one of the chapters of the book.

Finally, I would also like to acknowledge the editorial support given by Victor Bulmer-Thomas, Tony Bell, and Penny and Peter Simmons in the preparation of the final text.

Eduardo Posada-Carbó
ILAS, London.

LIST OF CONTRIBUTORS

Gustavo Bell Lemus was the first popularly elected Governor of the Department of Atlántico (1990–1993). He is the author of *Cartagena de Indias: de la Colonia a la República* (1991). He is currently completing his DPhil at St Antony's College, Oxford.

Belisario Betancur was President of the Republic of Colombia between 1982 and 1986. Before being elected President he had a long and distinguished public career. He is the author of many books and essays. He is currently the Director of Fundación Santillana para la América Latina.

Manuel José Cepeda was adviser to President César Gaviria on constitutional affairs. He was Ambassador to Switzerland and the United Kingdom, and to Unesco in Paris; he is currently the Dean of the Law Faculty at the Universidad de los Andes. He has published extensively on Colombian constitutional law, including *Los derechos fundamentales de la Constitución de 1991* (1992), and *Introducción a la Constitución de 1991, hacia un nuevo constitucionalismo* (1993).

Jesús Duarte completed his DPhil at St Antony's College, Oxford with a thesis on education and clientelism in Colombia. He is the author of various essays on Colombian education, including a chapter in M. Deas and C. Ossa (eds.), *El gobierno Barco. Política, economía y desarrollo social, 1986–1990* (1994). He is currently an officer at the Departamento Nacional de Planeación.

Alan Gilbert is Professor of Geography at University College London. He has published extensively on Latin American urban problems, including *The Latin American City* (1994), *In Search of a Home* (1993) and, with P. M. Ward, *Housing, the State and the Poor: Policy in Three Latin American Cities* (1985).

Rudolf Hommes was Minister of Finance during the whole period of César Gaviria's administration. As a co-founder of the journal *Estrategia,* he led a group of economists who became instrumental in the process of reform in Colombia. After the ministry he joined the Inter-American Development Bank. He is currently the Rector of the Universidad de los Andes in Bogotá. He is the author of various essays on the Colombian economy.

Gary Hoskin is Professor of Political Science at the State University of New York (SUNY) in Buffalo, USA. He has published extensively on Colombian party politics, including essays in M. Deas and C. Ossa (eds.), *El gobierno Barco* (1994) and F. Leal Buitrago and L. Zamosc (eds.), *Al filo del caos* (1995). He is the co-editor of *El Congreso colombiano* (1974).

Armando Montenegro was Director of the Departamento Nacional de Planeación during the whole period of César Gaviria's administration. He had previously advised the government on coffee affairs and on the monetary board. He is currently President of the Asociación Nacional de Instituciones Financieras, ANIF. He is the author of various essays on a wide range of Colombian subjects, and the co-editor of *Cusiana. Un reto de política económica* (1994).

Marco Palacios is Professor of History at the Colegio de México. He was Rector of the Universidad Nacional and Director of the Instituto Colombiano para la Educación Superior (ICFES). He has published extensively on Colombian history and politics, including *El Café en Colombia* (1978) and *Entre la legitimidad y la violencia: Colombia, 1875–1992* (1995).

Eduardo Posada-Carbó is Lecturer in History at the Institute of Latin American Studies, London University. He is the author of *The Colombian Caribbean: A Regional History, 1870–1950* (1996) and editor of *Elections Before Democracy. The History of Elections in Europe and Latin America* (1996). With Walter Little he is co-editor of *Political Corruption in Europe and Latin America* (1996).

Jorge Ramírez Ocampo was Minister of Development during the administration of Alfonso López Michelsen. He is currently President of the Asociación Nacional de Exportadores, Analdex. He is the editor of *Una aproximación al futuro: Colombia, siglo XXI* (1991).

Alvaro Tirado Mejía is Professor at the Instituto de Estudios Internacionales in the Universidad Nacional, Bogotá. He has been Ambassador to Switzerland and Presidential Peace Adviser. He is currently the President of the Commission for Human Rights at the Organisation of American States. His many books on Colombian history and politics include, *Aspectos políticos del primer gobierno de Alfonso López Pumarejo, 1934–38* (1981) and *Hacia una concepción global de los derechos humanos* (1990). He is the general editor of *Nueva Historia de Colombia* (1989), 8 vols.

LIST OF FIGURES

LIST OF TABLES

PROLOGUE

COLOMBIA: FROM THE ACTUAL TO THE POSSIBLE

Belisario Betancur

One afternoon in September 1982, the telephone rang in the office of the Colombian president, at the Nariño Palace in the venerable Candelaria neighbourhood of Bogotá. A New York banker informed the president that his country's loan application for a new energy project had been turned down by the international banking community. 'But Colombia is up to date in servicing its foreign debt, honours its word, meets its payments and is not even going to request any restructuring', was the president's answer. 'That is so', replied the banker. 'Colombia is on time and a responsible debtor, but it is in a bad neighbourhood.' A month earlier, Mexico had suspended payments on outstanding debts; an action soon to be followed by Argentina, Brazil, and Venezuela. In Paris, a United States banker suggested that Colombia abandon the 'Latin Quarter' and move to the Champs Elysées, because it was being affected by the neighbourhood crisis. One does not need to be astute to deduce that the intention was to praise the former while denigrating the others. What was then forgotten, however, was that Colombia cannot be understood outside the Latin American context, and that Latin America cannot be understood without Colombia. The Colombian president also perceived that isolated efforts were not enough. To a large extent, we depend on the good or bad fortune of our neighbours, and even on that of other far more distant nations. What happened in Mexico in December 1994 and thereafter is a case in point.

So, armed with the stoicism acquired through long years of reflection and of living immersed in the inclement culture of despair, I shall attempt a journey to the present-day heart of Colombia, the country that inspired Bolívar's ideal of integration when he called the Amphictyonic Congress of Panama in 1826. This is a good point of departure for an in-depth look at what is happening in Latin America and the Caribbean – and, of course, in Colombia, the subject of this book. Occasionally the reader will notice that this prologue takes on a personal tone, brought on by memories and experiences, often heterodoxical, following the good manners of traditional wisdom: they are but provocations aimed at stimulating debate.

At the dawn of the twenty-first century, Latin America presents the profile of an intermediate continent, in which one sees the contrasts that characterise the world's poorest areas. There, the transition to modernity comes hand in hand with processes of rapid urbanisation, accentuating the bipolar features of large cities and middle-sized agglomerations. Incapable of overcoming the rural-urban conflict, the Iberian American city is becoming a stage on which heroic gestures for survival are mixed confusedly with the full range of sumptuous expenditure, where the establishment accumulates against itself the accounts that anarchy has prescribed, almost invariably with solutions such as chaos or mounds of impossible theories. All of this creates the syndrome of marginality, charged with despair and ungovernability. There boils the agar of subversion with its own dynamism, far beyond the catalysing ideologies of other times.

Never before in Latin American have there been so many sensitive and talented young people. Yet, there has also never been such a tremendous degree of confusion, due to the weak social consciousness of its traditional leaders. The capacity to discern and react is expressed in the voluntary trend to re-establish popularly elected democratic regimes, to development based on a market economy, and to the participation of a civil society that aspires to governing the government. However, the institutional reforms carried out throughout the region during the 1980s and the beginning of the 1990s were not accompanied by real changes in state structures – at most the reforms were theoretical. The state is somewhere in the middle of the road towards modernisation, obstructing it and slowing it down are clientelistic subterfuges or formulas transplanted wholesale, which only increase chaos and encourage destabilisation. Thus, we continue without an efficient state.

Furthermore, both *providencialismo* and *caudillismo* – a constant feature in the history of Latin America – continue to serve as a basis for social disorganisation. When the transition from colony to independence took place, the syndrome of *providencialismo* was also transplanted. It still lives with us in not a few of the expressions of civil and political life, under the name of *paternalismo*, according to the Colombian sociologist, Alfonso Esguerra Fajardo.[1]

For that very reason, there are common denominators of positive and negative 'signs of identity'. They do not make us better or worse, but show that, in unity and disagreement, we have sketched the blueprint for integration. This will give our voice tone and volume before the emergent globalised society, which formulates challenges and demands answers leading to a path full of uncertainties.

In this context, Colombia is a singular case which, to some extent, encapsulates the possibilities and limitations of the region. On identifying them, the social scientist, the plain analyst, or the communicator could well deduce the grand outline of a Latin America aware that integration, inserted in the preamble of the 1991 Colombian Constitution, is not just one of the paths but the only possible one.

And, for more than three decades, we have suffered guerrillas with no known agenda or direction, who wreak havoc, most especially in the international political arena, where they paint the picture of a civil war that truly does not exist. The situation is such that Colombians, with black humour, say that our guerrillas are already a part of the establishment they are trying to fight.

Now, when fashion forces us to refer daily to post-modernism, it should be noted that Colombia is a small world where one still finds both pre-modern and modern societies, as well as a post-modern one. It reflects the symptoms of what is in crisis and of what is being renewed – a trajectory of restlessness signalled by a search for new assurances.

Those who look in at Colombia from the outside world, where news and information are tainted by perverse sensationalism, will conclude that we are defined by drug trafficking, kidnapping, terrorism and guerrillas, coffee, bananas, human rights violations, patriotic flags, oil, the *gordas* of Botero's painting, and soccer, with the weight of the final calamity, winning what we should lose and losing what should have been ours. We exhibit a sort of predestination symbolised by 'the bread that gets burned at the oven door', in the words of César Vallejo. And so, more often than not, Colombia is the almost-made-it, the night before the project. And, later, frustration.

Arcadios and Aurelianos

Modern times have not been easy for Colombia. As we entered the twentieth century, we were caught off guard by the emotional bulldozing caused by the loss of Panama and the consolation prize of compensation from the United States. In addition, with a vigour then barely imaginable, the scientific, technical revolution and the dynamic industrial revolution also took us by surprise, disrupting the bucolic peace of our agrarian society, full of mythologies and inequalities and marked by the beliefs of a Western Christian civilisation, resisting the overwhelming winds of Enlightenment. Once immersed by the Enlightenment, we became rationalists towards the outside world and kept our beliefs and traditions in the intimacy of the family. We thus developed a society divided between feeling and thinking, between day-dreams and reality, between wanting and acting, between the rhetoric of purpose and concrete realisations. In sum, we were divided, split between what we desired and what we did. We were beings that travelled on the double rail of aspiration and disillusion; in our disillusion, as Borges regretfully warned, we left the delirium of our efforts and the nostalgia of feeling that we need not arrive. We did not synchronise thought and pragmatism in terms consistent with the new era. But we did advance. A thinker of the first quarter-century, Marco Fidel Suárez, would say that the destiny of humanity is to progress, suffering. Ahead of time, he placed our events within the framework of the 'global village'.

Fragmented beings petrify a fragmented society. These circumstances lead towards the establishment of boundaries of violence, described in their time by two lucid Colombian minds: Rafael Maya, in the 1930s, stated that in each of us there is something of the knight and something of the squire, recreating an old truth in his interpretation of Cervantes. Quijote and Sancho made absurd wars, open or masked, while they governed the ungovernable. In the 1960s, Gabriel García Márquez substituted this image. He observed how a debate rages in each of us between an Arcadio, a dreamer, imaginative and creative, and an Aureliano, exuberant, violent, immovable and resourceful, alternately fighting to destroy himself and to survive.

What has happened is that we have arrived at the breaking point, at the nodal point where paths split; where we still cannot clearly perceive on which road firmly to place our feet. The sojourner vacillates between theories and concrete pressures from the most powerful corners.

The signs of confusion become clearer with the spectacle of a nation in ferment: studying, making proposals of all sorts, working on a new society that bursts through all the tissues of reality, even though negative signs continue to bewilder us, although not enough to make us forget the warning of an ancient Egyptian sun dial, 'it is later than we think', a caution against our inconsistencies.

Let us recall one of them. There were great pressures for reform barely fifteen years after the ratification of the Constitution of 1886. Generally speaking, constitutions of the past were an expression of social immobility which sought to represent the slow accumulation of several cyclical crises. They were a formal treaty for settling disputes.

But once the basic charter was achieved, reality started to separate it from its text, because immediacy invariably placed its mark on us. Two military men made the synchrony. First, General and Doctor Rafael Uribe Uribe, whose difficult virtue of an intuitive intelligence enabled him to observe, between 1904 and 1907, that the key to the future lay in decentralisation and tolerance. Then, General Rafael Reyes, also in the first decade of the 1900s, established the basis of modernity with elemental measures such as the law guaranteeing representation of the minorities and the prevalence of the Constitution – although they were systematically ignored. The modern age would finally come into its own in the mid-1930s, during the first administration of Alfonso López Pumarejo.

The departments of the Atlantic Coast and Western Colombia, with governors Alberto Jaramillo Sánchez, a Liberal, and Fernando Gómez Martínez, a Conservative, picked up on the decentralising wave in the 1940s. I saw them and heard them in the Plaza de Berrío in Medellín, haranguing the *Paisas* of Antioquia, from the Gulf of Urabá to the cordillera of Tolima and northern Valle, to reclaim a justice from the central powers that, even today, has yet to arrive in its entirety.

For 80 years this idea struggled to make itself heard, until 1986, when Congress approved the popular election of city mayors. The leader of that movement was the then Minister of Government, Jaime Castro, later mayor of Santafé de Bogotá. The era of Arcadio made its entry into history and its development would shake the very foundations of the country. It would put the creative force of citizen participation in the front line, and it would free the voices of the ethnic minorities drowned out by pretexts, sometimes judicial, but almost always political. A new, demanding citizenry would emerge. The purpose of numerous institutions would be questioned, institutions which on being measured would be found lacking. This is what happened with not only political parties and labour unions but also the Catholic Church, the police, and even the guerrillas, as well as the basic institutions of the state, such as the courts, congress, even the very institution of the presidency. Everything was on trial and Colombia began to prepare itself for the magnificent though arduous task of making the nation change its course.

The real Colombia, in a historical vindicative move, began to demand the settlement of debts from the formal, legal country. The nation was sceptical and disillusioned about the formal country – that is, labour unions, education, the Catholic Church, obsolete industrialists, political parties. The political parties, born at the nation's inception, set up their tents in the civil wars, that is, amid inveterate and arbitrary loyalties. Federalism and centralism, free trade and protectionism, Catholicism and liberalism were the principles that divided their loyalties. But in 1854, Conservative centralist Mariano Ospina Rodríguez wrote a federal constitution. In 1886, Rafael Núñez and Miguel Antonio Caro led federalists and centralists in writing a constitution which stood for political centralisation but administrative decentralisation. And little by little, the conviction started to take shape that it was no better or worse to be Catholic because of Liberal or Conservative affiliation, since all parties consecrated the republic to the Sacred Heart of Jesus, by law; and, also, by law, they consecrated the country to the Virgin of Chiquinquirá. The Virgin's mantle was always blue in colour, symbolising the Conservatives, while the Sacred Heart of Jesus was always red, the colour that identified the Liberals. Historic frontiers disappeared without drama or tears; however, the door was cautiously but firmly closed against any new political formations, as the nonsense of parity in the National Front took shape. It was an escape mechanism to free the country from the military government of Rojas Pinilla, which only made it to the halfway mark in overcoming the ruling political parties. But the National Front distributed the booty of public power in an egalitarian manner between the Liberals and the Conservatives, as though there were no other Colombians.

In the meantime, labour unions got bogged down in fundamentalism; businessmen were thrilled with their benefits; in the Church, reformers were tossed out into the darkness; and, in general, a Manichean society exorcised those who had vision. Red or blue – beyond those colours, there was no salvation.

All of this rarefied the air of democracy and blocked the respiratory channels of civil society. For that very reason, two Liberal presidents – an engineer, Virgilio Barco, and an economist, César Gaviria – needed courage and *ignorantia iuris*, as well as the judicial cosmic vision of the Conservative magistrate, Hernando Gómez Otálora, for the Supreme Court to open the door towards an institutional change that would place the country in the third millennium. It was the Constitution of 1991, no longer rigid and immobile like other constitutions, but rather the fulfilment of some anxieties and the starting point of new hopes. I have to be careful here, because the new charter was the product of concessions made by dissimilar forces that bowed before the procedural at the cost of principles. We shall have to wait and see whether reality confirms or disproves of what was done in haste.

At the same time, the air of reform had been rarefied in that petrified society. The lack of social infrastructure – illiteracy, malnutrition, unemployment, dependency – affected society, protecting quietism with no way to satisfy society's ardent desires. These were the objective and impersonal agents of subversion, which would discover the voice of the personal and subjective agents – the guerrilla – for their expression. When this situation was denounced in the continent during the 1960s and 1970s, the representatives of the Colombian traditional establishment fired their cannons of disqualifications against the denouncers and even came to signal them out as 'desk guerrillas'. In Brazil, sociologist Fernando Henrique Cardoso was excommunicated. On reaching power in 1994, Cardoso stated that we had to free ourselves from old ideological dilemmas.[2]

The cohesion of the traditional political parties, based on loyalties from the pastoral country that Colombia had once been, exploded when rural migrants poured into the cities. And when modern options and methods of communication replaced old time loyalties with new adhesions, the rupture was complete. The disintegration of the political parties came about without waiting for an invitation. Traditional arrogance, despite the warning bells of the 1970 presidential election which juxtaposed the candidacies of Misael Pastrana, General Rojas Pinilla, Evaristo Sourdis and Belisario Betancur, refused to accept that its back was broken. But independent sectors and even migratory votes came in droves and exalted the options based on new majorities. The 1982 presidential election of the author of these lines was the result of a coalition, disparaging the old arrogance yet again. But the same arrogance continued to deny the sociological fact of the disintegration of the old order and the coming of newly established political parties.

In a short space of time, civic movements with diverse components appeared. Like card games in the *fondas campesinas* of rural Antioquia, the moment had come 'to shuffle and deal again'. Today, the traditional political parties do not know what they have, nor what they can count on beyond their own machineries. And this has brought them some very disagreeable surprises, like the one that rocked Bogotá in the 1994 local elections. An academic, totally outside the establishment, was elected mayor of this most Liberal capital city of Colombia, by an overwhelming majority.

Allow me to digress autobiographically a moment here: I have always referred to myself as a member of the extreme left of the right, that is, the extreme centre. Right and left continue to exist in Colombian politics, like attitudes. But they have not settled especially in either party, living a diluted existence in all of them. In a recent seminar in

Bogotá, Malcolm Deas recalled that his friend James Hoge dreamed of a viable centre-left party for England. For Colombia, it would be the extreme centre.

We find ourselves, then, at the moment of disintegration, on the eve of a reintegration in which we can, and must, wager everything. Anyone who knows how to read history will understand that these are the times in which conflict opens all doors, where nuances abound in the hidden faces of controversy. It is necessary to nurture the wisdom that just prior to their demise, things blind the unaware with their final splendour, that just before being extinguished, they shine with excessive brilliance.

The third millennium, the moment to choose a new path, must redefine the relationship between citizen, community and state. The state can no longer be the determining centre which absorbs everything, but must accept the idea of its new destiny that makes it into an instrument for creating a more humane society. It must be a state that accepts the reality that its power comes from being the animator of common good rather than the possessor of the goods for its bureaucratic and corrupt excesses, because those goods should be in the hands of the citizens and the community. It must be a state in the process of learning how to be a state, in the full judicial and social sense of the concept. It must be a state that begins to lead a process of recovering and enunciating new values, based upon which it is capable of responding efficiently to the challenge of establishing social priorities that facilitate community and of making sustainable development possible.

This is a tough job. The Aurelianos of yesterday still try, with an obsession converted into a hope for their survival, to muddy, delay, and make themselves believe that the inexorable day of change has not arrived yet. There converge paramilitary and guerrilla groups, terrorists and drug traffickers as well as all those who reap benefits from the conflict, contributing towards increasing the cost of the transformation.

On the other hand, the new emerging collective consciousness demands action against rhetoric and finds that access to change is too slow – a change that is still not even visible in any statistics which could provide a real guarantee. And still resources are misappropriated from directly benefiting the community because of the clientelistic practices of bureaucracy; 2.4 per cent of the GNP destined to healthcare ends up that way. Deficiencies grow in education, both in quality and coverage. A consolidated 52 per cent of the population lives in poverty and unemployment remains firmly in the two digit range, though it is difficult to evaluate this with any precision. Nearly 28,000 homicides are committed annually. Eighty kidnappings every month and a society with 950,000 registered firearms make the task of overcoming the past look like a test for the powers of Hercules.

In contrast, foreign debt barely reaches the 20 billion dollar mark. Payments are always on time and it continues to be managed prudently. New to the scene, one notices the birth and resurgence of social organisations which, numbering nearly 30,000, are working diligently for the common good. The organisation of a community well disposed towards not only demanding solutions but also providing them points to a dynamism that balances the confusion.

The most barbarous times of drug terrorism have passed, but that does not eradicate the existence of present day drug trafficking, the result of international non-solidarity. We all know that as long as we are incapable of designing a policy that will assure a pledge from all nations and until we initiate a common strategy to create a world commitment, we will continue in the infernal circle of having accusations as both producers and processors hurled at us, while we respond with similar accusations against consumers. Meanwhile, drug-produced money continues to circulate, generating, in some people's eyes, somewhat illusory indices of growth and, for others, tricks in the financial system, mysterious areas where no-one asks about the origins of things. Nevertheless, the fight continues without quarter despite an extreme domestic and foreign lack of understanding.

And, in addition, the hard, cutting reality of insecurity and subversive violence that costs the country 6,200 billion pesos every year. This subversion that, having lost its connection with the questionable ideals of yesterday – ideal after all – has no legitimacy; it cannot find the way out of the vortex of death and tends to join forces with the drug traffickers, more and more each day. Political violence, individual violence, economic violence, social violence, cultural violence, ecological violence, all of these are terribly real and we cannot make them go away by wishing them gone. These are the expressions of violence that define the 'era of the Aurelianos' gone awry, a misfortune that does not hide the paradox of a predilection for the peace, respect, justice, culture, nature, community and solidarity of the 'era of the Arcadios' that is just beginning. It is an exercise in synthesis, where partial enthusiasm encourages the composite of dreams.

The peace process of the Betancur administration experienced its ups and downs, particularly after the erosion caused by the M-19's capture of the Palace of Justice in 1985. After the difficulties during the Barco and Gaviria administrations, a new process, begun at the end of

1994 by President Ernesto Samper Pizano, initially progressed credibly and amply. We were tied to this hope for a peace that is coalescent, advantageous to all.

In the final week of September 1994, experts in armed conflict met in the Colombian city of Villa de Leyva. Among the members of the group were former Colombian Minister of Foreign Affairs Augusto Ramírez Ocampo, who served as the United Nations representative in El Salvador after twelve years of war, and Shafik Handal, co-ordinator of the guerrilla groups of that country. Their thesis, and my own experience there as President of the Truth Commission, which judged the atrocities committed during those twelve years of war, is that the difficult itinerary of peace with the Contadora Group and in Colombia may be synthesised in the following methodology or list of ten requirements for peace, which I presented in November 1994 in Paris before the Organisation for Economic Co-operation and Development (OECD):

1. The point of departure must be the unmistakable political will of both parties in the conflict to reach peace. This political will means that neither of the parties nor subjective agents will unilaterally suspend negotiations.

2. The existence of an objective mediator, agreed upon by both parties – perhaps, the United Nations – a mediator who sets the meetings, resolves the difficulties of the process and seeks the necessary resources for initiating the peace agreements and for their verification.

3. The mediation of the Catholic Church in countries like Colombia, where the majority of the population is Catholic, is a creative force, because of the credibility that the Church enjoys and because of the ease of communications between the parties in conflict.

4. The formation of a group of nations friendly towards the process which collaborates in smoothing out still existing difficulties.

5. An initial agreement concerning the humanisation of the war, and respect for human rights and international humanitarian rights.

6. The confidentiality of subjects discussed in the various hearings of the negotiations, which does not exclude confidential information given internally by the parties in conflict.

7. The venue for negotiations must not be where the conflict is taking place, but in a friendly nation or in the headquarters of the United Nations in New York.

8. Negotiators must have the capacity to immediately commit the parties in conflict, even though each may make any key internal consultations they consider necessary.

9. Both government as well as the guerrillas must have representation of their armed forces.

10. Given that in all armed conflicts in Latin America there are subjective or personal agents – guerrillas – as well as objective agents – a lack of social infrastructure, for example – a United Nations agency should be established in the respective country to verify that the Peace Agreements are being upheld and that the resources supplied by the international community for reconstruction are being used wisely.

On the other side of the coin, as I have already said, it is exciting to observe how a society navigates such storms. It dedicates itself with optimism to the task of reconstructing its 'justice', which wears the cloak of new institutions during a trial period. It is true that there are ups and downs, but with the persistence of those who have understood that without perseverance, no new creative reality is stable. Security and development depend on justice. Living together requires it and we must, despite the incomprehension within or without, continue to seek the appropriate design that will make society free and sovereign.

Everything in Colombia is now being questioned and in an interim state. We were not always a violent country. Malcolm Deas proved it historically in a dense essay presented at a seminar in Geneva and published in Bogotá.[3] Only occasionally has it been violent. Why is it so now? Here we have another fascinating topic for another book. Everything is changing in our country, and that is what the positive and negative, ambivalent surroundings portray of the situation we are facing. We are in the dark, and never is one so sure of light as when someone ignites a light in the dark, however small. And there are many lights being lit. I am wont to say that we are in the fourth day of the creation of the world, separating the waters for irrigation and assembling them to produce energy. Sometimes, I think we are navigating before that fourth day, perhaps even in working towards the creation of a new being, the symbiosis of our achievements and contradictions.

The challenges of reforming the state and society will give way to the creation of a new democracy which will constitute the true social, just state, as the preamble of the 1991 Charter prays. It will, with all its risks, consolidate the social market economy already in bud. It will create a state that will strengthen the internationalisation of the economy and propel the conquest of world markets. It will become a state that will make education the backbone of its plan, as in President Samper's announcement that the new oil resources from Cusiana will be dedicated to such education. In summary, it will be a modern state without the customary arrogance, or lack of moderation, or inefficiency of the past. Thus we may achieve a common destiny and provide a Latin American design for humanism that will make of feelings a way of thinking, and of thinking an attractive way to build and progress.

Together Aureliano and Arcadio represent two undeniable moments of our existence, complementing the cycle that allows us to leave darkness behind and go forth into hope after all these years of solitude.

The story goes that one day Melquiades, the wise man of all times, arrived in that paradigmatic Macondo that represents the new world. He came from the region of the jaguar, the caiman, the orchid, and the anaconda. And, being the sage he was, he did not want to impose knowledge or procedures on the people. He limited himself to making proposals and experiments until he succeeded in creating a new world of unheard dimensions, that would make survival worthwhile in a secure future.

Melquiades, planetary testimony in Colombia and Latin America, made the 'era of Arcadio' possible. Every moment this catalysing faith becomes more imperative to a people who awaken with the dawn, to look over their libretto of the seven days of the creation of the world. Because everything has yet to be done. Only that faith will make us accomplish what we most want to be when we cross the threshold of the third millennium: a vital part of the neighbourhood of an integrated Latin America, Bolívar's essential dream – 'Aureliano and Arcadio'. In his dreams, the Liberator epitomised the imagination, thought, and impetus that adorn today's Colombia, like the intricate weave of our grandmothers' bobbin lace, and that is what will make the country just and strong in the future. When God, or the gods, judge us worthy of one hundred years of happiness on Earth.

Notes
1. Esguerra Fajardo (1995).
2. Betancur (1990), p.15.
3. See Deas and Gaitán (1995).

INTRODUCTION

REFLECTIONS ON THE COLOMBIAN STATE: IN SEARCH OF A MODERN ROLE

Eduardo Posada-Carbó

'Latin America' – Moises Naim has observed – 'which has spent the last ten years demolishing the state, will spend the next ten rebuilding it'.[1] Naim was writing from his own experience. As a minister of industry in Venezuela, he was part of a government embarked on a drastic programme of reform geared at increasing the role of market forces in the economy. Popular reaction against the reforms took the government of Carlos Andrés Pérez (1989–93) by surprise. As serious as the riots in Caracas were the frustrated *coups d'état* led by army officers. At the root of these signs of political instability was 'the institutional devastation of the state'. In a critical self-assessment of the reforms undertaken by the Pérez administration, Naim concluded that 'market reforms require an effective state'.[2]

The experience of Venezuela was only unique in the level of violence that accompanied the implementation of the reforms.[3] Nonetheless, as most Latin American countries implemented ambitious programmes of economic readjustment – a radical shift from the tendencies prevalent since the 1930s – it soon became apparent that the role of the state in the region needed substantial reconsideration. Surprisingly for some, demands for state action came from the very advocates of liberalisation. Sebastian Edwards, chief economist for Latin America at the World Bank, came to similar conclusions to those of Moisés Naim: the consolidation of the economic reforms of the last decade requires 'the need to rebuild the state'. Although, adds Edwards, 'the new state that emerges in the years to come will have to be strong but very different from the state of the 1970s and 1980s'.[4]

Latin America is not of course alone in reconsidering the role of the state. To some extent, as Naim and Edwards amply demonstrate, the economic reforms in the region were the result of pragmatism: a reaction against frustrated past experiences, particularly encouraged by the deep crisis of the so-called 'lost decade'. External influences, however, were also present. Successful experiences in other countries, such as those from East Asia, and economic thinking developed in multilateral institutions had an impact on Latin America.[5] Developments in the United Kingdom were particularly relevant. Here the consensus around the welfare state built after the Second World War had not been 'seriously challenged at the intellectual level until the revival of monetarist theory and the political philosophy of the "new right" in the 1970s'. 'Since then', as Dieter Helm points out, 'the question of the proper role of the State has been one of the most contentious issues on the political agenda.' Helm focuses on 'the economic borders of the state'; his is an enquiry from economic theory. Current interest on the 'proper role of the state' embraces other disciplines as well: political science, philosophy, sociology, and history.[6]

The various essays in this book touch, therefore, upon a subject of current interest in academic and governing circles. The politics of reforming the state in Colombia ought to be appreciated, first, in this regional and international context. From this perspective, some of the problems faced by the process of reform in Colombia examined in this volume may be familiar to the student of similar processes elsewhere.[7] This book does not follow a comparative approach, but by offering detailed analysis on several aspects of the reform process, it does provide a Colombian dimension to the general debate. It also serves to identify the peculiarities of the Colombian experience. In the prologue, former President Belisario Betancur (1982–86) reflects on some of the paradoxes involved in the attempts at reforming the state in a society living in flux. His picture is one of genesis out of chaos: immersed in a deep political crisis, surrounded by threats from powerful criminal organisations – be they drug traffickers or guerrilla groups – and pressed by urgent social demands, a disintegrating society aims at reconstituting itself. Nevertheless there is something typically Colombian in this picture of extremes with elements of moderation – Betancur's self portrayal as a member of the 'extreme centre'. 'The economy is doing well, but the country is going wrong', expressed a leader of the private sector in the mid-1980s. Unlike the rest of Latin America, the process of reform in Colombia was not preceded by an economic crisis.[8] Nor has the country experienced a drastic change of political regime. Gradual change seems to be the hallmark of Colombian reforms, a pace probably conditioned by the very weakness of state institutions.

The historical roots of the weakness of the Colombian state is the subject of Marco Palacios's chapter. Palacios focuses on the crucial period of transition to independence: from the late colony to the early republic. He examines the shortcomings of the modernisation of the state and, in particular, pays attention to the continuities of the Spanish colonial state in New Granada – as Colombia was then called.

At the heart of his analysis is the problem of centralisation, a key feature of the modernising project. The frustration of the Bourbon reforms in New Granada implied the continuity of the 'Austrian' model of the state, linked to decentralisation or, in other words, to the survival of strong regional elites which controlled local power. In addition, Palacios suggests that these elites adopted the liberal discourse in an exclusive fashion, discouraging the development of citizenship. The modernising efforts after independence were confined to the domains of political economy, while the problem of state legitimacy remained unresolved. Palacios's picture stands in clear contrast with common interpretations of Latin American history – such as that of Claudio Véliz who, instead, has emphasised the development of a powerful centralising tradition inherited from the empire.[9] The emerging post-independence state in New Granada was not an element of internal cohesion. Quite the opposite, it was the focus of regional conflict. This decentralised legacy – the survival of strong regionalist interests in opposition to the central state – could be best appreciated by looking more closely at regional fiscal history, as Palacios suggests in the final section of his chapter.[10]

Palacios takes his analysis only to the mid-nineteenth century, although he hints at later developments. Indeed, if the project of a modern central state was frustrated in the first decades of independence, the problems were exacerbated with the radical federalist constitution of 1863. Thereafter, and for the next 22 years, nine different states – the country now renamed as the United States of Colombia – gave themselves different constitutions and adopted legislation independently from each other.[11] The role of the central state was limited to a minimum. In 1874 there were scarcely 1,450 public officers employed by the national government. In addition, the army with '1,000 or so of men', 'can scarcely be said to exist', observed the British Minister in Bogotá.[12] In such circumstances, the state could hardly guarantee internal order: more than 50 local 'revolutions' and three major national civil wars broke out between 1850 and 1885. The 1886 constitution attempted to readdress the problem of national unity by centralising state structures, including the army. 'Political centralisation and administrative decentralisation' was the compromising formula adopted by the architects of the regime inaugurated in 1886, Rafael Núñez and Miguel Antonio Caro. Whatever gains were made, the fragility of the Colombian state was again exposed with the outbreak of the War of the Thousand Days, which resulted in the secession of Panamá in 1903. The basic organising principles set up in 1886 survived these upheavals, although major reforms were introduced in 1910, 1936 and 1968. The latter, in particular, had clear centralising purposes. However, despite the centralist organisation adopted by the 1886 constitution and reinforced by its later reforms, the country continued to experience an effectively decentralised political life – a fact that has often been overlooked in the literature.[13] To a large degree, effective political decentralisation was the result of the role of the political parties which, since the mid-nineteenth century, shaped Colombian state and society.

Colombian politics developed around a lasting two-party system. As David Bushnell has observed, 'modern Colombia is unique in that the Liberal-Conservative dichotomy survived from the mid-nineteenth century to almost the end of the twentieth'.[14] In the second chapter of this volume, Gary Hoskin examines how these two parties evolved since the 1850s to the present. Hoskin's analysis focuses on party organisation, on the extent to which party structures served to articulate social interests with state functions. He identifies four major periods according to distinct types of party organisation: (1) the 'caucus-cadre model', between 1850 and 1930; (2) the aborted transition to mass-based parties, 1930–58; (3) the 'cartel model', 1958–74; and (4) a final period from the 1970s to the present, with the development of both the 'catch-all model' and of a movement to reform the existing political practices leading to the 1991 constitution. As with most models, Hoskin simplifies a more complex history. Nonetheless his is a useful typology, which helps us to appreciate some of the dynamic features of what is often portrayed as a static political system.

Particularly relevant are his observations on the parties' links with social interests and state structures. Following in Palacios's footsteps, Hoskin notes how the structure of power that accompanied the institutionalisation of the parties was regionally anchored. In the 'caucus-cadre model', parties are described as 'undisciplined coalitions of regional party leaders'. As the state remained a partisan one, its development somehow reflected the fragmented nature of the dominant parties. After 1930, according to Hoskin, the organisation of the parties changed substantially. National party directorates were remarkably active, although they could not ignore regional leaders.[15] Indeed, parties showed themselves to be stronger than the state. Their organisation, however, seemed to have collapsed together with that of the state during a period of intense sectarian conflict which led to the army takeover of 1953. Military control of the state did not last long. In 1958 parties were back in power, showing again their capacity to mobilise society while reinforcing the tradition of civilian domination over the country's affairs. The power sharing arrangement between the two parties, known as the *Frente Nacional* (1958–74), would determine new changes in the relations between parties, society, and the state.[16] Society became depoliticised as the inter-party conflict subsided. The state took on a more active role in developmental policies – an already existing trend which was consolidated after the constitutional reforms of 1968. Here Hoskin poses an interesting paradox. On the one hand, a divorce was effected between national party organisation and government agencies, as the executive took firm control over economic policy accompanied by the emergence of a technocracy. Nevertheless, public perceptions identified the parties with a state that became increasingly inefficient and corrupt.

There was, however, no contradiction between these two developments. It is true that some state institutions – such as the Ministry of Finance, the Departamento de Planeación Nacional and the Banco de la República – became the centres of technocratic feuds, but politicians did not lose their capacity as power brokers. Furthermore, as the state expanded its role in the economy and society, politicians reasserted themselves as middlemen. Clientelism grew rampantly. It did so through national agencies attached to the ministries – such as those linked to the ministries of development, mines, education, health, transport, and agriculture. It also grew through the local bureaucracies in the departments and municipalities. The growth of 'pork barrel' politics went hand in hand with the extreme fragmentation of parties. Thus the divorce between national party organisation and government agencies was translated into close links between strong regionally based political bosses and state institutions. More often than not these regional bosses were representative of an emerging breed of politicians who challenged the power of, and even displaced, traditional party leaders. Party politics, therefore, did not remain static. Moreover, the capacity of these political bosses to articulate the demands of an ever increasing urban society should not be underestimated, although it was above all a vertical articulation, typical of clientelistic systems.[17] In 1978, Carlos Lleras Restrepo warned his fellow Liberals that the party had lost touch with the labour unions and the students.[18] Yet *anti-clientelista* discourses, such as that of Carlos Lleras Restrepo, were never endorsed by the majority of the electorate. Furthermore, clientelism had some redistributive functions; according to Miguel Urrutia this would help to explain the absence of economic populism in Colombia.[19]

However, the Colombian political system, and above all the role of the parties and their representatives in the handling of state affairs, came under fierce attack from both within and without. The limits of clientelism in attending social demands became evident as the quality of social services deteriorated. Even those benefiting from the system came to realise the costs of what proved to be a highly inefficient way of managing resources. Luis Carlos Galán's *Nuevo Liberalismo* captured the reformist mood of the country, particularly among the middle classes of major cities. The election of Belisario Betancur in 1982, under the 'catch-all' model described by Hoskin, was another sign of discontent with the party system. Pressures from outside the system took on a violent form. Guerrilla activities expanded. New groups, such as the M-19, emerged, justifying their criminal actions on the grounds that the system was closed to the opposition. The dominant intellectual discourse did not favour liberal democracy, which was disqualified as 'formal', 'bourgeois' democracy. In addition, the development of drug trafficking and related violence posed serious threats to Colombian stability. In this conflictive scenario, as in Italy,[20] the *clase política* – an unfortunate common denomination which did not help the electorate to discriminate – became the source of all evils and wrong-doings. Despite this hostile atmosphere, the parties, above all the Liberal party, retained a surprising vitality, most evident in the election of President Virgilio Barco in 1986. Yet the assassination of three presidential candidates – including that of Galán – during the following presidential campaign, added further elements of frustration. The difficulties in governing Colombia were largely perceived as originating in the supposed lack of legitimacy of the state.[21] This was the dominant mood by the time Colombians went to the polls on 27 May 1990 to elect a new president, when the voters were also given the chance to decide whether or not they supported the idea of convening an Assembly to reform their long established constitution.

The process leading to the constitutional reform of 1991 has been studied in detail elsewhere and should not detain us here.[22] Suffice it to say that this reform did not come about abruptly. It was the culmination of a long process aimed at changing Colombian institutions, already in motion during the Alfonso López Michelsen administration (1974–78), the first post-National Front government. The process gathered momentum during the government of President Betancur, under which the popular election of city mayors was adopted together with other significant decentralising measures, and a negotiated peace settlement was discussed with guerrilla organisations – labelled the democratic *apertura*. 'Change, change, change', seems to have been the motto of Virgilio Barco's campaign, and his presidency also made serious efforts at reforming the system.[23] All these efforts were not without problems, including struggles among the various branches of the state. The Supreme Court of Justice, for example, had ruled unconstitutional the major reforms attempted by Alfonso López Michelsen and Julio César Turbay (1978–82). The constitutional reform discussed by Congress during Barco's presidency was frustrated by the evidence of pressures from drug traffickers. In the face of what appeared to be an institutional blockage, President Barco proposed a referendum to find ways to reform the constitution outside Congress. When President

César Gaviria took power on 7 August 1990, he had a popular mandate to convene a Constitutional Assembly. This time the Supreme Court cleared the way for sweeping changes. Originally called into being to reform the 1886 constitution within a limited framework, the Court ruled that the Assembly had ample powers. After four months of deliberations, in a process skilfully managed by the President and his Minister of Government, Humberto de la Calle, the Assembly produced a completely new charter.

The 1991 constitution redefined the Colombian nation in substantial ways. As Manuel José Cepeda makes clear in Chapter 3 of this volume, it also reformulated the idea of democracy, and introduced a new conception of the state and of the relation between the state and society. According to Cepeda, a key concept to understanding the philosophy behind the new constitution is that of 'participatory democracy'. This is somehow a logical result of a diagnosis of the Colombian crisis which gave emphasis to the supposed illegitimacy of the system. A fundamental aim of the reform was to strengthen the state, but this was above all envisaged through empowering the citizen, the people – the ultimate source of sovereignty. While the dominant values of the ancient constitution of 1886 were 'liberty' and 'order', Cepeda notes that the 1991 charter is now inspired by the values of 'equality', 'participation' and 'peace'.[24] The notion of the state that emerges from the new constitution is far from being that of a classical liberal state, fundamentally concerned with the rule of law, whose role was limited to that of a 'night watchman'. *Estado social de derecho* is the expression used to define the nature of the modernising Colombian state. In this definition Cepeda finds a middle ground between a liberal and a socialist notion of the state. As already mentioned, the new constitution reformulates the relationship between state and society. It also reformulates the relationship between the different branches of government, redistributing the functions of the executive and the legislative, while introducing new institutions in the judiciary. All these features of the reformed Colombian state are clearly described in Cepeda's chapter. Moreover, in a detailed and valuable examination of the Constitutional Court's rulings during the first three years of existence of the 1991 constitution, Cepeda demonstrates that the Court has gone far in developing the new charter.

Legitimacy is indeed a very complex subject.[25] Whether or not the reformers were correct in their diagnosis of the Colombian crisis, only history will tell. For the moment, it is important to identify the way state modernisation has been conceived, and discuss its theoretical and practical implications. If empowering the citizen is the key to modernisation, the reforms should fill the vacuum left open by the previous efforts, as discussed by Marco Palacios (Chapter 1). However while Palacios links modernisation with centralisation, the spirit of the reform goes in the opposite direction. As Gustavo Bell Lemus shows (Chapter 4), the move towards decentralisation has been at the centre of the process of reform. Indeed, decentralisation is seen as part and parcel of participatory democracy. Bell Lemus does not challenge the principle of decentralisation, deeply rooted in Colombian history. However, based on his experience as Governor of Atlántico, he examines the practical difficulties of giving life to ideals. He convincingly argues that decentralisation poses great political challenges, and questions the role of the political parties: as long as old clientelistic practices survive, the process of decentralisation – and with it modernisation – is bound to be frustrated. The issues of clientelism and decentralisation are further examined in this volume by Jesús Duarte (Chapter 6), looking in particular at educational policies. Duarte shows how historically the national authorities have had little control over educational policies in the regions, in spite of the centralising trend after the 1960s.[26] State efforts to introduce a more rational distribution of resources in the educational system have been frustrated by clientelism, a practice that, according to Duarte, seems to be expanding with decentralisation. Like Bell Lemus, Duarte argues that the major obstacles in implementing decentralisation are not of a technical but of a political nature. In the final analysis these two essays suggest that, confronted with problems of political culture, the contradiction between centralisation and decentralisation may be of a relatively secondary importance in the task of modernising the state.

The policy of decentralisation has now become wide ranging, including housing programmes. As Alan Gilbert observes in Chapter 7, the Gaviria government substantially increased financial transfers from the centre to the municipalities and departments. Local governments now play a larger role in housing programmes. But Gilbert's central concern is not decentralisation. Rather he critically reviews the Colombian housing policy during both the Gaviria and the Samper administrations, acknowledging some of their achievements but also raising some questions about the implementation of those policies.

Where the weakness of the Colombian state appears most evident is in its manifest incapacity to provide security. Certainly the Colombian state fails the Weberian test: it cannot make any successful claim to the 'monopoly of the legitimate physical force'.[27] With the highest homicide rate in the world – and a rate nearly four times higher than that of the second, Brazil – the state is far from performing its most basic duty: to guarantee the right to personal security. The problem has been aggravated since the late 1970s, as the activities of guerrilla groups and drug traffickers expanded. In analysing the nature of political violence, Malcolm Deas draws our attention to the significance of the Hobbesian idea of the sovereign.[28] Sovereignty is of course 'the very essence of the state': '. . . the form which gives being to the state; it is inseparable from the state; without it, the state vanishes'.[29] In theory, as Blandine Kriegel points out, sovereignty should 'articulate a threefold conception of the state: external independence, internal coherence, and supremacy of the law'.[30] Set against this, the Colombian state seems to be suffering from serious problems of sovereignty. Criminal organisations, particularly guerrilla groups and drug cartels in control of significant areas of the country's territory, obviously undermine the very notions of 'internal coherence and supremacy of the law'. Indeed, with a rate of impunity above 99 per cent, the rule of law is on the verge of disappearing.[31] Moreover, the lack of capacity of the Colombian state to prosecute its own criminals is having serious international consequences.

Given its past experience with violence and the magnitude of the current problem, the country has become the focus of scholarly attention. This has encouraged the development of a new discipline, the *violentología,* as Alvaro Tirado Mejía reminds us in his review of the various approaches to the subject (Chapter 5). Economic and social interpretations of the problem have hitherto dominated the field. Recent studies, however, point in another direction, giving more emphasis to institutional issues, although traditional interpretations have remained strong in some circles. Public attitudes also appear to be changing. While in the past security was relatively low on the scale of priorities for most Colombians – it was rarely a top issue on the agenda of presidential candidates – it has now been increasingly perceived as a fundamental problem, a major barrier to the achievement of other social, economic and political goals. To some extent the reforms to the judiciary introduced by the new Constitution and the Gaviria administration reflected these changes. In particular, the newly established Fiscalía has been instrumental in strengthening the judiciary, as demonstrated by its role in the so-called *proceso 8,000,* where leading members of Congress and other personalities have been prosecuted for their alleged connection with the drug cartels. The task facing the judiciary is certainly daunting. Arguably, here lies the key to state modernisation in Colombia.

That the rule of law is central to a notion of the state closely akin to liberalism is an idea with long historical roots in the country, dating back to one of the founders of the republic, Francisco de Paula Santander. Nevertheless, the belief that the role of the state ought not to be limited to the enforcement of the rule of law has also long been established. According to Alfonso López Michelsen, the Colombian experience with Anglo-Saxon liberalism was merely a brief nineteenth-century interlude; it does not represent the genuine traditions of the country, dominated by an authoritarian and socialising concept of the state.[32] Equally significant, however, has been another tradition also of colonial origin: the anti-statist tradition, or as the Chilean historian Mario Góngora put it, a tradition of 'liberty outside the state'. A history of the Colombian state – and of how it was conceived in intellectual and political circles – should take account of all these traditions and how they came into conflict with each other.

Like in the British experience, as shown by G. Peele,[33] the two major political parties in Colombia have been on the whole 'committed to a positive role for the state' _vis-à-vis_ economic development since the late nineteenth century, although there were significant differences in emphasis, and they took their inspiration from distinct intellectual traditions. Miguel Antonio Caro, a leading Conservative ideologue and acting-President of the country during most of the 1890s, was an open advocate of state monopolies while, as a doctrinaire anti-liberal, he opposed individualism and the free-market. Caro, however, believed that the priority of government was above all to maintain internal peace and order.[34] Yet Bernardo Tovar Zambrano has shown how Colombian state interventionism had its roots in the _Regeneración_ (1886–98), advanced during the administration of Rafael Reyes (1904–09), and was explicit by the First World War – all these were years of Conservative rule, when the social doctrine of the Catholic Church enhanced an anti-liberal stand.[35] Meanwhile the trend among Liberals was shifting away from free trade; defenders of classic liberalism such as Tomás O. Eastman were becoming increasingly isolated by the 1920s. By the time the 1936 constitutional reform took place, there were few challengers to the dominant notion of state interventionism, a mixed concept – the result of a combination of influences, all present in the letter of article 32 of the constitution, which defined the role of the state in the economy. In 1938, the Minister of Finance expressed in Congress his strong support for 'economic nationalism', the 'only effective means for the future'. The nationalist policy that he referred to, the Minister explained, was 'the expansion of national capital, encouraged, supported, and controlled by the state'.[36]

This is not the place to trace in detail the intellectual history of the state in Colombia, but let me just highlight some further relevant points. Since the 1930s, although with precedents in earlier decades, the idea of state modernisation became closely linked with economic development, in particular with its capacity to stimulate the process of industrialisation. As the economic borders of the state expanded, views of the state which stressed its role in preserving the rule of law lost some currency. In the 1940s, Alfonso López Michelsen, then a young university lecturer, expressed in his *El Estado Fuerte* that the future problems of the state would be alien to 'abstract concepts of the law'. The only public liberties that the future state would acknowledge, pointed out López, would be those 'without an economic content'.[37] López might have later changed his views but this influential work, reprinted in 1968 and widely read among students, illustrates the anti-liberal statist mood that prevailed in some circles. Dominant statist views, however, were far from following any exclusive orthodoxy. According to Salomón Kalmanovitz, influences from Marxism and German historicism were probably stronger than those of classical and neoclassical doctrines up to the mid-twentieth century, as expressed in the works of leading figures such as Antonio García and Luis Eduardo Nieto Arteta. But the impact of Keynesianism and 'new deal' policies was also significant, particularly among the Liberals who came to power in 1930. In 1950 these influences were strengthened by the World Bank mission which visited the country under the direction of Lauchlin Currie, whose views bore heavily on a new generation of economists and policy makers.[38] The goals of the mission were of a mixed nature: while it suggested some redistributive measures, it also paid attention to market forces. In addition to Currie's report, the influence of ECLA (Economic Commission for Latin America) became central to the policies of the 1960s and their subsequent developments. During the following decades, the significant inroad of dependency theory and the various currents of Marxist thought in the social sciences and humanities added to a dominant intellectual atmosphere that favoured the expansion of state activities.

This brief summary suggests that at least since the late nineteenth century, views of a positive role for the state in economic development, although in an eclectic fashion, tended to prevail among influential circles, including intellectuals, academics, and policy makers. Nonetheless, these views were never applied in an extreme form. They were tempered, if for no other reason, by the very structure of the Colombian economy: the consolidation of coffee – privately owned and mostly in the hands of nationals – determined to some extent the conditions of state-private sector relations. It is here where Rosemary Thorp finds the roots of those 'pragmatic interventionist policies' which have characterised Colombian economic management. According to Thorp 'the success and centrality' of the Coffee Federation's relation to the state – a relationship of 'reciprocity and symbiosis' – 'built into Colombian consciousness the positive dimension of the state's role'.[39] This 'pragmatic' approach meant, as Armando

Montenegro acknowledges in Chapter 9 of this volume, that Colombian state interventionism did not reach the levels of other Latin American countries.

Against this background of 'pragmatic state interventionism' and eclecticism, there have been some significant changes regarding the role of the state in the last decade, although it is difficult to identify a radical shift in the dominant intellectual trends of the past. No minimalist view of the state emerged from the 1991 constitutional assembly – a reflection of the mixed composition of this assembly. Yet two major and closely interrelated changes are worthy of attention. As law and order deteriorated to extraordinary levels, there has been an increasing concern to redefine the process of state modernisation. In some circles, a modern state is no longer identified by its capacity to direct economic development but, above all, by its power to guarantee security for all citizens. Subsequently, the role of the state in the economy has also been readdressed. This has resulted in a drive to encourage market forces while empowering the state with new regulatory institutions. Far from a case of simple 'retreating', as Christopher Pierson points out in analysing recent developments of modern states elsewhere, the Colombian experience has also followed a path of state 'restructuring'.[40] Armando Montenegro examines in detail the efforts of the Gaviria administration to deregulate significant areas of the economy while creating new institutions geared at strengthening the role of the state as regulator in a more competitive environment.

As already noted, Colombia did not suffer the deep crisis that affected other Latin American countries during the 1980s. However, it did face serious problems which motivated a process of readjustment since 1984, led initially by Roberto Junguito, Minister of Finance in the Betancur administration. As Rudolf Hommes shows in Chapter 10, fiscal and budgetary matters received further special attention in 1985, when the government convened a group of experts to examine the problems. These steps, according to Hommes, 'signalled the beginning of a process of institutional building' that is still under way, a process that 'has deeply reformed budgetary mores in Colombia'. Hommes looks at this process from a long historical perspective, highlighting the significance of institutions in fiscal performance. He also looks at the development of budget institutions in the broader context of the 1991 reforms, which redistributed functions among the various branches of state power. While the tradition of prudent fiscal policy, as suggested by Hommes, may help to explain Colombian macroeconomic stability and moderate growth, the more open economy encouraged by the reforms poses new challenges for economic and indeed for fiscal management.

It is too early to pass final judgement on the ambitious programme of economic reform launched during the Gaviria administration, but Jorge Ramírez's chapter (Chapter 8) is a fair and welcome attempt at a preliminary balance of the *apertura*. Ramírez reviews the major reforms, examines their impact on economic performance by 1994, and looks briefly at the prospects. Any balanced view of the *apertura* ought to consider some of the features that appear to identify the Colombian experience. As Ramírez reminds us again, we are dealing here with gradual change. As already suggested, fiscal policies and institutions had been reconsidered since 1984. Significant steps towards the internationalisation of the economy had been taken under the Barco administration, during which Gaviria held two major cabinet posts: Finance and Interior. Furthermore, the package of reforms came as no surprise to the electorate: there was no 'U-turn' as in Venezuela, Argentina or Peru. Fernando Cepeda has shown how the internationalisation of the economy was openly discussed during the electoral campaign, while Gaviria, as a presidential candidate, promised a series of significant measures regarding taxation, foreign investment, exchange controls, and labour legislation.[41] On March 1990, a document published by *Estrategia* – the results of a working group that became the core of Gaviria's team – was interpreted as the platform of the presidential candidate. Once elected, Gaviria faced opposition within his own administration regarding the speed of the reforms, but by 1991 the *gradualistas* lost out to those who preferred to accelerate the process.

There were, however, some setbacks. Perhaps the most serious was the frustrated attempt at reforming Telecom, as a result of strong opposition from the union, which led to the resignation of the Minister of Communications.[42] And whatever the achievements, the process has been somewhat halted as a new administration, led by President Ernesto Samper, took power on 7 August 1994. Since the days when he formed part of the Gaviria government, Samper has openly favoured a 'selective' *apertura* – an 'alternative model of development' – although we are not witnessing a radical reversal of the reform process overnight. Indeed there are signs for concern as populist trends within the Samper administration gain positions in power. However, Samper's Ministers of Finance – Guillermo Perry and José Antonio Ocampo – have not distanced themselves from the need to preserve that tradition of macroeconomic stability which has so far characterised Colombia. In addition, the independence of the Central Bank has also served as a safeguard for the continuity of prudent economic management.

There is no irony in a process of reform where the state withdraws from being a direct producer of goods and services and strengthens its regulatory role, as Christopher Pierson wants us to believe.[43] Among the theoretical perspectives underpinning the worldwide tendencies of restructuring the state, very few subscribe to the minimalist view of Wilhelm von Humboldt, that 'the state must pursue no other end than the security of its subjects'.[44] As John Gray has shown, liberals and their major exponents today, such as Frederick von Hayek, would agree that the state has some positive functions including, among others, 'the maintenance and improvement of institutions which sustain market processes'.[45] Or, as Hayek himself put it, 'the whole design of the legal framework within which competition works – the law of contract, the law of property, the general provisions to prevent fraud and deception. All these are entirely desirable activities.' Theoretical considerations aside, there are further reasons – beyond strict economics – to argue in favour of a course of state restructuring in the Colombian experience, where the limited, procedural role of the state takes precedence over its ever expanding functions.

There is little doubt that the breakdown of the rule of law is Colombia's major problem today, as it has been in the past decades. The lack of security – the lack of certainty regarding the enforcement of the law – is not only affecting the basic human right to live and other values such as justice and freedom, but also economic performance and the international relations of the country. The very principle of sovereignty is under serious threat. An agenda for reforming the state surely ought to start by recognising the fundamental significance of the rule of law in the formation of modern states: a rule of law that, by definition, implies a regime of general rules applicable equally to all but also government by rules – a state whose power is limited by law. But above all it should recognise that at the heart of the modern state is its capacity to guarantee personal security. Given the dimensions of the problem in Colombia, references to the Hobbesian state of nature are indeed relevant. What is most evident here is the absence of that state in which, as Kriegel put it, 'the sovereign's confiscation of all acts of war, his monopoly on the sword of justice, brings about individual security by means of the rule of law'.[46]

Alongside these considerations regarding a basic unfulfilled role of the state in Colombia, there is another reason to support a process of state restructuring. As various chapters of this volume make clear, clientelism has become a serious barrier to any attempt at modernising state institutions. The links between the rise and consolidation of clientelism and the development of the interventionist state have not been sufficiently recognised. With the expansion of state activities, the power of politicians over society also expanded. This did not result in a stronger state. Quite the opposite. It led to the fragmentation of the state through its 'privatisation': a process by which politicians managed state agencies for their own personal or partisan benefit, while society bore the costs of their operations. Corruption and inefficiency followed. This could partly explain why, for example, the process of privatisation of utilities has not been opposed by public opinion. Of course restructuring the state alone will not be the final solution to clientelism, deep rooted in political culture. But there is no doubt that a limited state curbs the arbitrary power of politicians and forces a rearrangement of their relationship with the electorate.

A decade of reform in Colombia has not been unfruitful, as the chapters of this volume demonstrate. The continuing problem of crime, and the crisis produced by the scandals surrounding the 1994 presidential elections, should not detract from the achievements of these reforms. Nevertheless, there are serious concerns about their prospects. As political and socioeconomic problems also arise elsewhere in the continent, there is a need for reconsidering even further the role of the modern state in Latin American societies. It is hoped that the publication of these essays, by exploring, from different angles, various aspects of the politics of reforming the state in Colombia, will contribute to a debate that will remain central to the future of the continent in the years to come.

Notes

1. Naim (1993a), p. 133.
2. Naim (1993), pp. 116, 130, 144, 152, 154.
3. Some other Latin American countries also faced social upheavals. However, as the cases of Mexico and Argentina show, mass demonstrations against the reforms were confined to the provinces, and they never reached the dramatic outcome of Venezuelan protests.
4. Edwards (1995), p. 304.
5. See Edwards (1995), ch. 3.
6. Helm (1992), p. 10. As Theda Skocpol reminds us, 'not long ago the dominant theories and research agendas of the social sciences rarely spoke of states . . . the state was considered an old-fashioned concept, associated with dry and dusty legal-formalist studies of nationally particular constitutional principles'; in Evans, Rueschmeyer and Skocpol, eds. (1994) (first published in 1985), p. 4. The title of this book – *Bringing the State Back In* – is in itself eloquent. For an interesting reconsideration of the history of the state from the perspective of political philosophy, see Kriegel (1995) (first published in French in 1989). For general introductions to current debates on the state, see Hall and Ikenberry (1989), Poggi (1990), and Pierson (1996).
7. For an overview of the reforms in Latin America, see Edwards (1995); for

Venezuela: Naim (1993); for Mexico: Serrano and Bulmer-Thomas (1995).

8. See Cepeda Ulloa (1994c), pp. 53–5.

9. This is also a common interpretation in other disciplines. According to the economist Douglas North, for example, typical of the Luso-Spanish legacy is a 'centralising bureaucratic control over all aspects of social life, the political system and the economy'; *Estrategia*, 30 June 1996, p. 16.

10. As Kriegel notes: 'Fiscal history, like legal history, reveals the gap between intentions to modernise and their flawed actualisation.' Kriegel (1995), p. 86.

11. 'The states received much more sweeping powers than in the Anglo-American model.' Bushnell (1993), p. 122. Strong federalist tendencies, already in evidence during the so-called *patria boba* (1810–16), reappeared effectively in 1853. From then federalism developed gradually until its adoption in the extreme form of the 1863 constitution. See Gilmore (1995). For the workings of federalist politics in one particular region, see Valencia Llano (1988). For the presence of the state in the provinces, see Deas (1993), pp. 175–206.

12. *Parliamentary Papers* (London, 1874), LXXIV, pp. 367–8.

13. For the workings of decentralised politics in a Colombian region, see Posada-Carbó (1996), pp. 213–51.

14. Bushnell (1993), p. 117. Unfortunately, the history of the Conservative and Liberal parties has been largely neglected among modern scholars. However, the origins of these two parties are discussed in Colmenares (1968), Helguera (1969), and Safford (1977). An exceptional work which examines in detail the development of party organisation during the nineteenth century is Delpar (1981). See also Abel (1987), and Deas (1973).

15. For an interesting account of clashes between the national Liberal leadership and politicians from Bolívar, see Romero Aguirre (1949), p. 251.

16. For the National Front, see Hartlyn (1988). The most perceptive analysis of party politics during the National Front is Latorre (1974).

17. See Losada (1984) and Leal Buitrago and Dávila (1991).

18. C. Lleras Restrepo, 'La reorganización del partido Liberal', *Nueva Frontera*, 19 Feb. 1979.

19. Urrutia (1991), pp. 369–91.

20. See LaPalombara (1987).

21. The idea that the roots of the Colombian crisis lie in the lack of legitimacy of the system is commonly accepted by most analysts. See, for example, Francisco Leal Buitrago's essay, 'El estado colombiano: ¿crisis de modernización o modernización incompleta?', in the latest edition of the popular volume *Colombia Hoy*, Melo (1995), p. 436; Bejarano (1994), p. 57; Pizarro León Gómez (1994), p. 86.

22. See Dugas (1993), pp. 9–76, and Cepeda (1993).

23. See Cepeda Ulloa's chapter in Deas and Ossa (1994), p. 50.

24. In addition to his chapter in this volume, see also his arguments in Cepeda (1993), especially pp. 16–7, 23, 25, 31–3, and 149–63.

25. See Beetham (1991).

26. The idea that 'in most countries decentralisation should be a fundamental

component of the modernisation of education' seems that have gained common acceptance. See Edwards (1995), p. 310.

27. Quoted in Poggi (1990), p. 73.
28. Deas and Gaitán (1995), p. 23.
29. Quoted in Kriegel (1995), p. 15.
30. *Idem*, p. 29.
31. According to Néstor Humberto Martínez, Minister of Justice under the Samper administration, the rate of impunity in 1996 was 99.5%. See Martínez (1996).
32. López Michelsen (1968), p. 17.
33. See his 'Contemporary Conservatism and the Borders of the State', in Helm (1992), p. 178.
34. See, in particular, Caro's 'Mensaje presidencial al Congreso de 1898', in Caro (1991), pp. 361–420. It is interesting to note that his *Escritos sobre cuestiones económicas*, edited in 1943, were introduced by the later President Carlos Lleras Restrepo, a leading exponent of state interventionism within the Liberal party. See Caro (1943), pp. iii–xii.
35. Tovar Zambrano (1984), p. 229.
36. Vargas (1938), pp. 154–7.
37. 'The role of government will be based, not on abstract legal principles, but on economic criteria to rationalise the production, distribution and consumption of wealth for collective benefit.' 'The science of the state . . . will become the most important economic science', López (1968), pp. 54–5.
38. See Kalmanowitz (1994), pp. 97–102, and Urrutia (1994c), pp. 111–21.
39. Thorp (1991), p. 199.
40. Pierson (1996), p. 126.
41. Cepeda Ulloa (1994c), pp. 43–51.
42. After his resignation, the Minister, Mauricio Vargas, published his memoirs revealing some intimacies of the process of reform, including the problems with Telecom. See Vargas (1993).
43. Pierson (1996), p. 106.
44. Von Humboldt (1993), p. 110.
45. J. Gray, 'Hayek on the Market Economy and the Limits of State Action', in Helm (1992), pp. 127–8. Hayek himself observes: ' . . . competition, which, if it is to be made effective, requires a good deal of government activity directed toward making it effective and toward supplementing it where it cannot be made effective', in Kresge and Wenar, eds. (1994), p. 111.
46. Kriegel (1995), p. 40. 'Liberty . . . begins with the protection of life secured by law', *idem*, p. 37. See also Kriegel's interesting distinction between 'human liberty and civil liberty', *idem*, pp. 35–43.

PART I

THE COLOMBIAN STATE:
HISTORY, PARTIES AND
CONSTITUTIONAL REFORM

CHAPTER 1

COLOMBIAN EXPERIENCE WITH LIBERALISM: ON THE HISTORICAL WEAKNESS OF THE STATE*

Marco Palacios

It has recently been noted that historical narratives without analysis are trivial, and that historical analyses without narrative are incomplete.[1] Let me acknowledge from the start that this chapter will not strike a perfect balance between these two.

In Colombia, as in the rest of Latin America, liberalism shaped the construction of the modern centralised state, the development of citizens' rights, and the definition of national identity. Although, ideally, these three processes should form part of the same project of modernity, they have followed divergent paths, which at times have been mutually conflictive. As a result, modernity has been itself inconclusive; this can be shown by looking at the fragility of the Colombian state.[2]

In this chapter, I re-examine some aspects of what is known as the Colombian encounter (or, more precisely, disencounter) with liberalism – the key to understanding the state's fragility.[3] To this aim, this chapter focuses on the complex period between the final crisis of the Spanish Empire and the consolidation of the Republic. It is here that we can identify the emergence of Colombian modernity and the roots of Colombian political traditions. It is difficult not to identify in later periods of the country's history the convergence of all these substantial elements: a plurality of social hierarchies, a struggle over political territories and a legitimising constitutionalism.

From today's perspective, a look at this founding period is relevant. The collapse of Soviet communism and the end of the Cold War have left some results similar to those following the French Revolution and the Napoleonic wars, which were so crucial to Spanish American independence. Today, as in the second decade of the nineteenth century, the principle of sovereignty and the relations between state and nation are being questioned. Similarly we speak of a new international order. Within the national states, we witness the reappraisal of regions, be they historical provinces or ethnic communities. If we follow Samuel Huntington, this is taking place in tandem with a 'third wave' of

* Translated by Patricia Roberts

democratisation throughout the world. This is the general international context under which the state in Latin America is undergoing a process of reform. In this chapter, I attempt to provide a historical perspective on this process of reform in Colombia.

In the first section, I outline some of the challenges of Latin American modernisation in a comparative perspective. In particular, I want to highlight the difficulties of modernisation in the face of traditional societies. I also want to emphasise the centralising character of the project of modernisation and how this was frustrated by the continuity of 'the Austrian model of the state' in Colombia. The second section will analyse some of the features of traditional society in New Granada, while the following two sections will look at how those features survived the movement of independence. Prominent among these was the survival of entrenched regional elites and their network of interests. These two sections will also serve to identify some of the contradictions encountered by the liberal modernising project in Colombia. In the final section, I explore further the argument that the development of citizenship was curtailed by the way the liberal discourse was adapted by the Colombian elite

Modernity as a Project

An oil-painting (c. 1840) hangs in the Quinta de Bolívar in Bogotá, measuring 94 x 120cm., in commemoration of the Battle of Boyacá, painted by José María Espinosa (1796–1883), 'the most important figure in ninteeth-century Colombian art'.[4] In the foreground, to the left and right, we see a thatched hut and a tiled peasant's cottage; the mountain range, set against cloudy skies, marks the horizon, whilst in the centre, the cavalry and infantry, in an imposing formation, charge the enemy with a bold display of courage. Heavy gunfire lights up the countryside as smoke rises from the cannons, silhouetted against the white clouds.

This description does not correspond to the historical event. This is official, patriotic iconography. The fundamental qualities displayed are honour and optimism. It was the only way in which a patriot could conceive of the struggle for national independence: as a heroic deed conjured up in the most modern guise, though with no attempt to conceal the poverty that surrounds it. The incongruity between the ideal of liberty and the poverty and inequality which were prevalent in the country, framed in Espinosa's rural landscape, evokes the allegory of the

Colombian state and its constitutionalism. It is the allegory of the struggle for modernisation.

According to current historiography, a titanic struggle was waged between the forces of modernity and those of anti-modernity and pre-modernity in nineteeth-century Latin America. Bushnell and Macauley conclude that 'by the 1880s the liberal order seemed more or less established in Latin America, and its creators had good reason . . . to be satisfied with their handiwork'.[5] This could be considered an optimistic conclusion after the event, but at the outset there were few reasons for optimism. As John Lynch points out, although independence was a great upheaval which destroyed the links that bound Spanish America to Spain, together with the framework of colonial government, it left the foundations of colonial society intact.[6] Those same foundations have been a formidable impediment to the processes of modernity.

Centralisation has been a fundamental aspect of the modern state. In Europe, such centralisation operated through different institutional channels, and had a long-term effect upon political values. For example, in France, it redounded upon the monarchy, and in Great Britain, on parliament. In this context, some historians use the terms Austrian and Bourbon – the two dynasties which dominated the Spanish empire in America – to distinguish a state which was 'passive' *vis-à-vis* civil society, from an 'interventionist' state.[7] According to John L. Phelan, the first of these types could be epitomised in the famous sentence 'obedezco pero no cumplo' and the second in the 'blind obedience inspired by the Louis IV model',[8] embodied by ardent civil servants such as the *Visitador* Juan Francisco Gutiérrez de Piñeres. Bourbon Spain would go on to adhere to the French model.

As Samuel Huntington notes, the United States did not experience a revolution promoting the centralisation of the modern state (one of the components of what he terms modernisation). The American colonies retained the principles of the English (unwritten) constitution from the sixteenth century, including that of local government, one of the most highly prized in a modern democracy.[9] In this regard, it is claimed that the strength of federalism in the United States can be traced to the preservation of the political model of the Tudors, the English equivalent to that of the Austrias, rather than to the configuration emanating from their independence. The pinnacle here was an 'elected monarch', responsible for the institution of the presidency – possibly the chief contribution to constitutionalism made by the United States.[10]

As in the United States, independence in New Granada was not a revolution. Here, constitutionalism came hand in hand with the disruption of regionalist prerogatives brought about by attempts at Bourbon modernisations. It was developed following the Napoleonic invasion of the Iberian Peninsula, finding its subsequent expression in the language of revolutionary France and of the Constitution of Philadelphia.

But the key to institutional continuity in the United States was ultimately the fact that they were 'born as modern states'. Citing de Tocqueville, Huntington agrees that 'American society was born modern', and that therefore it:

> was never necessary to construct a government powerful enough to make it so. An antique polity is compatible with modern society but it is not compatible with the modernization of a traditional society.[11]

What should be our understanding of the statement that the United States was born 'modern'? This should mean that it was not feudal. However, until the eve of the Civil War, the system of slavery in the United States was the largest in the world, in terms of its relevance to demography, geography, and economic output. But what we have termed a centralising state revolution did occur in the United States with the triumph of the Union in the Civil War which abolished slavery – although not racism.[12] Subsequently, the Civil War unleashed the drama of North American modernity, in a fundamental sense: the development of citizenship.

Traditional Society in New Granada

In what sense was New Granada a 'traditional society'? New Granada, as in the majority of the dominions of the Empire, was characterised by the plurality and segregation of racial, social and political hierarchies. It also revealed a remarkable degree of territorial segmentation, perhaps more than any other of the administrative divisions of the Empire.[13]

Any description of 'traditional society' in New Granada must take into account two entangled phenomena which would go on to obstruct the project of liberal modernity: territorial fragmentation and the plurality of prevailing social, racial and class hierarchies around 1800. A century later, Colombia would preserve the same basic organising principles.

Let me address the second aspect first. From the top downwards we find the following hierarchy: the Viceroy and the viceregal bureaucracy; the ecclesiastical hierarchy; the urban aristocracy, made up of Spanish merchants and almost always related by marriage to big land-owners, merchants and *criollo*[14] miners who, from the seventeenth century onwards, had gradually ennobled themselves through the pur-chase of titles, offices or privileges, and had taken control of the town councils during the following century. The lowest level was constituted by the plebeians, a kind of commonality which, to paraphrase Abate Sieyes, 'was nothing', although it 'ought to have been everything'. In the upper echelons of the commonality were the middle- to small-size property owners dedicated to trade, mining and various kinds of agri-culture and animal husbandry, whilst the lower echelons were made up of poor whites and *libres* (freed slaves).

A juridical order which had been imposed at the time of the Spanish conquest culminated, in spite of any formal changes, in a system of so-cial and racial values and prejudices which was not destroyed by independence. This system prescribed the place which each individual would hold according to ethnic principles (ethnic with reference to any group united by race and culture). This system evolved from being a simple one in the sixteenth century to a complex one in the eighteenth, when it became difficult, biologically and culturally, to classify any in-dividuals. Even so, the population was organised hierarchically: whites, Indians, blacks and the *castes*: *mestizos*, often of Indian and white race; *pardos*, also people of mixed race; *mulattos*, of mixed black and white race; *zambos*, of mixed black and Amerindian race; and so on, succes-sively. The travellers who during the Enlightenment journeyed through Spanish America, noted the symptoms of what would come to be known as a 'pigmentocracy'.[15]

This system of ethnic segregation conditioned (in Althusser's sense of the word) the categorisation of the lower ranks in terms of class: ur-ban artisans (Indians, blacks and *mestizos*), *mestizo* and native peasants (the latter from individual communities or property-owners), and slaves from the mines, plantations and great estates, and rural and urban do-mestic service.

Social order was also conditioned by territory. Up until the end of the nineteenth century, and in some areas until well into the twentieth century, Colombia, in spite of being considered a politico-geographical unit, had no well defined internal or external borders, but rather vast ar-eas of transient status, known as 'frontiers' in historical sociology. These frontiers may be grouped under the headings 'open frontiers', giving access to resources (uncultivated land owned by the state, the *baldíos*) and 'closed frontiers' (usually vast unproductive *latifundios* or large estates). Throughout the nineteenth and twentieth centuries, the occupation of empty land has been a cause of both dynamism and conflict, as it had been from the time of the Spanish conquest: the promised land of the *mestizo*, the *freemen*, the poor white and the runaway slave.

A complete sample of the socio-racial hierarchy described above could only be found in the main cities (Santa Fe, Cartagena, Popayán). As we go down the scale in the urban hierarchy (such as in the cities, towns, *mestizo* villages, Indian villages, local bailiwicks), the socio-racial hierarchy varies. Furthermore, cities were at a significant distance from one another, and the social and political character of each varied according to the composition of its population. The most obvious distinction from the sixteenth century onwards was between those settlements in the mountain range known as the eastern Cordillera, with its rural population of indigenous character, and the mining region of the west, its labour base being made up of black slaves. Cities and towns were surrounded by a hinterland consisting of politically and administratively subordinated rural nuclei. But in the greater part of the territory, it was the various types of sparsely-populated urban nuclei which predominated. Here, the interaction between different social strata was very tenuous and sporadic. Such nuclei rarely had taxes levied on them by a public administration system, nor did they often benefit from its services. But with the exception of the undiscovered tribes of the Amazon and the Orinoco, and the settlements of free *mulattos* and slaves in the Chocó – according to Sharp,[16] not even the most rural and frontier societies were completely outside the urban web.

It is, therefore, essential to give even more rigorous and careful attention not only to the network of regionalist interests which led to the creation of the urban elites, but also to the relationships between the provinces themselves. This patchwork of regional interests merits re-examination and perhaps a new typology. If we pay greater attention to the list of elements which made up the European classes (including the *criollos,* and to the socio-racial, cultural and legal order of the majorities (from which the *mestizos*, the largest group at the end of the eighteenth century, wished to escape), we can observe an extraordinary degree of geographical dispersion and heterogeneity.

The importance of territory in political attitudes can be studied by focusing on the dynamic tension which arose from the system of power relations emanating from town councils. The political networks expanded in the eighteenth century, as described by Margarita Garrido.[17] They recall the classic account of the political formation of ancient

Rome by Foustel de Coulange. Disregarding its religious basis and the traditional legacy of the Roman practice of *clientelismo*,[18] in New Granada this latter phenomenon increasingly appeared to be the main thread running through municipal life, as if it were the forerunner of a specific political world, or a potential means of subversion of the patrician order.

However, it is necessary to establish whether this situation occurred universally, or whether certain conurbations were characterised by an idle oligarchy which was indifferent to the management of local affairs. Such indifference would then manifest itself in the form of an incompetent town council, as was the case of Santa Fe (Bogotá) during the eighteenth century.[19] Yet it is at this point that the gulf separating the 'administration' from 'politics', which grew wider during the nineteenth century, first opened up. A classic example is provided by the *santafereño rosca* clique, gathered around Jorge Miguel Lozano de Peralta, the Marquis of San Jorge, whose interest lay in a kind of proto-national power, rather than in municipal government. In this sense, civil servants of such dissimilar character as Gutiérrez de Piñeres and Caballero y Góngora viewed the *rosca* as the potential enemy. And in all probability they saw a decisive enemy in the rise of the *comuneros*, the rebel movement of El Socorro in 1781.[20] In the century of the Enlightenment, such a hierarchical structure in the regions was the subject of attempted reform by a modern and functional bureaucracy which, *inter alia*, influenced the ecclesiastical order (the expulsion of the Jesuits) and the political *status quo* (measures taken to exclude *criollos* from government).

In many provinces, with the exception of almost all those from Antioquia and Santander, land was the asset most likely to guarantee a position at the top of the social ladder. All in all, however, the class structure of the 'white republic' was quite fluid, as is corroborated by the interrelated lineages which gradually created a '*criollo* aristocracy'. But in the face of social and geographical mobility of elite families, it is important to identify the continuity of some forms of social power, as shown in the research on Popayán (1730–1830) by Guido Barona.[21]

Independence: Transition and Ambiguity

Historiography, 'old' and 'new', has been slow to deal with two aspects which could assist us in defining the sociopolitical transition: a) the secularisation of the *criollo* elites, by virtue of the Enlightenment, and its concern with natural sciences, with political economy and with the principles of 'the liberty of the moderns', inspired by the French Revolution and the American Constitution and the Constitution of Cádiz; b) the *comunero* rebellion of 1781, and whether or not this rebellion was a forerunner of independence. The debate over the latter should not stop us here. Suffice it to say that this rebellion, a subversive and anti-fiscal alliance which stretched far beyond local and provincial confines, and which surpassed ethnic boundaries, had a dual historical sense. It was a clear expression, in the conservative mould, of popular resistance to the menacing emergence of the centralising modern state, and one which was shared by *criollo* sectors of the local elites. It was also a revolutionary manifestation aimed at increasing political participation which, as such, remained in the collective memory of the people, in addition to placing the values of the viceroyalty temporarily in jeopardy.

Following Huntington and Phelan's arguments, it should be possible to re-examine the continuities of the 'Austrian state', especially as it is well known that the modernising centralist reforms of the Bourbons failed in New Granada.

The *comunero* movement in principle signalled the origins of the modern Colombian state: it expanded the sphere of politics, it politicised what under the *Ancien Régime* seemed impossible to politicise, and it showed the way forward to direct citizen participation. In that period, 'citizen' was one of the favourite terms of the Spanish enlightenment in Madrid. A citizen with civil rights but without political ones: an agent of market forces, a subject of the monarch.

François-Xavier Guerra interprets the revolution for independence in Spanish America in the following terms:

> Everything points, in effect, to a single revolution which began with the great crisis of the Monarchy brought on by the royal abdications of 1808, and ended with the consummation of the independence movements in the Americas. This is a global crisis which, like the crisis of the Soviet empire which we have recently witnessed, reconceptualises its overall political structure, and ends by bringing about its own disintegration. The revolutionary process with which we are here concerned and which can be succinctly defined as a 'Hispanic Revolution' has, as it were, two faces, each of which complements the other: the first represents the break with the *Ancien Régime*, the transition to Modernity; the second represents the disintegration of that vast political conglomeration which was the Hispanic monarchy, that is to say that it represents the revolutions towards independence.[22]

The Napoleonic wars, like the First and Second World Wars, the collapse of communism and the end of the Cold War, signalled a systemic crisis in the international order. A perceptive analysis of these crises notes that victorious coalitions have attributed the origin of the various crises to the emphasis which the defeated coalition had given to a specific concept of sovereignty. Postwar orders have then built upon that belief.[23]

It is important to stress that the ideological agitation of the period of independence could not have been indifferent to the Napoleonic 'exporting' of the French Revolution, the defeat of Napoleon, the Congress of Vienna (1814–1815) and the Holy Alliance (1815). According to all accounts, Napoleon came armed with the civil code – a centralising weapon to be used against medieval legal particularism and feudal institutions – and with an administrative reform which made a clearer distinction than ever before between a 'public' and a 'private' domain. The former swept away the patrimonial concept of the state, since it discharged specific 'functions' within a differentiated hierarchical structure, and had clearly defined 'responsibilities'. The latter was precisely that of the Civil Code. Napoleon also arrived with an army of conscripts, of French citizens, which was in the process of revolutionising the theory and practice of war but which, above all, was the symbol of the people in arms, the idea of all nations as peoples sharing a common destiny, the natural home of the state. This was not fearsome Jacobinism but the exaltation of bourgeois individualism, of nationalist feeling and of the modern public administration.[24]

The 'Spanish American encounter with liberalism' was mediated by a new vocabulary, including the concept of popular sovereignty. The establishment of the new states demanded that this enduring concept should be made explicit,[25] in spite of the extraordinary changes which had taken place in the functions and also the formal, material, social and political structures of the state.

It is worth recalling that from the Peace of Westphalia (1648) onwards, the international order was founded upon the notion of states which were theoretically equal, subject to the control of a prince *(princeps),* whose dominion over a territory *(dominium)* is recognised and whose authority over the population of the same territory *(imperium)*[26] is acknowledged. Within international law, *dominium* was equivalent to the concept of property, as defined in private law. A prince had dominion over a territory with all its inhabitants (in Castilian-Indian law, according to 'natural law' and 'positive law'[27]). The sovereign right to the American possessions enjoyed by the Catholic Monarchs, Ferdinand and Isabella of Spain, is understood in this sense, within the terms of the Papal Edict of Alexander VI (1493).

The custom of denoting inhabitants as 'souls' dates from the *Ancien Régime*. Until recently, many official texts referred to a 'y' municipality consisting of '*x*' souls. But with the French Revolution the 'souls' began to be considered as 'citizens', denoting a vital component in the nation, with a common destiny, the true foundation of state sovereignty, and therefore, of the territorial limits of the state.

Thus a tension, which is latent to this day, was set up between an understanding of sovereignty which lends emphasis to *imperium*, which is to say to the people who constitute the nation, and that which emphasises *dominium*, or the sovereign power of a prince over his territory, regardless of the principle of nationhood.[28]

In the period of independence, the elites of New Granada revealed a deep desire to understand the principles behind the apparent dynamism of international development. They wanted to be part of this new world of opportunities: independence was, precisely, an evident result of the reconfiguration of the international order, harnessed by the advance of Napoleonic troops through Europe.

The fleeting period of peace brought about by the virtual abdication of the Viceroy Amar y Borbón (who, according to the historian Restrepo, failed to show the same courageous and intrepid spirit as his wife)[29] proved to the *criollos* that it was irrelevant whether Spain was guided by the liberal principles of the Constitution of Cádiz or by the traditional practices of Charles III and Charles IV, or the 'Desired One', Ferdinand VII. For them, the supreme objective was to break the colonial bond with the Empire.

Thus a point of no return was reached. The process served to consolidate what would later come to be known as the principle of self-determination. Sovereignty was proclaimed; as in the French Convention this was defined as 'one, indivisible, sacrosanct and imprescriptible'.[30]

The international borders of the new states were defined by the *criollo* elites in accordance with the principle of *uti possidetis iuris* which, incidentally, took no account of the indigenous settlements and communities which normally inhabited and inhabit these same territories. In other words, the *criollos* adopted a notion of sovereignty based on the *dominium*, in the hope of constructing the nation out of the new Republican state.

The *patria boba* (1810–16) was a fertile era for constitutional experimentalism. Independence did not give way to a social revolution. Conflict instead arose from the endeavour to redefine territorial authority. For this reason, the various agreements proclaiming independence – those of 20 July by the Extraordinary Meeting of the Town Council of Santa Fe, by the Federation of the United Provinces of New Granada (1811), by the various provincial constitutions which adapted it later to their own conditions, and that by 'centralist' Cundinamarca – shared a common concern to legitimise sovereign authority over a specific geopolitical territory.

Constitutional experimentalism was not the only reason for the chaos brought about by the *patria boba*. The disorder of 1810–16 had other causes. The New Granadan provinces which claimed sovereignty after 1810 had not experienced the far-reaching administrative reorganisation under the Bourbons known as the *intendencia*, undergone by the majority of new Spanish American states. There prevailed a kind of 'provincial egoism',[31] which had already taken shape in the seventeenth century. Behind the conflicts of the *patria boba*, there was a history of a partisan struggle between the aristocracy and their clients, which revolved around the establishment of regional prerogatives as the new state was constituted. The federalism underlying the *patria boba* was not the same as that of mid-century Radicals: that expression of the ideal of Tocquevillian civic spirit, which sought to distinguish between the positive forces of political centralisation and the negative forces of administrative centralisation. The federalists of the decade of 1810 represented the dismantling of the apparatus of the Spanish state. They aspired, quite simply, to protect traditional regionalism under 'republican' auspices.[32]

The gulf between what was the province, in legal terms, and the regionalist forces, became even greater, and conflicts in the sphere of political representation were not long in coming. From the foundation of the constitutional republic to the present day, Colombians have elected legislative and electoral bodies. For the greater part of the 180 or so years which have elapsed since the cry for independence, such bodies have elected the President and the supreme tribunals of judicial power. Since the beginning of the republic (up until the Constitution of 1991, which granted representation to the indigenous people, opened the way for representation of 'black peoples' and created a system of national jurisdiction for the election of Senators), these bodies have possessed a geographical base which has not always been in harmony with the principles of political representation.[33] These bodies now stand accused of being hotbeds of clientelism and corruption.

All these constitutions were proclaimed in the name of the people, though in reality they were the expression of an oligarchic and patrician tradition. The citizen has hardly ever figured in the history of the nation: either (s)he forms part of a project for democracy in the future, or is reminiscent of a putative civic age now past. In a brief treatise addressed to the Santa Fe Junta in 1810, Antonio Nariño emphasised this contradiction:

> It is said that the people, in its precipitous state of revolution, is reassuming sovereignty. But in what sense does the people exercise it? It is contested that it does so through its representatives. Yet who appoints these representatives? The people itself. And who summons the people? When? Where? Under what conditions? This is the question to which, in its most rigorous and strictest application, nobody can respond.
>
> A simultaneous uprising of all the citizens of a province, at a single moment, and with the same aims and objectives, is a purely abstract thing which is, at heart, impossible. What we have witnessed in our midst has been practised according to the laws of necessity: a handful of enlightened and reputable men have appropriated a part of sovereignty in order to take the first steps in the restitution of that sovereignty to the people.[34]

Whenever the terms 'enlightened' or 'reputable' were questioned by the new protagonists of the social domain (the free men and their descendants), political conflict was relentlessly exacerbated.

The state of New Granada was inspired by the abstract principles of liberty and sovereignty, but in failing to recognise that the social substance of the nation was made of its citizens, it also failed to take cognisance of the cultural foundations of nationhood. The political rights of *mestizos*, natives and Afro-Colombians implied a prior recognition of their cultural values, but they were considered primitive and premodern by the liberal elite. The iconography of the 'revolution' was founded upon the construction of an artificial and precarious system of patriotic symbols drawn from indigenous culture yet lacking in any authentic character.[35]

The ideal which inspired the *criollos* was, as Frank Safford argues, among others,[36] to construct a culturally white Colombia. In spite of that symbiosis between politicisation and the advance of the *mestizos* which had been apparent since 1810, such an ideal successfully infused every cultural, geographical and institutional sphere of nineteenth-century Colombian life.

The Experiment of 'Gran Colombia'(1819–30): Nations or States?

When the armies of Ferdinand VII disembarked in New Granada and Venezuela in 1815 and 1816, following the plans of the Spanish reconquest, the different sections of the *criollo* aristocracy still disagreed about matters such as those raised in the brief treatise by Nariño (mentioned above). Even the very ferocity of the pacification of Morillo, who led the Spanish army, initially divided them, only to unite them later.

Some conservative trends were present. 1815, the year of Napoleon's defeat, marked the return to 'the international balance of power', emanating from the territorial sovereignty of the continental dynasties dating from before the French Revolution. The Bolívar ideal of liberty and constitutionalism, along with the stance taken up by the European allies of Spanish American independence, would thenceforth take on a conservative tone.

In the final analysis, the question of the form of state to be adopted remained to be resolved. Bolívar, relying on his charisma and military strength – since 'his victories, covered in glory, overcome old envies and rivalries' – gained the political initiative. His plan to 'lend a solid, enduring basis to the Republic'[37] led to the Fundamental Law of Colombia (Angostura, 1819) and to the Constitution of the Republic of Colombia (Cúcuta, 1821), underwritten by the Nations of New Granada and Venezuela.[38] However some fundamental questions had to be addressed: How was the nation defined? What kind of modern and national public administration could emerge from this process? What type of national army was going to be adopted? To what extent would the 'nation' continue to be shaped in a struggle leading to the levelling of classes and races?[39]

The war of independence and its impact on society were in turn affected by changes in the 'balance of international power', and the financial demands of the war effort. It is in the context of the Holy Alliance that we can gain a clearer picture of the brief experiment which took place in Gran Colombia, properly defined as a 'military and diplomatic necessity', which ceased to exist as soon as it fulfilled its purposes.[40] It was an experiment which could also be viewed in the light of a sharper definition of the Bolivarian ideals of territorial sovereignty and centralism, which followed the Bourbon model. Some of Bolívar's actions, like his secret conversations with José de San Martín – the leader from the River Plate – in Guayaquil (1822), could be best appreciated if we take into consideration the continuities of the *Ancien Régime*. The national rights of the Peruvian people appeared to have been conceived by both leaders in terms of the 'Northern' and 'Southern' spheres of influence of South America.[41] In a well-known passage, written in 1826, Bolívar developed the idea of a strong presidential system, illustrating it with the metaphor of Louis XIV: 'The President of the Republic figures in our Constitution, like the Sun rising . . .'[42]

The *criollos* of New Granada, Venezuela and Ecuador, however, refused to conform to the Bolivarian model. The question of how they defined their identities remains to be investigated.[43] But it is noteworthy that the disintegration of the *patria boba* and the institutional fragility of the new political order, was followed by a national movement based perhaps on a notion of culture as defined by some anthropologists:[44] a rapprochement of values and customs within a territory, entrenched in turn by three centuries of Spanish domination. The ethnic element disappeared from the constitutions. The state was defined as the reflection of a political order, outside the realms of culture.

The elites of 1830, in the same vein as those of the *patria boba,* adapted themselves to the principle of *uti possidetis iuris* in order to demarcate the borders of the new national states, following the disintegration of Gran Colombia. They also managed to agree on the way each new state should individually pay the foreign debt contracted jointly from London bankers in the 1820s.[45] They also achieved diplomatic recognition from the powers that mattered: Great Britain, France and the United States.

Against a background of twenty years of conflict, the dissolution of Gran Colombia was a peaceful event. The *criollos* secured domination but failed to achieve hegemony.[46] They remained at the top of the new constitutional republics where, ideally, national communities were defined by territorial borders. The demarcation of these, in spite of frequent disputes, had no apparent effect on Colombian sovereignty – at least until the secession of Panama in 1903.

The legal transition to the new order posed perhaps more problems than the territorial one, although the transformation of the legal framework is one of the least researched aspects of the period. Republican sovereignty could not erase the record of the legal past, constructed upon three centuries of Catholic monarchy.[47] There were here some liberal inroads. Apart from constitutionalism and the so-called classic political economy (which tends to be exclusively identified with free trade) a further fundamental expression of liberalism was the Napoleonic Civil Code. As in other Latin American countries, this Code was adapted by different members of the Confederación Granadina in the mid-nineteenth century.[48]

None the less, from very early on, these liberal inroads were not devoid of contradictions. In a letter sent to Páez (Bogotá, 26 August 1828), for example, Bolívar supported a legal system based on 'our' customs, religion, origins, institutions and history, while he criticised the existing Colombian legislation, 'which has had no salutary effect because it is based on foreign texts, totally alien to us'.[49] These ideas shed light on some of the problems raised in the transition to a new legal order. The nineteenth century can be seen as the age of 'law against custom', the age of faith in the magical power of legislative bodies, the age of constitutions and codification in the new states.[50] In addition, changes in population and the economy were believed to erode customs. Bolívar took side with 'customs' and 'national rights'. However, he also drew attention to a dimension overlooked by the historiography: the greater social importance and historical continuity of private law. In his address to the Bolivian Constitutional Assembly, Bolívar observed that 'the true liberal constitution lies in the civil and criminal codes; . . . the Tribunals exert a most terrible dictatorship through the tremendous instrument of legislation . . .. Sometimes political organisation matters little, provided that the civil organisation is perfect.'[51] While liberalism encountered opposition in some areas, there was a large degree of consensus among the elites in the realm of private law. For example, the Conservative regeneration (1885–1900) accepted the civil and mining codes passed during the Liberal, federal period (1863–85), without reservations.

The Contentious Encounter of Colombians with Political Rights

The ideals of liberty and equality and the balance of public powers had to spread through the whole range of different social hierarchies which were the legacy of the colonial period. In order to survive, liberalism desisted from establishing culture as the defining characteristic of the nation, as already suggested. Subsequently, citizens' rights were curtailed and the popular sectors came to be viewed in the same way as the indigenous peoples had been during the colonial period: as minors.

Modernisation, from that moment on, was circumscribed within the domain of political economy, under the belief that the market would define social relationships and go on to forge new and modern social classes, alien to those socio-racial hierarchies of the colonial period. In reality, these hierarchies became covertly interwoven with the new social elements engendered by capitalist development.[52]

The encounter with the idea of citizenship raised enduring traumas. In the post-independence period, the precariousness of resources held by provincial elites, and the primitive nature of an economy which did not allow them to prosper within an authentically liberal order, reinforced the colonial heritage. As a consequence, the new state, in spite of its legal rhetoric and legal framework, could maintain itself only if it subjected the people to the old social order, and the provinces to the old tried and tested methods of colonial rule. Yet liberalism managed to take hold within the electoral map of the country: in places such as Cauca, by mobilising popular forces – blacks and *mulattos*, the so-called *obandismo*;[53] or in Santander, where an ethnically more homogeneous upper class adapted it in order to consolidate traditional social ascendancy, a process which has been described by Richard Stoller.[54]

In this final section, I would like to shed light on the question of how regional dynamics, the expansion of citizenship and the consolidation of the state were interrelated. Two doctoral theses, the first on the subject of tithes between 1764–1833, and the second on the province of Santander between 1830–70, offer valuable contributions to this subject. These theses demonstrate the density and rich complexity of relationships between the new nation, the surviving regions from the previous regime, and the emerging Colombian individual. They also describe the functioning of political economy in relatively closed territories – areas which in 1810–50 could not have been 'born liberal', as was the case in post-independence Argentina[55] – and how these were linked to the political centre. There emerged a more complex and realistic socio-political picture, which can help us to understand how liberal principles worked, in practice, in the construction of the national state.

Maurice P. Brungardt analysed the auction of *diezmos* or tithes (a levy on agricultural production for internal consumption, such as potatoes, corn, peas, beans, livestock) in 32 provinces in the interior of the country, which he grouped into six large regions: the Llanos Orientales, the Valleys of Cúcuta, the Magdalena slopes of the Eastern Cordillera Oriental, Guanentá and the Upper Magdalena. He drew up a complete series from 1764 to 1833.[56] The privatisation of the collection of tithes changed little during the early years of the republic. The tax was collected by professionals who went to the various districts during the festivities of St Peter and St Paul, the *novenas*, to bid for the commission before the respective authority – a *juez colector*. The auctions were held on 29 June (the day of the patron saints), and the tithe collector usually paid the first quota on Holy (Easter) Saturday the following year. As in the former Colony, the organisation of taxes reflected the boundaries of the ecclesiastical and parochial areas of jurisdiction. Throughout the Eastern Cordillera ('el reino'), some 500 tithe collectors, or *diezmeros* were bidding in approximately 1,000 auctions. During the period of the *novena*, they would set up commercial links, obtain credit, either in order to take part in the auction which opened with a first bid worth two thirds the value of the tithes collected during the previous year, or in order to acquire their basic equipment: beasts of burden, a steelyard with which to weigh loads and a set of scales to weigh light produce.

Brungardt brings to light a system open to competition. The *diezmero* who won the bid for a group of districts (*veredas*) had to leave collateral in mortgage, and the collecting judge had a vested interest in the competition because he obtained, overall, 4.5 per cent of the value of the bid.[57] In spite of the narrowness of the approach he brings to bear on the political network of the *diezmos* or tithes, it seems clear that these were a republican reproduction of clientelistic networks first established during the colony by notable local families. Brungardt states that 'prominent Colombians amassed part of their fortunes as collecting judges', and he quotes the cases of Manuel Samper (the uncle of Manuel and José María Samper, two prominent nineteenth-century figures) in Guaduas, Joaquín Ricaurte in Bosa, and Luis and Domingo Caicedo in Purificación.

Malcolm Deas has dedicated himself unremittingly to the task of unravelling these interconnected networks. As in similar agrarian societies throughout the world, be they in twentieth-century China or in nineteenth-century France,[58] from the peasant landscapes of New Granada there emerge social figures who, by virtue of their values and aspirations, transcended the limits of rural society, upon which their interests, nevertheless, depended. Figures who are given special attention in the fine analytical studies of Deas,[59] and who are also carefully studied by Richard Stoller: the priest (who, we assume, owed the same devotion and loyalty to the Pope as the Confucian public servant to the Emperor), the tax collector, the ubiquitous *arriero* (mule driver), all three of colonial origin; or those overtly republican figures such as the *cacique* or electoral boss, the *tinterillo* (unqualified lawyer) or the school master. Each and every one of them was of a peculiarly local and municipal character.

We are dealing here with the mouthpieces of an order which accepts the principles of citizenship but is incapable of applying them. There is little daily interaction on a local level between the different strata in this hierarchical society. Political life, in the majority of town councils and districts, was literally fragmented until republican politics created a system of symbols, values and 'national' allegiances – a system of partisan identities, a political culture in the sense in which the term 'culture' has been used above.

Stoller analyses the Province of Socorro, one of those regions which was ill-equipped to accept liberal economic policy. The proud elites of this region understood, from the outset, that a liberal order granting autonomy to the poor represented a threat to their interests. Their geographical location and their lack of control over natural resources forced the families of traditional elites to reinforce their control over the population. They were also forced to accept the centralism of the constitutions of 1832 and 1843 as the lesser of two evils.

Thus, until the middle of the century, the administration of tax monopolies (chiefly over *aguardiente* – locally produced alcohol – and tobacco) constituted the main institutional links between the Socorro elites and the national state.[60] The reforms which took place in the middle of the century definitively abolished the levy on tobacco. However, the monopoly over *aguardiente* remained. In Socorro, as in other regions, clientelistic networks developed around the auction of this tax. These networks had a great flexibility to operate within all the different possible electoral systems. They were clearly in evidence from the 1830s up to the 'dictatorship' of Rafael Reyes (1909). In the 1890s, they had provoked the exasperation of President Miguel Antonio Caro. They managed to survive to the present day in the corrupted state-owned (departmental) alcohol factories.

Stoller's figures show that between 1834 and 1849 tax receipts per inhabitant in the Socorro province did not seem to have diminished. They also show that the central state could keep more than 60 per cent of all taxes collected in the Province, apart from salt tax and *diezmos*.[61] Intra-regional rivalries played an important part in settling the handling of fiscal matters; this was the case with the long-standing dispute between Socorro (the municipality, which gave the name to the province) and San Gil for the primacy of the province, which predated the republic. The ruling classes of San Gil had long benefited from the privileged tax position of their municipality. The advantage enjoyed by San Gil was due to its location on the River Fonce, or rather its control of the bridge which was an indispensable thoroughfare for thousands of travellers and tons of merchandise subject to obligatory tolls. This was the cause of resentment from its neighbouring towns, including Socorro. The advent of independence linked this inter-municipal conflict to the dynamics of national conflict, in a relatively unpredictable fashion. This became evident during the War of *Supremos* (1839–41) which in turn transformed the proto-liberalism of Santander into liberalism, when the province was 'bound to an *obandista* mystique, to a political discourse which was at once nationalist and popular'. But this liberalism also smoothed the way for the elites to strengthen their political role and to control the local guerrillas, such as the 'guerrilla of Dulcei'.[62]

San Gil, a victim of the interplay of cantonalist rivalries and electoral alliances, found itself without representation in the national congress of 1851. It marked the precise moment when the liberal revolution had started to come into its own, and heralded a period in which the cultivation of tobacco and the manufacture of straw hats served temporarily to stave off stagnation in the economy of Santander. This was the 'mid-century revolution' when Colombian liberals emphasised the difference between 'independence' and 'liberty', meaning that the colonial structures were still standing and that it was necessary to bring them down. Salvador Camacho Roldán, one of the key figures of this period, was later to consider that 'the great reforms of 1849–57', with their preface in the Mosquera Administration (1845–49), had signalled 'the transformation of the feudal colonial world into a democratic republic'.[63]

The dispute over the foundations of the political economy, the struggle between 'feudalism' and 'democracy' unfolded unexpectedly, in San Gil, in the form of social conflict. In fact, as a countermeasure to the impending electoral tendencies of 1851, the elite of San Gil decided to present the intra-provincial political struggle as a struggle, in Stoller's words, 'for the social significance of the republic and of the liberal party'. But when they adopted this strategy and highlighted the social conflict revolving around the inter-municipal dispute, they unleashed a deep political crisis, rooted in the class struggle, on their own doorstep.

The language of liberalism, constrained by the legal vocabulary of the elite, was appropriated by the artisans and their ideologue, the priest José Pascual Afanador, a native of Pinchote, a municipality to all appearances oppressed by San Gil. This 'red' priest was the author of a work entitled: *Democracia en Sanjil o Cartas del ciudadano José*

*Pascual Afanador Dirijidas a los señores de la Nobleza Sanjileña,
sobre la naturaleza y efectos de un Programa* (Socorro, 1851).[64] This
text possessed the plebeian clarity, and reflected that exalted citizen,
long feared by the patricians of the decade of 1810. Though the ruling
class of San Gil succeeded in aborting the artisan movement, and in
neutralising and co-opting its class enemies, the questions posed by liberalism did not disappear.

After the Melo coup (1854), and the spread of *Melismo* through
Eastern Colombia, liberalism – which for the intelligentsia of the capital was linked to questions of political economy and taxation – took on
an anti-colonial undertone in these provinces, a discourse against op-
pression. As such, it became a threat to the fundamental values of the
hierarchical and anti-citizen order, to what Stoller (in common with
Deas) so aptly calls deferent society. Once it had given expression and
significance to the civic and political aspirations of a radicalised, social, popular power base, then the liberal discourse had become
subversive. And so it was that at the time of the two-party coalition
against Melo which had emerged during the civil war of 1854, the San
Gil elite found a pretext for changing their allegiance to the Conservative party, without further ado, and without breaking off personal
relations with the liberals of the provincial elites.[65]

This type of research carried out by both Brungardt and Stoller
should be extended to further areas of investigation. They will serve to
reach a better understanding of: a) the nature of political relations (in
both directions) between the central government, the provinces and the
municipalities; b) the networks which are set up between politics and
the various entrenched and premodern social hierarchies; and c) the
conditions under which potential citizens emerge.

Conclusions

In this chapter I have left out the material bases of politics: demo-
graphic, geographic and economic factors, except when dealing with
regional economic policies and fiscal matters. Let me go back to
Huntington's essay:

> The Latin American experience . . . is almost exactly the reverse of that of the
> United States. After independence the United States continued essentially
> the same political institutions it had before independence, which were per-
> fectly suited to its society. At independence the Latin American countries

inherited and maintained an essentially feudal social structure. They attempted to superimpose on this social structure republican political institutions copied from the United States and revolutionary France. Such institutions had no meaning in a feudal society. These early efforts at republicanism left Latin America with weak governments which until the twentieth century lacked the authority and power to modernise the society. Liberal, pluralistic, democratic governments serve to perpetuate antiquated social structures. Thus in Latin America an inherent conflict exists between the political goals of the United States – elections, democracy, representative government, pluralism, constitutionalism – and its social goals – modernisation, reform, social welfare, more equitable distribution of wealth, development of the middle class.[66]

This is not the place to embark on that long debate on 'feudalism vs capitalism in Latin America'. For the purposes of this essay, what is here described as the 'Newgranadian traditional society' can be compared with Huntington's 'feudal society'. From this perspective, 'traditional' or 'feudal' refer to some conditions of social domination, economic backwardness, technological stagnation, low population density and a highly sparse population in a fragmented and hostile topography. All these factors constrain the size and location of modern economic development.

Colombian political history suggests the resilience of the Austrian model of the state. This is proved by the short life of all experiments with centralisation, Bourbon, neo-Bourbon and liberal. Whenever one looks at the various modernisation efforts already attempted at the end of the eighteenth century – reforms of the tax system, public administration, education, mining, commerce and agriculture – the result has always been unsatisfactory. From those early reforms there emerges the figure of the enlightened Viceroy, compromising his principles, retreating from the modernising path. After independence, such leading figures would look more powerless, even pathetic: Bolívar in his last years, Miguel Antonio Caro and Rafael Núñez at the end of the nineteenth century, Alfonso López Pumarejo and Carlos Lleras Restrepo during the twentieth century. Common to all was their frustrated attempts at reforming the state.

However, these have all been attempts at modernising without fully accepting the attributes of modernisation. This is what I refer to as the Colombian (dis)encounter with liberalism. In the final analysis, all these constitutional reforms, from the *patria boba* to the most recent constitution of 1991, have resulted out of agreements from above, to solve conflicts within the elites. Other elites were included in the last agreement: elites from the guerrillas were allowed to sit in the

Constitutional Assembly, and elites from the drug-trafficking industry were able to negotiate a constitutional ban on extradition of Colombians. Nevertheless, it should be emphasised that in all cases the majority is still treated as minors, while its mandate is merely disputed by politicians and their parties. Obsessed by capitalist 'efficiency' and 'modernisation', the leaders of the 'new' Colombian state – like those of the Bourbon state at the time of the *comuneros* revolt – have failed to address the problem of legitimacy. In the short term, their pragmatic approach may be fruitful to those in power. But in the long run, the project of state modernisation runs the risk of, yet again, being frustrated.

Notes

1. This idea has been attributed to Kant, cf. White (1987), p. 12.
2. See Palacios (1994), pp. 5–33.
3. It is worth clarifying that liberalism in the context of this chapter does not refer to the Colombian Liberal Party.
4. González (1994), p. 7.
5. Bushnell and Macauley (1988), p. 286.
6. Lynch (1986), p. 356.
7. Knight (1993).
8. Phelan (1978), p. 244.
9. Huntington (1966), pp. 395–6.
10. By constitutionalism I mean the set of principles which put limits on political power.
11. Huntington (1966), p. 396.
12. See McPherson (1988).
13. See McFarlane (1993).
14. *Criollo:* of European descent, born in a Spanish American colony (translator's note).
15. On this subject the work of Mörner (1974) is still obligatory reading.
16. Sharp (1976), pp. 192–3.
17. Garrido (1987), pp. 37–56, and (1994).
18 In the sense of the Roman practice whereby plebeians (*cliens-clientis*) received patronage from patricians in return for favours (translator's note).
19. Brubaker (1960).
20. Phelan (1978), pp. 68–70.
21. Barona (1995), pp. 252–2.
22. Guerra (1995), pp. 195–96.
23. Barkin and Cronin (1994), pp. 107–30. See also Cobban (1945), a work written under the influence of the Second World War and which points in the same direction.

24. From the ample bibliography on this subject, see: Seton-Watson (1977), Smith (1983), Gellner (1983), and Hobsbawm (1990); see also Anderson (1993).
25. On the enduring nature of the notion of sovereignty, see the analysis by Krasner (1988), pp. 66–94.
26. There is a rich literature, from Hobbes to Hegel, on the different principles of legitimacy or 'justicia' on which that international order was based, and which took on the most diverse forms: *pactus, societatis, unionis*. See Bobbio (1989), pp. 39–67.
27. This, ultimately, was the point upon which De Las Casas based his formidable allegations regarding the illegal Spanish dispossession of the Indians' legal right to dominion over their lands in the Americas. Within the abundant literature on this theme, see Pennington's admirable account. Pennington (1970), pp. 149–61.
28. See Barkin and Cronin, (1994), pp. 108–15.
29. Restrepo (1942), vol. I, p. 108.
30. Pombo and Guerra (1951), vol. I, p. 240.
31. Restrepo (1942), vol. I, pp. 205–7.
32. Safford (1972) makes the point that republican political alignments could be explained, to a great extent, by their colonial roots: that is, by the position which the urban centres had come to occupy by the end of the colonial period. This is one of the seminal contributions which this author makes to the debate. Colmenares (1989) appears to share this view.
33. Possibly the only attempt to establish representation of the legislative bodies along corporate lines, in the fascist style, was the abortive Constitution proposed by Laureano Gómez during his presidency (1950–53).
34. Pombo and Guerra (1951), vol. I, pp. 101–2.
35. König (1994), pp. 236 *et seq.*
36. Safford (1991), pp. 1–33. See also, Urueña (1994), pp. 5–25.
37. Restrepo (1942), vol. V, pp. 177–8.
38. Pombo and Guerra (1951), vol. III, p. 67.
39. *Ibid.*, vol. V, pp. 196–7.
40. Deas (1985), pp. 507–38. Gran Colombia was formed by Colombia, Venezuela, Ecuador and Panama; the union lasted from 1819 to 1830.
41. Restrepo (1942), vol. VI, pp. 74–9.
42. Taken from his speech to the Constitutional Congress of Bolivia, 'Discurso al Congreso Costituyente de Bolivia', May 1826, in Bolívar (1947), vol. II, p. 1223.
43. A number of valid hypotheses and suggestions regarding the 1809 elections of deputies to the Cortes (parliament) of New Granada, what the author defines as 'the *criollo* network', can be found in Garrido (1994), pp. 93–109. On national symbologies, see König (1994), pp. 202–313.
44. According to Geertz, 'the concept of culture . . . denotes an historical transmitted pattern of meaning embodied in symbols, a system of inherited conceptions expressed in symbolic forms by means of which mankind communicates, perpetuates and develops its knowledge about and attitudes to life'. See Geertz (1973), p. 89.
45. See the relevant chapters in Dawson (1990), and Marichal (1989).

46. See Palacios (1980), pp. 1663–89.
47. The subject has barely been studied. For some introductory suggestions, see Bravo Lira (1992); on Colombia, see Means (1980), esp. pp. 3–61. It is symptomatic of the subject that the assiduous student of the evolution of jurisprudence such as Nieto Arteta in 1938–39, should have been completely mistaken in his diagnosis, as Cataño (1991) makes clear; see esp. pp. 66–8.
48. Taking up as it does the fundamental principles of Roman law (over property, contracts and bequests) the Code is also presented as the only kind of law which is possible. In common with the economic laws of the classical economists, rights consecrated within the Code are in the nature of reality. See Bobbio (1989), pp. 127–34.
49. Bolívar (1947), vol. II, p. 445.
50. The first codification of a truly national type was drafted by Lino de Pombo (1845).
51. Bolívar (1947), vol. II, p. 1225.
52. An analysis of the complex transition from 'caste' to 'class' in the town of Atánquez, in the foothills of the Sierra Nevada of Santa Marta, can be found in Reichel-Dolmatoff (1956), pp. 435–46. A fundamental contribution to the subject is to be found in García Mejía (1989).
53. See Escorcia (1983), and Pacheco (1992).
54. Stoller (1991).
55. Halperín Donghi (1988), pp. 99–116.
56. Brungardt (1974) and (1990), pp. 164–93.
57. The indices provided by Brungardt could be refined. As the author himself points out, any increase in the value of the auction bids must take into account the increase in population, in inflation, or the substitution of export crops (which were not taxed, such as sugar cane, cocoa, animal skins) with crops for internal consumption. The series of tithes in central Colombia, the 'realm' of the Colony, reveal that within each district, or between districts, there were significant differences. For example, the dynamism of animal husbandry in the plains, between 1764 and 1813, and its collapse after the wars of independence, are plainly evident. A similar tendency, though much less pronounced, can be observed in the Valleys of Cúcuta, where the war destroyed the slave cocoa plantations.
58. Fei and Chih-i (1948) and Weber (1987).
59. I refer, in particular, to Deas (1973), pp. 118–40; and (1983), pp. 149–73, reproduced in Deas (1993).
60. Stoller (1991), fig. 5.1, p. 131.
61 *Ibid.*, pp. 129–48.
62. *Ibid.*, p. 203.
63. Camacho Roldán (1923), p. 26.
64. Reprint: Bucaramanga (1990). Introduction by R. Stoller.
65. Stoller (1991), ch. VII.
66. Huntington (1966), p. 410. This argument has recently been restated – though not necessarily taken from Huntington – by Guerra (1992).

CHAPTER 2

THE STATE AND POLITICAL PARTIES
IN COLOMBIA *

Gary Hoskin

Between 1990 and 1995, Colombia experienced an unprecedented period of intensive political change, as reflected in the conduct of seven national elections and the drafting of a new constitution. This outpouring of democratic activity represented an effort to move from a limited, elitist democratic regime to one based upon more extensive popular participation and a more equitable distribution of societal resources. Quite obviously, Colombian elites, following a highly institutionalised pattern with respect to efforts to restructure power relationships, opted for political reform as a means of enhancing the diminishing legitimacy of the political system. This reform effort, which gathered momentum during the Betancur administration and continued through the Barco and Gaviria governments, generated formidable opposition from traditional politicians and other elite groups, but finally emerged triumphant with the convoking of the Constituent Assembly and the promulgation of a new constitution on 4 July 1991.

The most widely postulated reason for the emergence of a profound political crisis relates to the belief that political party elites failed to modernise the political system in a manner congruent with the dramatic transformations that occurred in society during the post-war period, particularly with respect to economic development and societal modernisation. Perhaps no Latin American country has experienced the magnitude of change that Colombia has sustained since the Second World War.[1] Traditional party leaders, so the argument goes, grew complacent during the National Front period (1958–74), and were unwilling to restructure the political system in a manner congruent with a rapidly changing society.[2] However, this mono-causal interpretation is overly simplistic for a variety of reasons. First, the extent and rapidity of societal transformation that occurred during the National Front and its aftermath created a very distinct society in comparison to its predecessor, altering civil society fundamentally and contributing to the mounting illegitimacy of the political system, especially after the resumption of inter-party competition at the national level in 1974. Yet each post-National Front president from López to Gaviria sponsored political reforms oriented towards modernising the political system, with limited success until the promulgation of the new constitution.[3]

Moreover, the Liberal and Conservative parties maintained their electoral hegemony in the post-National Front period, averaging around 93 per cent of the vote, which certainly did not constitute much of a stimulus for political reform from their perspective. This electoral monopoly was facilitated by the malapportionment of Congress, which grossly overrepresented rural interests, the clientelistic system that increasingly became the axis of political party behaviour during the National Front, and continued sharing of governmental offices until Virgilio Barco assumed the presidency in 1986 (both subsequent presidents, Gaviria and Samper, have continued the tradition of coalition cabinets).

In addition to the foregoing system-specific reasons for the failure of Colombian parties to adapt sufficiently to changing realities, on a more theoretical plane political parties almost inevitably change more slowly than their environments because the initial conditions surrounding their formation tend to impact heavily on their organisational structures, reflecting what Lipset and Rokkan label the 'freezing' of party systems.[4] Especially in the absence of a credible challenge to realising its goals, winning elections in the case of political parties, any organisation will resist changing its behaviour.

Moreover, political parties not only defend the structure of power but likewise are constrained by it. As Max Weber argued, the structure of parties necessarily is quite diverse, and varies according to the structure of communal action that it seeks to influence, acting in accordance with the organisation of the community in classes or strata and, above all, the structure of domination that prevails within the community.[5] Panebianco elaborates upon this argument as follows:

> Organisations differ enormously from one another. But whatever their activities . . . each of them invariably also serves to guarantee, perpetuate, or increase the social power of those who control them, i.e., of the elites that guide them . . . The striving for or the defence of this power is an important component in the continual conflicts with 'ALL' organisations, regardless of their category or type, and regardless of the functions they serve (or are supposed to serve) within the social system.[6]

Thus it is unrealistic to expect the behaviour of Colombia's traditional parties to deviate significantly from the policy preferences of those who dominate the society, considering that the parties reflect those interests. Changes in party behaviour are dictated, to a considerable extent, by alterations in the structure of domination. The current organisational chaos in Colombian parties reflects clearly the transformations in the structure of domination, as well as extensive environmental uncertainty associated with the multifaceted violence[7] and the still uninstitut-ionalised rules of the democratic system reflected in the new constitution.[8] However, these factors provide an opportunity for parties to restructure their organisational behaviour, a process that has been initiated but remains inconclusive at this point.

I shall argue in this chapter that Colombia's traditional political parties have always demonstrated, at least retrospectively, a remarkable capacity to adapt their behaviour to changing environments, as mani-fested in their continuing, though diminished, electoral hegemony. After discussing briefly Katz and Mair's models of party organisation that stress both the way in which parties represent societal interests and their relationship to the state,[9] the following sections discuss, chrono-logically, five stages in the development of Colombian parties: (1) the caucus-cadre model, 1850s to 1930s; (2) the aborted transition to mass-based parties, 1930s to 1958; (3) the cartel model, from 1958 onwards; (4) the 'catch-all' model, from 1974 onwards; and (5) reactions to the cartel model and political reform, from 1991 onwards. Finally, in the conclusions, I shall offer some generalisations about the probable im-pact of the reforms on the behaviour of Colombian parties. I shall argue that Colombian parties, both in terms of their representational functions and their relationship with the state, are in the throes of significant change which, undoubtedly, will result in the restructuring of Colom-bian parties and perhaps the party system as well.

Models of Party Organisation

Modern democratic government is difficult to conceptualise without political parties, for they perform critical linkage functions between civil society and the state, not only transmitting demands emanating from civil society to government but also relating formal governmental structures to civil society. Sigmund Neuman did not exaggerate when he wrote that 'The viability of a party system becomes a test for the stabil-ity of a social and political order.'[10] Yet if political parties are pivotal structures in democratic systems, why are they under assault around the globe, with citizens expressing their deep discontent at the polls and academics lamenting the decline of parties?[11] The answers, according to Katz and Mair,[12] are rooted in the evolution of political party structures that reflect, on the one hand, the changing relationship between parties and civil society with respect to the manner in which parties represent societal interests and, on the other hand, the relationship between parties and the state.

The thrust of the criticism directed towards contemporary political parties focuses upon their representational function or, more specifically, their failure satisfactorily to represent civil society before the agencies of the state. The validity of this criticism hinges upon four interrelated presuppositions: (1) that parties are not capable of identifying the interests of the electorate; (2) that parties do not have the organisational capacity to translate those interests into electoral victories; (3) that the interests of party organisations are not isomorphic with their supporters; and (4) that parties do not have the capacity to translate societal interests into public policy.

With the expansion of suffrage and the increasing differentiation of civil society, the task confronting political parties of identifying voter preferences became increasingly complicated, yet development of sophisticated survey techniques has simplified this endeavour considerably. Thus, assuming sufficient resources, political parties can isolate voter preferences and develop appropriate strategies to win elections. In this respect, the structures of political parties have adapted historically to changing environments in order to win control of government. Drawing upon the party literature, Katz and Mair capture this dynamic well by developing a dialectical model of party structures.[13] The first party structures, with their locus of power in parliamentary bodies, were of the caucus-cadre variety, followed by the emergence of mass-based parties which, in turn, generated a structural reaction of the cadre parties, and eventually mass-based ones as well, in the form of 'catch-all' parties.[14] Finally, the contradictions associated with 'catch-all' parties generated the cartel model of parties, whose principal mission was the retention of governmental power through inter-party co-operation and material support from the state.

Thus enters the third proposition about political party representation, namely that the interests of party organisations do not necessarily coincide with the societal interests that they supposedly represent. In other words, political party organisations may well place more emphasis upon maintaining or gaining governmental power than in performing the linkage function between civil society and the state, thereby creating a scenario in which political parties are accused of promoting their own self-interests at the expense of their constituents. If parties neglect their representation function excessively, this may undermine not only the legitimacy of the parties but also the political system as well which, in turn, will prompt a restructuring of parties or their displacement by new parties or movements.

Finally, the representational function associated with political parties will necessarily be undermined if they are incapable of translating societal interests into public policy. This fourth proposition about party representation revolves around two principal variables: (1) the extent of political party discipline, especially within parliamentary bodies; and (2) patterns of governmental decision-making. If political party discipline is weak or non-existent, then the probabilities of translating the demands of civil society into public policy are minimised and the parochial interests of politicians will prevail. Patterns of decision-making in the political system are equally important, in the sense that political parties must be plugged into the policy-making process if they are to represent their constituents well. As Katz and Mair point out, '. . . the capacity of a party to perform the brokerage function depends not only on its ability to appeal to the electorate, but also on its ability to manipulate the state.'[15] This may well not be the case because of the concentration of power in the executive branch of government at the expense of parliament, one of the pivotal institutional loci of representation in democratic systems.[16] In short, for parties adequately to represent civil society, parliaments must not be tangential to policy-making. This is not to deny the representational functions of presidents, only that they often differ from those expressed by parties in legislative bodies. Presidents supposedly represent interests that go beyond their respective political parties and, in so doing, may rely more on technocrats than on political party leaders in policy formulation.

We now turn to models of Colombian party structures that have evolved since the formation of the two traditional parties around the middle of the nineteenth century. The four models analysed by Katz and Mair are applicable to the Colombian case, yet there are differences in terms of the transition from one model to another and the sequencing of the models. The classic caucus-cadre model corresponded perfectly to Colombian parties until the 1930s when the Liberal Party sought to build a mass-based party dependent upon the mobilisation of workers and the peasantry, along with *la clase popular* in the 1940s. However, the attempt to institutionalise a mass-based Liberal Party was incomplete, and the cadre model ultimately prevailed. With the creation of the National Front, the cartel model emerged as the traditional parties relied increasingly upon the state to maintain their viability through clientelistic practices. Only after the expiration of the restrictions on inter-party competition at the national level in 1974 did Colombian parties seek to appeal to a broader electorate than their traditional clienteles, thereby moving, however intermittently, towards the 'catch-all' model. The clientelistic-cartel model that developed during the National Front generated formidable opposition from civil society that culminated in the 1991 *Constituyente*, which undermined the pervasive clientelism and corruption of the political class, forcing parties to seek, as we shall see below, other forms of state support. In summary, the structure of contemporary Colombian parties represents a fusion of the cadre, 'catch-all', and cartel models, with only the mass-based model not now figuring prominently.

The Caucus-Cadre Model – 1850s to 1930s

Colombia's political history is almost synonymous with the two-party system; its evolution, stages, and changes usually refer to the variations in the relations between the two traditional parties.[17] 'With a few exceptions, parties have not only represented Colombian history, they have also made it, which is something quite distinct.'[18] Irrespective of which party controlled the presidency, inter-party relations have been marked by periods of one-party hegemony, coalitions between the two parties, and forceful competition between them that produced the civil wars of the past century and *la violencia* of this century. Each of these models of inter-party competition has impacted heavily upon the structure of party organisation, as the parties responded to changing environments in their efforts to fortify their electoral bases and gain control of the government.

The first stage of party development corresponds with the caucus-cadre model, which was embedded in what Katz and Mair refer to as '. . . the liberal *régime censitaire* of the late nineteenth and early twentieth centuries, with its restrictive suffrage requirements and other limitations on the political activity of the propertyless'.[19] In this model, parties are conceptualised as a bridge between civil society and the state, although this is somewhat misleading because '. . . the people who made up the politically relevant elements of civil society and the people who occupied the positions of power in the state were so closely connected by ties of family and interest that even when the two groups were not simply coterminous, they were heavily interpenetrating.'[20] Parties consisted of Burke's 'groups of like-minded men' in pursuit of the public interest. In this context, there was little necessity for highly structured party organisations to mobilise the electorate or relate societal demands to the formal structures of government.

During their formative years Colombia's two traditional parties were not highly organised. However, there did exist an informal structure in both parties which was based upon regional power and adhesion to a caudillo. Party behaviour revolved around local notables and activities were rooted in clientelism. The transcendental goal of the parties was to obtain power and in so doing the representation of interests was almost invariably overshadowed by the contest itself. The rivalry for domination of the state was paramount; partisans followed their leaders in search of power. *Caudillismo* and localism marched forward, side by side, in the formation of Colombia's two major parties. From the outset, the phenomenon of *caudillismo* constituted a more significant source of political mobilisation than that associated with interest representation. The two parties were groups of individuals who struggled to obtain the *botín de poder*. Party membership became a sectarian commitment to the party. Pronounced inter-party competition oriented towards control of government went beyond the purely political domain of elections and Congress – it incorporated armed conflict into the game. Conservative and Liberal chiefs surrounded themselves with partisans throughout the country and engaged in civil war. This was the typical form of party mobilisation during the last century; the struggle for power was manifested in civil wars and political recruitment occurred through *caudillismo*. Both political parties mobilised partisans irrespective of their social status, thereby developing very early *policlasista* memberships.

During their early years no major ideological differences separated the two parties; instead, party differences revolved around disputes involving programmatic, representational, and church-state conflicts.[21] The Conservative Party represented landowning and clerical interests; the Liberal Party reflected the interests of businessmen, lawyers, and artisans.[22] Political party programmes were rooted in doctrinaire principles that were in vogue then, derived largely from currents of European thought and adapted to the interests of sectors represented within the parties. Clearly, the Conservative Party defended ideas associated with the most traditional sectors of the society; its programme promoted a clerical orientation, religious education, and the creation of a strong state. In contrast, the Liberal Party talked about freedom of association, freedom of educational choice, political decentralisation, non-interference of the state and church in social organisation; these were principles that corresponded with the artisan societies, then the most modern sector of Colombian society. Several of these principles in dispute were questions of wide magnitude that have survived to the present. However, both traditional parties altered their programmes and the interests they represented in response to environmental change. This capacity for adaptation constitutes one of the prime characteristics of the traditional parties, at least until the post-National Front period. The structure of power in Colombian parties that accompanied their institutionalisation was anchored in regional and local political leaders, who joined together to form party coalitions at the national level that were imbued with extensive factionalism from the outset. As is typical of cadre organisations everywhere, the locus of party decision-making was concentrated in Congress, not in the extra- parliamentary structures of the traditional parties. National party leaders, drawn almost exclusively from the upper class during this phase, thus presided over rather undisciplined coalitions of regional party leaders whose interests did not always coincide with each other or with the national leadership.

The Transition to Mass-based Parties – 1930s to 1958

With the consolidation of the Conservative Party hegemony that emerged after the Thousand Days War at the turn of the century, the Liberal Party counteracted by incorporating socialist principles into its ideology and platforms and appealing to specific social strata, moving toward a mass-based model of party organisation. With the Conservative Party division in 1930, the Liberal Party won the presidency, and deepened its commitment to reforms oriented towards seeking the support of newly emerging groups, such as labour unions, the peasantry, and industrialists. Alfonso López Pumarejo's *Revolución en marcha* was oriented towards the enactment of governmental policies designed to represent those interests. The Conservative Party reacted forcefully to Liberal efforts to create a permanent electoral majority by fortifying its organisational strength through solidification of its traditional clienteles throughout the country, especially landowners and those strongly identified with the Catholic Church. The inter-party rivalry intensified when a split in the Liberal Party enabled a Conservative, Mariano Ospina Pérez, to win the presidency in 1946, along with the subsequent movement of the Liberal Party, under the leadership of Jorge Eliécer Gaitán, in more populist directions. The result was a civil war, known as *la violencia*, which was primarily an inter-party feud that resulted in the death of over 200,000 Colombians.

During this period the role of Colombian parties was considerably more significant than is presently the case with respect not only to *el país político* but also with respect to *el país nacional*. Party sectarianism was extremely pronounced, and Colombians were discriminated against (*tratos discriminatorios*) on the basis of their partisan affiliations. Both political parties became much stronger organisationally: (1) carnets were issued to party members; (2) party organisations served their members in a protective sense by helping them find jobs, in both the public and private sectors, distributing material favours, and defending their followers from partisans of the opposition; (3) party directorates were not only maintained between elections but were also hubs of political activity at all times; (4) ideological differences between the parties were quite pronounced and expressed in rather primitive terms, revolving around such abstractions as communism, the Church, centralisation-decentralisation, and the role of the state; and (5) both parties were eminently successful in mobilising their partisans, largely on the basis of traditional socialisation patterns and clientele relationships, as witnessed by *la violencia* and the electoral process. The traditional parties, in short, displayed a remarkable organisational vitality.

Interactions between political parties, interest groups, and the state were characterised by a much higher degree of integration during this period than is presently the case. Parties were more powerful than the state; the parties were not only responsible for staffing the three branches of government but they also constituted the locus of decision-making in the political system. Parties, likewise, tended to overshadow interest groups as autonomous actors. Interest group behaviour during this time reflected two salient features: (1) an embryonic stage of development; and (2) a close identification of groups that did exist with one of the two parties. The Church constituted a pillar of the Conservative Party, the military became politicised and reflected partisan favouritism, and labour unions identified with one of the parties. Peak associations worked through the parties as well to realise their political ambitions. Thus the mounting identification of the two parties with specific sectors of civil society, and favouritism towards those interests when in control of the government, contributed to the intense inter-party warfare that ultimately eluded the control of national party leaders, resulting in *la violencia* and the decision of leaders of both parties to support a military coup headed by General Gustavo Rojas Pinilla. When Rojas Pinilla belatedly sought to restructure the political system and continue his 'populistic authoritarian' rule, Liberal and Conservative leaders closed ranks and backed a military coup in 1957, seeking to restore the hegemony of *el país político*. That did not occur, however, for a new model of party behaviour and organisation emerged during the National Front.

The Cartel Model – 1958 to the *Constituyente* and Beyond

A very different model of political parties emerged during the National Front as a consequence of the coalition agreement itself and of the development process. One of the principal goals envisioned for the National Front was to *depoliticise* the society through curbing inter-party competition, parity in the distribution of bureaucratic and legislative posts, and alternation in the presidency. In this respect, the National Front was quite successful, in part because of the conscious cultivation of a *non-sectarian style* by major party leaders.[23] National Front presidents projected images of governmental rather than sectarian leadership.

This non-sectarian style contributed to the weakening of party organisations, for inter-party competition was throttled and the parties were not forced to engage in extensive mobilisation of the electorate, other than that associated with intra-party factionalism. In contrast to the previous stage of party development, party organisations at all levels of the hierarchy became more intermittent, less active, and oriented principally towards the electoral arena and not governmental policy making. This attenuation of party organisational activity is reflected clearly in national party directorates, which were formerly permanently functioning bodies that were continuously at the core of political activity (Laureano Gómez, for example, used the Conservative Party directorate as a forum for conducting his intensive partisan fights). The *jefes naturales* distanced themselves from the directorates, preferring instead to accept an embassy or orchestrate political strategy and tactics from their private studies or maybe from a congressional post. The lack of correspondence between the *jefes naturales* and the composition of the directorates clearly underscored the diminishing importance of party organisations as arenas of political decision-making. The

Alianza Nacional Popular, ANAPO, constituted an obvious exception, with Rojas Pinilla and his daughter María Eugenia dominating that party organisation.

The National Front coalition envisioned a depoliticised society emerging not only within *el país político* but also within the *país nacional*, largely through bipartisan support for developmental policies and the marginalisation of political parties from the policy-making process. In this respect as well, the National Front enjoyed considerable success. The political and governmental arenas became increasingly distinct, in terms of both recruitment channels and behavioural patterns.[24] Political parties no longer maintained extensive lists of supporters from which government bureaucrats were appointed, particularly at the upper levels. The *país político* became preoccupied almost exclusively with the electoral process at the national level and departmental politics. Congress remained the core of the political arena, but the institution became more and more isolated from the policy process, in large part because of the 1968 constitutional reforms, which transferred budgetary powers from Congress to the president, in exchange for the institution-alisation of the *auxilios parlamentarios*, or funds allocated to each congressperson with virtually no strings attached. This was a mutually beneficial arrangement, for the president increased his control over state expenditures and legislators gained permanent access to resources necessary to maintain their electoral fiefdoms.[25] The distance between the *país político* and the *país nacional* narrowed during presidential elections, but they moved into distinct orbits thereafter, leaving the president with the increasingly difficult task of governing.

During the National Front the role of the state was fortified considerably as a consequence of the developmental policies pursued by coalition governments. As the number and importance of autonomous decentralised institutes multiplied, the line ministries became less important in the policy process, even though the latter remained most salient for politicians jockeying for positions in future elections. The expansive state was accompanied by mounting reliance upon *técnicos* to manage the development process, a tendency reinforced by the increasing dependence of the state upon financial assistance from international agencies, which emphasised a depoliticised development process. Technocratic government became institutionalised by the end of Carlos Lleras's administration (1966–70). Another ramification of this depoliticised model consisted of the mounting importance of interest groups in the political process; they generally detoured around political parties and Congress, preferring instead to develop their own forms of interaction with the executive branch of government.

In summary, the mass-based model of Colombian parties that was solidifying during the post-1930 period was undermined, in large part purposefully, during the military and the National Front governments, and the cadre model reasserted itself. However, some new wrinkles emerged as the state-centred model of economic development became institutionalised and the parties gravitated increasingly towards a reliance upon state resources, especially clientelism and *auxilios parlamentarios,* to maintain their electoral fiefdoms. Despite the marginalisation of the parties in the policy-making process, the distance between the traditional parties and the state narrowed in terms of public perceptions; the parties became identified with the state, as postulated in the cartel model.

The Emergence of the 'Catch-all' Party

Although restrictions placed upon inter-party competition at the national level were removed for the 1974 elections, the basic contours of the National Front remained with respect to sharing of governmental offices, as dictated by Article 120 of the Constitution, which guaranteed that the party coming second in the election would receive a proportional share of bureaucratic posts. Consequently, each Colombian president, with the exception of Virgilio Barco (1986–90), formed coalition governments, thereby perpetuating the cartel model that emerged during the National Front. State subsidies to the parties continued in the form of *auxilios parlamentarios*, distribution of bureaucratic posts, and mounting corruption in government.[26]

The two traditional parties continued their electoral hegemony during this period, as reflected in the electoral returns for the *Cámara* shown in Table 1. Excluding the 1991 and 1994 elections, the two-party proportion of the vote averaged 93 per cent during the National Front period and thereafter (1958 to 1990), with their percentage falling to 90.9 between 1974 and 1990. Despite the electoral domination and sharing of governmental posts, incentives did exist for restructuring parties for reasons associated with inter-party competition.

Table 1. Electoral Returns for the Cámara (1958–94)*

	Liberal %	Conservative %	Other %	Total Votes	Abstention %
1958	57.7	42.1	—	3,693,939	31
1960	58.1	41.7	—	2,542,651	42
1962	54.5	41.7	3.7+	3,090,203	42
1964	50.5	35.5	13.7+	2,261,190	63
1966	52.1	29.8	17.8+	2,939,222	56
1968	49.9	33.7	16.1+	2.496,455	63
1970	37.0	27.2	35.5+	3,980,201	48
1974	55.6	32.0	9.5+	5,100,099	43
1978	55.1	39.4	—	4,180,121	63
1982	56.3	40.3	—	5,584,037	59
1986	47.6	37.0	6.6+	6,912,341	56
1990	59.0	32.1	—	7,631,694	45
1991	44.2	22.3#	8.8+	5,486,636	65
1994	47.0	23.2#	29.8+	5,576,174	67

* All the electoral data are taken from the 1990, 1991, and 1994 publications of the
Registraduría Nacional del Estado Civil.
+ From 1964 through 1974, this vote is for ANAPO, which used both traditional party
labels through the 1970 elections. For the 1986 elections, this vote is for the New Liberal
Party, headed by Luis Carlos Galán. To be consistent with previous years, this vote probably
should be added to that of the Liberal Party, particularly since the New Liberals joined the
Liberal Party in 1989. For the 1991 elections, this vote is for AD-M-19. The 1994 vote in
the other category consists of all those votes not cast for either major party, 5.8% for those
classified as 'others', 2.8% for AD-M-19, 0.8% for coalitions, 0.7% for Unión Patriótica,
and 19.7% for 19 distinct minor parties on the ballot.
The Conservative vote consists of four factions, the Social Conservatives, the National
Salvation Party, the National Conservative Movement, and Independent Conservatives.

Since the 1930s, the Liberal Party has dominated Colombian elections, averaging 52 per cent of the *Cámara* vote between 1958 and
1994, in comparison to 33.6 per cent for the Conservative Party during
the same period (including ANAPO's Conservative votes through
1970). If relevant ANAPO and New Liberal votes are tallied with their
respective parties, the Liberal Party registered an absolute majority of
the votes cast between 1958 and 1990. The Liberals' majority status
also extended to the presidential arena as well (even with Betancur's
victory in 1982, the combined Liberal vote for Alfonso López
Michelsen and Luis Carlos Galán exceeded 50 per cent).

Thus the Conservatives faced a classic dilemma of parties to the
right of centre, namely how to mobilise a sufficient number of voters
beyond their traditional core to win elections. Their response consisted
of moving in the direction of a 'catch-all' party, appealing to voters

across the political spectrum and social structure on the basis of their
policy preferences rather than their partisan identifications. Every Conservative Party presidential candidate since the resumption of
inter-party competition in 1974 has utilised, with varying degrees of intensity and success, this mobilisation strategy. Alvaro Gómez tried to
conduct a supra-party campaign in 1974, with little success given his
close identification with the Conservative Party, but Belisario Betancur
mastered the strategy in order to win the presidency in 1982. Andrés
Pastrana went so far as to disavow the Conservative Party label in his
almost successful bid for the presidency in 1994, running under the label of *Andrés Presidente*. In light of their majority electoral status, the
Liberal Party has moved much more slowly towards the 'catch-all'
model. Virgilio Barco won handily in 1986 by conducting an eminently
Liberal Party campaign. In the classic 'catch-all' model, parties move
towards the centre of the political spectrum, becoming less distinct in
terms of ideology and policy distinctiveness, rely increasingly upon the
mass media to mobilise voters, and appeal to the policy preferences
rather than social identities of the electorate in order to win elections.
'Elections are properly choices between teams of leaders rather than
contests among closed social groupings or fixed ideologies.'[27]

> While there remain differences among parties with regard to their receptive-
> ness to inputs from differing groups, and with regard to the policies they are
> prepared to defend . . . most groups expect, and are expected, to be able to
> work co-operatively with any party that is in power.[28]

The emergence of the 'catch-all' party, especially among the Conservatives, has been facilitated by the recruitment patterns of the traditional
parties virtually from the outset that cut across the social structure
(each was based upon *policlasista* memberships) and were anchored in
one-party hegemonies at the municipal level.[29] Additionally, the diversification of civil society and the waning of traditional party
attachments during the period after 1958, facilitated electoral mobilisation on the basis of policy preferences rather than blind, inherited
partisan loyalties so characteristic of the pre-National Front period.
However, the choices presented to voters, both in terms of ideology and
policy, became increasingly constrained as the traditional parties maintained their electoral hegemony and gravitated towards the centre of the
political spectrum.

The Assault upon the Cartel Model – The *Constituyente* and Beyond

The narrowing of the boundaries between the parties and the state, along with the seeming resistance of traditional party leaders to change, prompted a vehement reaction from civil society, as manifested during the 1980s by the persistence of guerrilla opposition, the emergence of Luis Carlos Galán's *Nuevo Liberalismo,* and, ultimately, the convoking of the *Constituyente.* The pervasive violence associated with the guerrilla, drug cartels, paramilitary organisations, and common criminals further undermined the legitimacy of the political system and discredited the *clase política,* which seemingly was more interested in maintaining its clientelistic practices and electoral fiefdoms than in promoting policies that would increase political stability and socio-economic development. The popularity of Congress, the principal arena of *el país político,* plummeted when the second round of President Barco's constitutional reform was thwarted in December 1989. Within this context of mounting discontent with traditional politicians, a group of university students distributed a seventh ballot, *la séptima papeleta,* during the March 1990 elections, calling for the convocation of a constitutional convention. The electorate approved it overwhelmingly. Even though the Constitution permitted only one route to constitutional reform, through Congress, the Barco government decided to support the initiative and, through the use of extraordinary powers, authorised the National Electoral Council to count the ballots in the May 1990 presidential election of those favouring or opposing a Constituent Assembly. Eighty-nine per cent of the voters supported the initiative. In an historic decision rooted in an expansive interpretation of sovereignty and partisan politics, the Supreme Court upheld the constitutionality of the proposal. Subsequently, Colombians went to the polls in December 1990 to select delegates to the Constituent Assembly, which met continuously from February to July 1991. The new Constitution became the supreme law of the land on 4 July 1991.[30]

The composition of the *Asamblea Constituyente* deviated significantly from traditional party alignments in Colombian legislative arenas, thereby extending the space for political reform. This resulted from the manner of delegate selection (from a national constituency rather than by departments), an extremely low turnout (26 per cent participation rate),[31] significant opposition from *la clase política,* and the political opening associated with the incorporation of the M-19 guerrilla movement into the political system. The traditional parties (Liberal, Social Conservative, and Independent Conservative) commanded only 47.1 per cent of the Assembly votes, which exaggerated their influence because the Liberal bloc was by no means highly disciplined (the 25 Liberal members were elected on 20 separate lists). Consequently, because no single group was capable of setting the agenda or imposing its will, a tripartite leadership emerged – Horacio Serpa (Liberal), Navarro Wolff (AD-M-19), and Alvaro Gómez (*Salvación Nacional*). Thus, from the outset, the reformist, anti-traditional party orientation of the Assembly became apparent, spearheaded by the AD-M-19 delegates and other non-traditional representatives, often supported by the Gaviria government. One of the central thrusts of the crusade against the cartel model of Colombian parties revolved around efforts to undermine the clientelism, nepotism, and corruption rampant among the *clase política*, along with extending opportunities for new parties, social movements and groups to gain access to elected office.

With respect to Congress, the new Constitution dictated rules that abolished alternates (*suplentes*); eliminated *auxilios parlamentarios*; placed restrictions upon foreign travel; clamped down on absenteeism; declared ineligible for election those persons who held government office during the previous twelve months or have relatives holding public office; prohibited congresspersons from holding other jobs in both the public and private spheres (university professors were the only exception). Quite clearly, the new Constitution forcefully attacked the clientelistic bases of the political class, removing financial incentives traditionally at their disposal to maintain their electoral bases and enrich themselves at the public's expense.

In contrast to the 1886 Constitution, which invested sovereignty essentially and exclusively in the nation, the 1991 Constitution proclaimed that sovereignty emanated solely from the Colombian people. Consequently, the framers drafted a document designed to maximise opportunities for expression of the popular will that went well beyond the representational process. More specifically, the Constitution (Title IV, Chapter 1) created the bases of a participatory democracy with the following methods for the people to exercise their sovereignty at every level of government: the vote, plebiscites, referenda, popular consultations, open meetings (*cabildo abierto*), legislative initiative and recall.[32] Moreover, the new Constitution augments the means by which the people may amend or replace it – through Congress[33] or a constitutional convention, initiated either by Congress and subsequently approved by the voters or by popular initiative. Congress passed the enabling legislation, and the Constitutional Court declared most of it constitutional in April 1994.[34] The statute authorised the President of the Republic to create a fund to finance the implementation of the law.

If we assume that participatory democracy will become institutionalised, what are the likely consequences for political party behaviour? Quite frankly, the ramifications are likely to be minimal in the short term, with the greatest impact possibly emerging from an increased accountability of government officials to their constituencies and a reduction in the gap between voter preferences and public policy. This does not necessarily involve any dramatic restructuring of political parties, especially if the traditional parties retain their electoral hegemony. Any transformations of the parties or party system will likely be indirect and delayed, in part because the institutional arena of the political class, Congress, is not effectively plugged into the decision-making process, although Congress is becoming more assertive in policy-making. However, the implications of popular participation should not be minimised in terms of governmental decision-making, deepening the democratic political culture, and enhancing the efficacy of Colombian voters.

The reformist thrust of the Constitution was directed specifically at the political parties as well (Title IV, Chapter 2). All citizens were guaranteed the right to establish, organise and develop political parties and political movements, along with the right to affiliate or withdraw from them (Article 107). Social movements and 'significant' groups of citizens also were given the right to nominate candidates for public office. The National Electoral Council was empowered to extend *personería jurídica* to those parties and movements that presented valid petitions with at least 50,000 signatures, received that number of votes in the last election, or elected representatives to Congress. With the elimination of *auxilios*, the Constitution moved in a new direction in support of the cartel model of parties in three respects: (1) State financing of electoral campaigns of parties and movements with *personería jurídica*, as well as other parties, movements, and 'significant' groups whose candidates receive a specified proportion of the vote, as determined by law.[35] (2) The National Electoral Council was authorised to place a ceiling on campaign expenditures, both public and private, and parties were required to make their campaign contributions public. (3) Parties and movements recognised by the state were provided access to the state's communication media at all times. However, those seeking to impose internal democracy upon Colombian parties were frustrated because Article 108 specified that under no circumstances can the law establish any controls over the internal organisation of parties or political movements, or require party membership to participate in elections. The implementing legislation for Title IV, Chapter 2, the Basic Statute of

Parties and Political Movements, was passed by the *Cámara* in 1992 and the Senate in 1993. In a very detailed, theoretical discussion of the role of political parties and movements, along with their relationship to the state, the Constitutional Court issued its decision on the constitutionality of the Basic Statute on 4 March 1994, nullifying portions of the legislation.[36] Incorporating the Court's revisions, the Basic Statute was promulgated as Law 180 (23 March 1994).[37] The legislation provided a detailed and expansive framework regulating the relationship between parties and the state, extending well beyond the Constitution in several respects.

In most instances, the Court upheld the constitutional stipulation that the state should not interfere in the internal affairs of parties and movements. The internal organisation and functioning of parties and movements were to be governed by their own statutes,[38] and citizens were extended the right to challenge any party decision believed not to be in accordance with party statutes. The Court expunged the word democratic from the programmes that parties and movements present to the National Electoral Council for recognition because it undermines pluralism. However, the Court did uphold the provision that requires parties and movements *democratically* to debate and approve their proposals but *only* for those involving state funding.[39] In addition, the Basic Statute dictates that all parties and movements establish Councils for Ethical Control of their membership, an annual internal audit of its finances, and an external audit of state funds allocated to them. The Basic Statute extended beyond the Constitution in the sense that it not only provided for state funding of campaigns but *also* for parties and movements with *personería jurídica* or with representation in Congress. With respect to financial support of parties and movements, monies are distributed yearly from a fund, indexed for inflation, based upon the contribution of $150 pesos for each registered voter, not to fall below $2,400 million pesos. Congress stipulated that these funds would be distributed as follows: (1) 10 per cent equally between all parties and movements; (2) 50 per cent between parties and movements in proportion to the number of seats in the last election for Congress; (3) 10 per cent for organisations within parties (youth groups, women's organisations, labour unions); and (4) 30 per cent for parties and movements in the realisation of their goals. The Court nullified the 10 per cent allocation for internal organisations, along with the specified activities listed under the fourth category, among them the provision that at least 50 per cent of these funds listed be allocated to regional and local organisations. Much to the chagrin of the locally oriented *clase política*, the Court declared unconstitutional the provision (Article 12, Paragraph 1) which stated that at least 70 per cent of the funds in the first three allocations be assigned to regional and local organisations.

Article 13 outlines the amount and destination of public funds for electoral campaigns from the national to the local level. Presidential candidates are to receive $400 pesos per vote during the first round, $200 for the second; congressional candidates $400; mayoral and council candidates $150; and gubernatorial and deputy candidates $250. Once again, these funds are indexed for inflation. In anticipation of state funding, candidates are given access to lines of credit from banks three months before the election. Significantly, candidates can receive state subsidies only through their respective parties or movements, excepting independent candidates or those belonging to organisations without *personería jurídica*. In addition, the National Electoral Council is authorised to limit and control private contributions to political campaigns as well.

Two other provisions of the Basic Statute likewise will affect Colombian parties. First, the National Electoral Council was authorised to conduct primary elections for parties and movements, *consultas internas*, in presidential, gubernatorial, and mayoral elections. The Constitutional Court ruled that the outcomes of these elections would be binding upon the parties, unless otherwise specified in the petition requesting such an election.[40] Second, parties and movements with *personería jurídica* were allotted free access to state controlled media at all times to promote their philosophies and programmes, and immediately prior to elections to sell their candidates, allotted in proportion to their representation in the *Cámara*. Moreover, guidelines were established to prevent discrimination against candidates and parties in terms of their access to privately controlled media.

The Constituent Assembly also altered the rules for allocating seats in Congress, which may have an impact on the behaviour and success of political parties and movements. It approved the 1985 census thereby forcing Congress to reapportion itself, changed the representational bases for both the Senate and the House, dissolved the old Congress, and scheduled new congressional elections for October 1991. Instead of using departments as the principal electoral unit, a fixed number of senators (100 plus two elected from indigenous communities) were to be elected on a nation-wide basis, thereby undercutting the rural orientation favouring the traditional parties that formerly prevailed in the Senate. However, the creation of nine new departments in outlying areas and the separation of Santafé de Bogotá from Cundinamarca, seriously jeopardised the 'one-person one-vote' principle and the representation of urban voters in the *Cámara*.

The new rules for allocating seats in the *Cámara* clearly favour the traditional parties. First, the creation of ten new electoral districts that, with the exception of Bogotá, are sparsely populated, along with the continued over-representation of the smaller departments, enhances the electoral chances of the traditional parties. Thus 89 per cent of the legislators elected to the *Cámara* in 1991 from the nine new departments were affiliated with one of the traditional parties, or a faction thereof. Second, the traditional party hegemony tends to be weaker in the more urban departments, precisely those electoral districts that are under-represented. It is the urban districts that are most likely to present non-traditional candidates, which diminishes their electoral chances because of the representational distortions in these departments. In summary, apportionment of seats in the lower house suggests that the traditional parties manipulated the electoral rules to maximise their competitiveness, indicating that most members of the Constituent Assembly were not as vehemently devoted to undermining the traditional parties as their rhetoric might have indicated.

However, loading the dice in favour of the traditional political class in the *Cámara* supposedly was counterbalanced by the electoral rules for the Senate, which was to be elected from a national circumscription. This type of election offers greater opportunities for non-traditional groups to elect candidates, though it by no means eliminates the capacity of traditional parties to formulate regional lists that are capable of winning. Nonetheless, new parties and movements have a better chance of winning seats in the Senate than in the *Cámara*, as a result of the relatively low threshold for electing a senator. Thus in the 1991 Senate election, the quotient for obtaining a seat was 26,868 votes, and a Liberal won a post with a residual of 21,064 (the last seat assigned in 1994 required 20,702 votes). Considering that most elected senators head their respective lists, this enhances the electoral probabilities of non-traditional groups.

How have the political reforms affected political parties at the polls, as reflected in the 1991 and 1994 congressional elections? Have the traditional parties maintained their electoral domination? Are new parties and movements gaining more access to governmental posts? Before seeking answers to these questions, two factors should be underscored. First, as revealed in Table 1 (see page 57), the abstention rates vary dramatically, increasing notably for the 1991 and 1994 congressional elections. Second, the National Electoral Council printed the ballots for the 1991 elections for the first time, which may explain the dramatic surge in the number of blank and null ballots – 12.7 and 8.6 per cent respectively for 1991 and 1994.

Tables 2 and 3 (below) show the percentage of the vote that parties registered in the *Cámara* and Senate elections, along with the distribution of seats by party in the legislature. Although the Liberal vote declined in both houses between 1990 and 1994, it should be pointed out that the Liberals received their highest proportion of the vote in 1990 since the beginning of the National Front. In short, the Liberal Party has not suffered immensely at the polls. The Conservative Party vote has declined as well, even aggregating the vote of the various factions, falling 8 per cent in the *Cámara* and 10 per cent in the Senate between 1990 and 1994. The two-party hegemony has declined to around 76 per cent in both houses in the two most recent elections, in comparison to around 93 per cent between 1958 and 1990. Note the dramatic increase in the vote for other parties in both houses since 1990.

Table 2. Distribution of the Vote and Seats for the Cámara (1990–94)*

	Liberal		Conservative+		Other	
	%Vote	*%Seats*	*%Vote*	*%Seats*	*%Vote*	*%Seats*
1990	59	60	33	33	8	8
1991	51	54	26	26	24	20
1994	51	56	25	34	24	11

* *The percentage of the partisan vote is calculated by excluding the blank and null votes, and the seat percentage excludes those for black communities.*
+ *The Conservative vote and seats include the National Conservative Movement, National Salvation, and Independent Conservative factions.*

Table 3. Distribution of the Vote and Seats for the Senate (1990-94)*

	Liberal		Conservative+		Other	
	%Vote	*%Seats*	*%Vote*	*%Seats*	*%Vote*	*%Seats*
1990	59	58	33	34	8	8
1991	51	56	25	22	23	22
1994	52	56	23	25	26	19

* *The percentage of the partisan vote is calculated by excluding the blank and null votes, and the seat percentage excludes the two for indigenous communities.*
+ *The Conservative vote and seats include the National Conservative Movement, the New Democratic Force, National Salvation, Conservative Renovation, and Independent Conservatives.*

Because the formula for translating votes into seats favours the traditional parties, the decline in the allocation of seats to them was not as pronounced as the decrease in their votes, as revealed in Tables 2 and 3. The Liberal Party has retained its majority in both houses, while the Conservatives have increased their percentage of seats in the *Cámara* while it has declined in the Senate. Note the dramatic increase in 'other' seats for the 1991 Congress, and the notable decline in 1994, especially in the lower house. Clearly, the traditional politicians are experts in utilising the electoral laws to their advantage.

Finally, although I shall not develop this theme here, the impact of the administrative, fiscal and political reforms initiated during the Betancur government and consolidated in the new constitution will significantly affect political party behaviour.[41] Conceptualised at the outset as a means of restructuring Colombian democracy from the bottom up, the evidence to date suggests movement in that direction. Participation rates in mayoral contests since 1988 have exceeded those of other elections, civic and independent candidates have made inroads into the traditional party vote, and mayors enjoy considerably more independence than before from national and departmental leaders. Reforms at the departmental level are moving more slowly, but with the popular election of governors in 1992, departmental politics may likewise become more pluralistic and participatory. Nonetheless, as the chapters in this volume by Gustavo Bell and Jesús Duarte suggest, realisation of the full potential of decentralisation for promoting governmental efficiency will be a lengthy process by reason of the pervasiveness of clientelism in departmental and municipal politics.[42]

The traditional parties have been forced to meet increasing competition from civic and independent candidates at the local level, forcing them to re-evaluate their electoral strategies. The bulk of elected civic candidates were generally from smaller and medium-sized cities. In the 1994 elections thirteen civic and coalition candidates were elected mayors in large cities (seven in 1992). Metropolitan mayors retained their traditional party labels until 1992 when a civic candidate, Padre Bernardo Hoyos, won the mayoral race in Barranquilla. His successor in 1994, Edgard George, likewise was a civic candidate, and the new Cali mayor ran on a coalition ticket, although listed as a Liberal on the ballot. But perhaps the most phenomenal mayoral election in 1994 occurred in Bogotá, where another civic candidate, Antanas Mockus, handsomely defeated, with 64 per cent of the vote, the Liberal Party nominee. As a consequence of the electoral successes of civic and independent candidates at the local level, it is not inconceivable that a civic candidate may become competitive in presidential contests, perhaps as early as 1998.

Conclusions

The Colombian political system, along with its political parties, is currently experiencing the pains of transition from a representative to a more participatory democracy. From their inception, Colombia's traditional parties have adapted to their changing environments, developing different structures to win elections. Beginning with caucus-cadre organisations in the nineteenth century, the parties moved towards the mass-based model in the 1930s that was aborted during the National Front. The cadre model reasserted itself in conjunction with the emergence of a cartel model based upon inter-party competition and state funding through clientelism and corruption. Restoration of inter-party competition in 1974 forced the Conservative Party to take the initiative in altering its electoral strategies to overcome the Liberal majority, giving rise to the 'catch-all' model in which appeals were directed to voters on the basis of their policy preferences rather than the blind sectarianism that permeated society before the National Front. Thus, a hybrid model emerged in the post-1974 period consisting of a combination of the cadre, 'catch-all', and cartel models. But mounting popular discontent with the *clase política* and its close identification with the state prompted a revolt against this hybrid model of Colombian parties that culminated with the promulgation of the 1991 Constitution.

What are the probable consequences of the political reforms upon Colombian parties? Will the parties and the party system undergo a dramatic transformation? Although the brief time elapsed since the adoption of the 1991 Constitution and subsequent implementing legislation caution against generalisation, the evidence is mounting that the parties are adapting to their new environments in several respects. First, the cartel model was preserved in terms of state support not only for political campaigns but for party organisations as well. The Constitutional Court nullified the efforts of the *clase política* to make these subsidies the functional equivalent of the outlawed *auxilios parlamentarios* when it ruled that the state cannot allocate these funds specifically to regional and local party organisations, leaving that decision to national party directorates. Quite clearly, state subsidies for parties and movements, including free access to the state controlled media, will have the effect of reinforcing those groups represented in Congress.

Perhaps an even more important ramification of the new constitution and the Basic Statute for political parties revolves around the possibilities of restructuring political party organisations, making them more accountable, participatory and transparent. *Consultas internas*, already adopted by the Liberal Party and currently under discussion in the Conservative Party, open the process of selecting candidates more fully to party members. Assignation of state subsidies to national party directorates, rather than to individual candidates or sub-national party organisations, enhances the prospects for centralising party decision-making, possibly leading to increased control over the nomination process, tighter party discipline, and a decrease in factionalism. State control of private contributions to parties and movements, along with internal auditing and publication of party and campaign finances, should contribute to increased transparency of parties' activities. Additionally, the two major parties have complied with the Basic Statute in terms of establishing Ethical Councils designed to instil greater public morality among their members (the Liberal Party has already sanctioned several of its adherents). Finally, the various methods for direct participation in government decision-making, especially the *voto programático* and recall, should enhance the accountability of political parties. For the above reasons, as well as the increasing number of civic movements and independent candidates, Colombian political parties will move away from the closed leadership structures of the cadre variety and their heavy reliance upon clientelism towards more open, participatory organisations that may well involve more extensive and differentiated party structures than was formerly the case. Colombia's traditional parties have always adapted to changing environments in order to realise their principal goal, namely winning control of government. This does not imply that the traditional parties will not suffer defeats at the polls or make the transition smoothly to a participatory democracy, but considering their historical record, I am hesitant to pronounce their demise.

Notes

*.   For their assistance in providing materials for this chapter, I want to thank the Political Science Department of Los Andes University, Fernando Cepeda, and Stephen Taylor.

1.   Leal Buitrago and Dávila (1990), p. 18.

2.   See Hartlyn (1988) for an analysis of the problems involved in moving beyond

the consociational scheme in Colombia. The standard reference work that links traditional party politicians with the lack of political reform is Leal Buitrago (1984).

3. For an overview of the political reforms in the post-National Front period, see Santamaría and Silva (1984), and Orjuela (1992), pp. 27–84.
4. Lipset and Rokkan (1967).
5. Weber (1964), p. 693.
6. Panebianco (1988), pp. xii–xiii.
7. For an extensive discussion of contemporary violence in Colombian society, see Alvaro Tirado Mejía's chapter in this volume (Chapter 5).
8. See Cepeda's chapter in this volume regarding the efforts to implement the new constitution (Chapter 3).
9. Katz and Mair (1995), pp. 5–28.
10. Neuman (1956), p. 1.
11. See, among others, Lawson and Merkl (1988).
12. Katz and Mair (1995), pp. 5–6.
13. *Ibid.*
14. After gaining access to power, the mass-based parties also moved in the direction of 'catch-all' parties as a result of their becoming a part of the political establishment and the changing nature of the electorate, in the sense that they were no longer able to win elections solely on the basis of appealing to the groups and social strata that they represented originally.
15. Katz and Mair (1995), p. 14.
16. For an excellent discussion, both theoretical and empirical, of executive-legislative relations, see Shugart and Carey (1992).
17. Latorre (1974), pp. 251–71.
18. *Ibid.*, p. 276.
19. Katz and Mair (1995), p. 9.
20. *Ibid.*, p. 9
21. For an analysis of the development of Chilean parties during their early years, in which church-state relations figured prominently, see Scully (1992).
22. With respect to the formation of Colombian parties, see, among others, Molina (1970), Colmenares (1968), Tirado Mejía (1979), Safford (1977), Delpar (1981), Deas (1973), pp. 118–40, and González (1982).
23. The roots of this non-partisan approach can be traced to the Rojas Pinilla government. Although Liberal and Conservative party leaders participated in his government, party organisations as such were displaced, as *patria* took precedence over *partidos*. The arena of the traditional parties, Congress, was dissolved and replaced by a constituent assembly.
24. See Hoskin (1980), pp. 105–30.
25. See Hoskin et al. (1974) and Shugart (1992).
26. For a superb discussion of administrative corruption in Colombia, see Cepeda Ulloa (1994a).
27. Katz and Mair (1995), p. 14.
28. *Ibid.*, p. 13.

29. Pinzón (1989).
30. See Dugas (1993), Hoskin (1994), and Dugas (1994).
31. For a discussion of the reasons for the high abstention rate, see Dugas et al. (1991), pp. 207–9.
32. For a more detailed analysis of the participatory thrust of the new constitution, along with the Constitutional Court's decisions supportive of participatory democracy, see Cepeda in this volume (Chapter 3).
33. Constitutional amendments by Congress can be initiated by the government, Congress, departmental assemblies, municipal councils, or 5% of those registered to vote.
34. For the statute and court decision, see Cepeda Ulloa (1994b).
35. State financing of political campaigns began with the 1990 presidential elections, but its legal basis stemmed from a presidential decree.
36. Corte Constitucional, 'Sentencia No 089, REF: Expediente P.E.-004', Magistrado Ponente: Eduardo Cifuentes Muñoz (Bogotá, 2 Mar. 1994).
37. Ley 130 del 23 de Marzo de 1994, 'Por la cual se dicta el Estatuto Básico de los partidos y movimientos políticos', Consejo Nacional Electoral (Santafé de Bogotá, Mar. 1994).
38. Basic Statute, Article 7.
39. *Ibid.*, Article 12, Paragraph 3.
40. Corte Constitucional, p. 55.
41. For more extensive analyses of decentralisation in Colombia, see Gaitán and Moreno (1992); Dugas et al. (1992); and Hoskin (1995).
42. G. Bell, 'The Decentralised State: An Administrative or Political Challenge?'; and J. Duarte, 'State Weakness and Clientelism in Colombian Education'; Chapters 4 and 6 in this volume.

CHAPTER 3

DEMOCRACY, STATE AND SOCIETY IN THE 1991 CONSTITUTION: THE ROLE OF THE CONSTITUTIONAL COURT

Manuel José Cepeda

If men were angels, no government would be necessary.
If angels were to govern men, neither external nor
internal controls would be necessary.

James Madison, *The Federalist Papers*

Since July 1991, Colombians have been living under a new Constitution adopted by a popularly convened and elected Constituent Assembly. The 1886 Constitution, one of the oldest in Latin America at that time, was repealed after a process of intense public deliberation – the most open, pluralistic and democratic in Colombia's history. Even active guerrilla groups were invited to participate as an incentive to their demobilisation.

The purpose of this chapter is to describe both the conception of participatory democracy embodied in the Constitution and its interpretation by the Constitutional Court in Colombia. The idea of strengthening participatory democracy was the only popular mandate given to the delegates to the Constituent Assembly when it was called by popular vote on 27 May 1990. This idea led to a change in the concepts of state and society; it also led to a change in the nature of their relationship.[1]

Focusing on the Constitutional Court's role in the development of the Constitution is particularly relevant. Only six years have passed since its adoption, and it is obvious that what the Constitution says is still closer to national purpose than national reality. It is the Court's natural role to implement the Constitution. In contrast, Congress may be somewhat reluctant to go as far as the Court in the development of constitutional laws which were not of their own making. In fact to some extent the reforms were intended to curtail the privileges of 'the traditional political class' – in other words, congressmen. Furthermore, as often happens after an ambitious reform, the years following the initial enthusiasm are marked by disappointment among those who expected quicker results, and by the concerted efforts of the 'losers' to stop or reverse the changes. Therefore, the Constitutional Court has become the key player in the transition from the old legal order to the new constitutional system.

Some caveats about the scope of this descriptive chapter are in order. It does not attempt to make an evaluation of the functioning of the Constitution nor does it pretend to justify or criticise constitutional ideas and institutions. It only presents an overall picture of three years of Constitutional Court decisions with the hope that it will contribute to put key underestimated elements into the debate about the worth of all these constitutional efforts. Finally, no space is given to the description of the process that led to the creation of the Constituent Assembly. Suffice it to say that from President Barco's proposal of holding a plebiscite in January 1988 to the proclamation of the Constitution on 4 July 1991, the country experienced a very complex process, characterised by a combination of imagination and pragmatism. President Gaviria's leadership translated an abstract general idea[2] into the seventy-two-members flesh and blood Assembly, and a mood of reconciliation and modernisation into the first Colombian Constitution enacted by consensus of all political forces, four former guerrilla groups and representatives of social groups, notably of indigenous peoples.

Participatory Democracy and the Constitutional Court

The new Constitution introduced radical changes to political life in Colombia. The main objective was to promote participatory democracy, that is, the transfer of powers to the citizens to enable them to be directly and effectively involved in those fundamental decisions in which they have an interest, both in the public and the private spheres. The other main aim was to strengthen the judicial power. In the end, the whole Constitution was changed.

The idea of participatory democracy was promoted with the argument that traditional representative democracy was insufficient to sustain the legitimacy of the country's institutions, and that citizens wanted to be more involved in the decision-making process but lacked the necessary channels to present their views effectively. For the middle class, this idea of participatory democracy interpreted their distrust of congressmen and political bosses, and their rejection of privilege and corruption. The process that led to the creation of the Constituent Assembly was seen both as an example of the virtues of participatory democracy and of its practical viability. The entire Constitution is best understood as an instrument to promote this principal idea. Let me review the major changes.

First, every conceivable institution of direct democracy was introduced. They may operate at the local or regional level, but also at the national level. A referendum could be used to veto legislation already adopted or to approve bills that have been neglected by the representatives of the people. It can also be applied to constitutional amendments. The President, with the advice and consent of the Senate, may call national advisory referendums on any issue. The recall of popularly elected mayors and governors is defined as a political right. Any citizen can demand the removal of congressmen by the Council of State, a national judicial body, on the grounds that they have violated specific prohibitions stated in the Constitution.

Second, several constitutional clauses provide for the democratisation of political parties, labour unions, professional colleges, universities, public administration and other power holders. Previously they did not have to respond to democratic principles of participation and accountability.

Third, in order to transfer power to each individual, a generous Bill of Rights was adopted. It includes civil, political, social, economic, cultural and collective rights. Special emphasis was given to ecological issues and the right to a healthy environment. New institutions, like the Ombudsman (*Defensor del Pueblo*), and the Constitutional Court, were created to assure the effectiveness of these rights. Expedient and special procedures to protect rights were also created – *acción de tutela*[3] is the most important one. The state of siege, the greatest symbol of human rights restrictions, was abolished, although temporary emergency powers may be used. Congress may regulate the use of those powers by the Executive – accountable to both Houses. All emergency decrees must be automatically reviewed by the Constitutional Court through a fast-track procedure.

Fourth, to promote pluralism, assure electoral fairness and provide equal political resources to the power contenders, several reforms were introduced, including direct popular election of governors, a special constituency for ethnic minorities, and free access to television for candidates and parties.

Obviously, Colombia is still far from being a participatory democracy. The electoral reforms are just beginning to show their first results.

Up to April 1994, no direct democracy instrument had been applied, although several party and social organisation leaders, as well as the President himself, have proposed issues to be submitted to the people on several occasions. Three popular initiatives at the national level had been introduced by the citizens to Congress. One of them became law (the anti-kidnapping statute). Nonetheless, the statutory law enacting direct democratic institutions is already in force. Some previous consultation of social organisations before the adoption of administrative regulations and during the preparation of key bills has already taken place. *Acción de tutela* has been massively used by all kinds of citizens, with an impetus that not even the more optimistic expected. It has complemented the traditional *acción popular*, which allows citizens to challenge any law. They have both placed the Constitutional Court in the front line of the development and implementation of the Constitution.

An overview of the Constitutional Court decisions leads to the conclusion that the idea of participatory democracy has inspired all the main judicial opinions, not only implicitly but also explicitly. However, the judicial implementation has gone much further. The Court has strictly reviewed any attempt by the legislator to curtail citizens' participation. The most important decision made by the Court in this respect refers to the statutory law adopted by Congress to enact the different instrument of participatory democracy: popular initiatives, referendum, plebiscite, recall, *consulta popular* and *cabildo abierto*. The Court upheld the law, but ruled out the articles which had previously created judicial control of the use of those institutions, including control of the popular initiative by the Council of State. Although the Council of State review would only have had mainly advisory implications for the groups which promoted the initiative, the Court saw it as a deterrent for the participation of citizens. It is also worth underlining that the Court refused to enlarge its own review powers.

The Court also placed a barrier to the continuation of old practices which would diminish the impact of direct democracy institutions. It ruled out the possibility of appointing a governor or a mayor to replace the recalled one, as the statute upheld, if less than one year of the three-year mandate remained. The Court said that a new election should be held after any successful recall. The winning candidate should then govern for a whole three-year term. The only aspect of the Court's decision limiting the instruments of direct democracy was the unconstitutionality of plebiscites delegating sovereignty to supranational organisations. Plebiscites, according to the Court, can only be used by the President to seek a popular pronouncement concerning its own already existing powers. Other conditions for the application of popular initiatives and recall were upheld. They did not represent an obstacle to the exercise of the new political participation rights since they only channel and set minimum procedures on them.[4]

In 1994, the Court also reviewed another statutory law developing one of the Constitution's innovations, *voto programático* (programme voting). Of the four points declared unconstitutional, only one is substantial. The Court did not allow the statute to specify the criteria that each candidate had to follow to elaborate his/her programme, even though they were quite general. In the Court's view this was against pluralism, which had to be interpreted widely in a participatory democracy.[5]

In a blunt attempt by Congress to restrict the practical application of the new participatory democracy institutions, a law created new conditions for the use of citizen actions requesting the withdrawal of specific congressional mandates *(pérdida de investidura)* to the Council of State. According to the law ruled out by the Court,[6] such actions could only be adopted if there was a previous criminal sentence condemning a congressman of stealing public money or abusing his/her influence. If the actions were backed by the other reasons stated in the Constitution, that would not constitute a crime; a previous congressional authorisation was needed. The obvious purpose of these conditions was to create an almost insurmountable barrier for citizens to have direct access to the Council of State. Had these conditions survived, it would have been almost impossible to declare the loss of any congressional mandates, as has already been done in about fifteen cases.

In another context, the Court has also cleared ways of participation to young student associations. A new law setting up the general framework of the education system created national, departmental and municipal advisory bodies integrated by both public officials and private representatives of organisations and associations linked to education. Representation from students' associations, however, was originally excluded. The Court upheld the statute, but on the condition that these advisory bodies opened their doors to student organisations interested in presenting their views in special sessions.[7]

Of course there is no unanimity on the meaning of participatory democracy. The Constitutional Court has been flexible in allowing different perspectives to influence the development of the Constitution. But it has been very careful to stop corporatist misunderstandings. The

Court explicitly said that the state cannot 'exert control over the diverse orders of social life', nor can private powers 'assume state management through diffused corporatist networks'.[8] In another case, the Court declared the National Council of Bacteriologists to be unconstitutional. This body, which included public and private representatives, had powers to set professional standards and criteria for academic programmes. It also had the power of creating entry barriers for non-bacteriologists in the administration of laboratories, the development of biotechnological research and other activities which could be well performed by other scientists as well.[9] Since several professionals have organised themselves in similar corporate bodies approved by law, the full implications of this case are yet to be appreciated.

Two other aspects of participatory democracy have received wide attention by the Court. Although political parties and judicial actions to enforce constitutional rights are typical of representative democracy, the Court has been very active in reinterpreting their functioning in the light of participatory democracy in Colombia. The first, the writ of protection for human rights known as *tutela,* is the best example. The Court has interpreted *tutela* as an instrument of resistance against arbitrariness. It has opened it specially to groups and individuals who do not usually have a voice or a representative in the political arena, and therefore have to use the judicial forum to assert their interests. Legal conditions to exercise *tutelas*, the number and kinds of rights enforceable, and the formalities in the judicial procedure have been interpreted widely and generously in favour of such silent majorities. Now they speak with a strong voice in what can be called a strategic alliance of the powerless with the judges to protect fundamental constitutional rights. Between November 1991 and April 1994 more than 60,000 *tutelas* have been decided all over the country.[10]

The second typical institution of representative democracy interpreted by the Court from the perspective of participatory democracy is that of political parties. On three different occasions, the Court reviewed the law that set up the framework for the institutionalisation of political parties. In 1993, the Court repealed an article of the 1985 statute which, arguably to avoid manipulation, prohibited the publication of opinion polls one month before election day; according to the Court, this restriction contradicted a principle of trust in the people, considered crucial in a participatory democracy.[11] The Court, nevertheless, allowed the prohibition to stand on election day. It used a participatory democracy argument rhetorically summarised by saying that on such an occasion, 'all voices should be silenced because it is time for the people to speak'.[12]

The key decision about political parties is the judicial review of the statutory law which, in 54 articles, regulated aspects such as registration of parties, presentation and selection of candidates, public and private finance, disclosure of accounts of parties and campaigns, propaganda and opinion polls, special rights for opposition parties to access mass media, party members' ethics and enforcement by the National Electoral Council.[13] The Court upheld the right of social organisations to present independent candidates, it outlined ceilings on contribution and spending, and guaranteed access to television for minor and opposition parties as well as other rules designed to open the political process. On the other hand, it held unconstitutional several articles which in the Court's view were against pluralism. It even went to the brink of banning the exclusive use of colours by the parties which had registered them, an audacious decision in a country where red and blue have, for more than a century, been associated with the Liberal and Conservative parties.[14] From the same perspective the Court repealed a prohibition on negative campaigning, but it opened the way for a future less generic ban and for case-specific prohibitions.[15] I will not go into other details of this decision, but let me highlight a critical aspect of it. The law established criteria for the distribution of public party funds – funds directed to stimulate participation of civil organisations within the parties, and promote programmatic activities and party organisation at the regional and local levels. The statute assigned different percentages of the available resources to each party according to its achievement of those ends. According to the Court these quotas hindered the process of democratic approval of the overall budget by party members.[16]

Thus with one exception – the anti-kidnapping popular initiative[17] – it is reasonable to conclude that participatory democracy institutions have been advanced by the Court. Now it is up to the various social forces to give them life. Since Congress has not approved the necessary law to enact the constitutional clause created to stimulate the organisation of civil society,[18] the Court has also tried to interpret other parts of the Constitution in a way favourable to the awakening of individual and group initiatives. This is the subject of the following section.

The Constitutional Court and Civil Society

The Constitution does not use the expression civil society, although the expression was often heard in the debates at the Assembly. The phrase also appears frequently in the Court's opinions. Nevertheless, the Constitution introduces innovations in its treatment of 'society'. Separating itself from the tradition of constitutions that concentrate on limiting state power, the 1991 charter contains several articles directed to the empowerment of citizens and social groups, to the protection of the vulnerable, and to the distribution and limitation of power within society itself. Since its main philosophy is participatory democracy, society becomes the key player not only at election time but permanently.

In some articles the Constitution follows the trend of other recent constitutions or international documents. Pluralism is not only protected in the political process but also in ethnic, religious and virtually all features of social life. Solidarity is considered a pillar of democracy. Equality is defined in substantive terms not merely as formal equality before the law. Affirmative action in favour of individuals and groups is authorised. Social rights include protection for women, adolescents, the elderly, children and the handicapped. Society is thus viewed not as a set of individual citizens but as composed of different groups with diverse needs and interests. The Constitution protects them specially. Indigenous peoples were protected in their cultural, territorial, and participatory rights. This was also true of the black population, although to a lesser degree. Peasants, consumers, and users of public services are also mentioned and protected by the Constitution. Entrepreneurs are not overlooked nor are 'the marginalised or formerly discriminated'. Unusual constitutional concepts were introduced in an effort to give everybody a place in the Constitution: for example, persons in conditions of 'especial economic, mental or physical weakness'. Another, more alien to constitutions, is the concept of guerrilla groups, mentioned in three transitory articles granting extraordinary powers to the President to adopt reforms following a peace process with the rebels.

Other aspects of the Constitution are innovative even in the light of recent international treaties or constitutions. They have in common a concern for private power exerted over private citizens. Firstly, the Constitution introduces a few clauses which affect the distribution of social power, in particular the right of access to property, the possibility of using *tutela* against private powers, and the extension of the right of petition to private organisations. Secondly, the Constitution has several articles concerning the democratisation of private organisations, such as professional associations and trade unions. The due process clause is framed in such a way that it can be extended to punishments imposed by private authorities, such as a teacher or a school director. Thirdly, the

Constitution provides for state stimuli of Non-Governmental Organisations (NGOs) and grass-root organisations. Their autonomy is protected since the Constitution's basic philosophy is not corporatist but to promote an equilibrium among the forces of society. Fourthly, special participation rights are given to some of these categories of citizens mentioned above. The most articulated ones recognise indigenous peoples' rights to be consulted in the decision-making process concerning the exploitation of natural resources within their territories, and women's rights to participate in the higher levels of public administration. Finally, the Constitution not only protects individuals but group or community rights. For example, freedom of religion and the prohibition of discrimination on a religious basis, which are individual rights, are complemented by 'equality of all churches and confessions before the law'.[19]

Of the two thousand Constitutional Court decisions delivered in the three years between 1991 and 1994, most of them implemented those articles related to 'society'. I will of course not mention all of them. But even being very selective, one runs the risk of being tedious. The abundance of decisions related to issues where the concept of 'society' is concerned may be explained by the impact of *tutela,* and by the fact that the Constitution reflected the wide social composition of the Assembly. Let me begin with some general cases. Then I will concentrate on the protection of vulnerable groups, indigenous peoples' rights, women's rights and the limitation of private power.

The Court has taken seriously the values of 'solidarity' and 'pluralism' that inform the constitutional clauses concerning society. The most interesting case concerning the principle of 'solidarity' is a *tutela* decision in which a woman claimed her right to protect a child given to her, without due official authorisation, by the priest who found him abandoned near his church.[20] 'Pluralism' has also been promoted by the Court in several aspects of social life. The most significant change in this respect is the cases concerning not only the separation of church and state, but also the respect of diverse images of the sacred realm. The most polemical was the decision to annul the main clauses of the 1974 *Concordato* with the Holy See. The Court's decision was based on the defence of liberty of conscience and of equality among all churches and faiths. According to the Court the privileges enjoyed by the Catholic church in Colombia could not continue under the new Constitution.[21]

Other cases, less notorious and controversial, are also significant in the promotion of pluralism, including one in which the Court explicitly quoted ethnic minorities' rights to invalidate the 1950s law which provided for an annual ceremony in the National Cathedral where the President of the Republic participated officially in the consecration of Colombia to the Sacred Heart.[22]

Among the several vulnerable groups protected by the Constitution, the Court has paid special attention to the mentally and physically handicapped, but adolescents, prisoners, domestic workers, and homosexuals have also benefited from the new constitutional law.[23] For example, the mentally and physically handicapped, when going to vote, cannot be obliged to be accompanied by a member of their family nor can they be excluded from teaching activities if their physical limitations do not allow them to perform other non-academic activities within the school.[24] The Court has not only prohibited the restriction of the ordinary rights of the handicapped. It has deduced positive special rights for the handicapped that go far beyond the traditional negative conception of rights as barriers against abuse of authority.[25] The decisions concerning homosexuals are very significant in the Colombian context. They have arisen in the police, as a result of claims against the exclusion of homosexuals for disciplinary reasons. In one case, the Court granted the *tutela* arguing that 'the condition of homosexuality in itself cannot be a reason for excluding someone from the institution'.[26] The Court held that disciplinary codes in these kinds of institutions could only sanction the practice of sexual behaviour – be it homosexual or heterosexual – if it took place within the official buildings. Nevertheless, homosexuals should not declare or manifest their sexual preferences, and authorities cannot oblige them to do so.[27] Before the 1991 Constitution, homosexuals were not criminally punished but could be sanctioned for disciplinary reasons and excluded from the practice of their professions. The Court had ruled unconstitutional such laws. Therefore, these *tutela* cases represent a complete change both for the status of homosexuals and for their role in professional activities.

The Court has indeed been very active in promoting sexual equality, and protecting women in weak positions within society. The most advanced case dealt with the recognition of the economic value of women's housework. The case of Ester Varela is worth attention. She had worked for 25 years by the side of her male companion. They never formally married or established any legal kind of partnership. When he died, the house was given by a civil judge to the dead man's only sister, according to civil succession laws. The Court reversed the Supreme Court decision challenged by a *tutela* filed by Ester Varela. According to the Court 'housework is essential to the economy even though it is indirectly linked to the process of development and the accumulation of capital, . . . the home was the fruit of the joint efforts of the two household partners', and, therefore, it belonged to Ester Varela.[28] Since, in Colombia, more than half of women live with men outside marriage, the Ester Varela case has profound social implications to remedy their economic insecurity.

Another common discriminatory practice against women dealt with by the Court is linked to pregnancy. Examples abound: teenage girls expelled from state schools because they are pregnant, parents pressed to take their daughters out of private schools for the same reason, and university students not readmitted because they temporarily interrupted their first semester to give birth. In all these cases the Court granted the *tutela*.[29] A more critical problem affecting sexual equality and women's personal autonomy is what can be called systemic discrimination resulting from values, prejudices and deeply entrenched patterns of relations. The Court has gradually been more sensitive to this less discussed but more profound problem. In a 1992 case, for example, the Court considered it justified that daughters of military men, whether single or married, were granted more social welfare benefits than their sons, because in our society they are 'frequently dependent on men'.[30] This approach has, of course, a risk of perpetrating stereotypes. Fortunately, in another case the Court warned against such attitudes. It held that 'the social stereotype that women are not the principal source of household income' cannot prevail. The Court then ordered the social security registration of a husband dependent on his wife's income, even though the relevant statute did not contemplate this possibility.[31]

The pinnacle of this line of argument was a Court decision declaring constitutional the new social security law which establishes a lower pensionable age for women than for men. The Court said that since there was a systemic and cultural discrimination against women, even those who went out of the house to work had the burden of domestic activities, because society was still organised on a 'masculine basis'.[32] Additionally, since equality was not defined in formal terms but had a substantive content, the state could not be neutral in the promotion of sexual equality. The state has a duty to 'overcome secular injustices' by taking 'affirmative action measures' in order to transform reality.[33]

The most divisive issue about women's rights, however, has been abortion. It is not necessary to stress its importance. The Court upheld a fifteen-year-old statute that penalises women who have abortions. The right to life was paramount, according to the Court, in a decision in which the above considerations about the way society was organised and women's autonomy were not mentioned. In this case, the three dissenting magistrates recalled this line of argument. They also underlined that the Court had not reviewed the constitutionality of other articles of the Code that criminalise abortion in extreme cases such as rape. No doubt the situation of violence in Colombia, which undermines the value of life, led the Court to defer to 'legislative criminal policy'.[34]

These cases – on the handicapped, homosexuals and women – reflect modern constitutional law tendencies. Those concerning the limitation of private powers go even further. As noted above, the Constitution contains several clauses directed to redistribute power within spheres of private life and to reduce the lack of equilibrium in private relations. Civil law and police measures sometimes may serve this end. But since they were inspired in the past by a perspective insufficiently sensitive to weak persons or groups, *tutela* has filled the vacuum.

The Constitution contemplated three general hypotheses in which *tutela* could be used against a private party: when it is in charge of a public service; when its behaviour seriously and directly affects collective interests; and when it is in a situation of superiority (the other person being in a situation of subordination or defencelessness).[35] The definition of the specific cases in which *tutela* could be used was to be determined by the law . It was first applied in 1992, opening the way to *tutela*s among private parties and, at the same time, setting clear conditions and limitations.[36] The Court applied them at the beginning, then interpreted them widely, until finally, in 1994, it struck down two of the most important limitations.[37]

It is interesting to see in what kinds of private relations the Court has granted *tutela*. A brief review of some of the cases is revealing: (a) a widow against two priests who authorised the transfer of the buried body of her husband at her son's request; (b) a parapsychologist against a famous journalist who described her in a book as a skilful witch; (c) a sick man against a hospital which did not allow him to leave until he paid the bill; (d) a student against his teacher because he punished him by taping his mouth closed with scotch tape; (e) two daughters against their mother who published a book, 'Perdute', accusing them of immoral behaviour; (f) a labour union activist against his employer who refused to give him the possibility of working extra time and earning more money; (g) a woman worker against her employer who transferred her to another city in spite of her children's need to receive daily care; (h) a family against a very noisy industry; (i) a rural community against a pig industry which contaminated their water sources; (j) an urban community against a food industry which generated terrible smells; (k) a suburban community against a bus company which refused to maintain the only service that went to this community because it was not profitable; (l) a man against an express mail company which did not deliver a package addressed to him in time; and (m) a private individual and a public official against television and radio programmes as well as newspapers, alleging that they violated their privacy, or that they published false information about them, and therefore wanted rectification.[38] The kinds of abuse of power were very varied – physical, economic, territorial and religious. But in almost all of those cases under review, the Court decided in favour of the weak.

The most frequent cases have arisen in three sorts of situations: when the protection of the environment is at stake, when a businessman's credit is unfairly curtailed, or when the mass media publish false factual information about an individual. In this last situation, the Court has established conditions to protect freedom of expression and of the press. In the most significant case, the Court refused to grant a *tutela*. It held that it was part of the autonomy of a TV news station to decide what was newsworthy. In this case, the M-19 candidate wanted to participate in the presidential debate preset by the news stations between only the Liberal and Conservative candidates.[39]

Limitations have also been established in other cases. In essence, *tutela* cannot be used against a private party when another judicial procedure is available. However, when there is great inequality among the parties and an immediate risk to a fundamental right, the Court has accepted the possibility of using *tutela* as a transitory and urgent means. From a more substantive viewpoint, the Court has rejected *tutela*s in relations in which there was not an inequality of bargaining power (a singer against a record company), or no economic dependency (a father against his self-sufficient wife and children). In addition, even if there is a power inequality, *tutela* cannot be used when no fundamental right is at risk (a community could not stop the construction of a hotel).[40]

Indigenous peoples' rights have been protected through *tutela* in an unsuspected way. This area of the Court's activity is, without doubt, one of the most innovative. In its first decision on the topic – the Cristianía case – the Court stopped the construction of a highway and noted that the preservation of the integrity of the community was a protected constitutional interest, even though no individual fundamental right was violated. In such a way, a judicial instrument conceived to protect individuals, according to the liberal tradition, was transformed into a tool to protect community rights, according to the traditions of the ethnic minorities themselves.[41] In another case – the Chimcuambe – the Court ordered INCORA (the Institute for Agrarian Reform) to proceed to the creation of one or several *Resguardos* to solve a distribution of land conflict between two indigenous communities. The Court upheld the right to the creation of a *resguardo* (collective property), constitutionally protected by the principle of ethnic and cultural diversity.[42] Later, the Court took an additional step in strengthening indigenous rights. A company, without the appropriate public agency permit, was exploiting a particular forest; the indigenous authorities had apparently given their consent in exchange for working materials and money. The Court granted a *tutela* filed by the indigenous community. It, as such, had rights independent of its individual members. In this case, the Court clearly stated that collective rights did not belong to the members of the community but to the community as a whole. Only for indigenous peoples does the right to life include a right to collective subsistence, and only for them is the right to ethnic, cultural and social integrity a fundamental right. According to the Court, individual rights as well as general principles became communitarian rights from the perspective of the indigenous peoples.[43] The doctrine does not go so far as to disregard other constitutional countervailing interests, such as fighting against organised crime. Therefore, the Court did not order the removal of a radar installed in an airport situated along a *resguardo*. It did not accept the cultural integrity protection argument. Rather, it underlined that the community had agreed to its installation and that its members were paid workers in the process.

Two additional cases concerning linguistic rights are also relevant. In one an indigenous political candidate was granted the right to speak in his native language through an official communication system, even though there was as yet no legal rule giving official status to his language. In the other, a law required public servants in the Caribbean islands to speak both Spanish and English. A Spanish-speaking public servant challenged the law arguing that it violated the constitutional prohibition to discriminate on the basis of language. The Court upheld the law, noting that it provided for a delay, so that Spanish-speaking public servants had time to learn English.[44]

The above considerations suggest that the concept of the state has changed along with the new philosophy that inspired the Constitution and guided the Court on the long journey of spreading new constitutional values all over society. The following and final section devotes further attention to the concept of the state as understood by the 1991 constitution and to its interpretation by the Constitutional Court.

The State after the 1991 Constitution

The fundamental purpose of the Constituent Assembly and the government was to strengthen state institutions. This was also Rafael Núñez's objective in 1886 but he did it from an authoritarian perspective, albeit a republican one. In 1991, President Gaviria's perspective was different, as was the country's and the delegates' mood.[45] The strengthening of state institutions this time was to be achieved by promoting other values, such as efficiency, accountability, representativeness and responsiveness. That the state's strength lay in its legitimacy not in its arbitrariness, in its capacity to achieve results accepted by the community not in its power to impose orders, was a common belief among Colombian reformers.

The horizontal and vertical distribution of powers, the branches of government themselves and the territorial entities, were transformed following this view. In a broad move towards federalisation, the autonomy of the territorial entities was guaranteed, local democracy was promoted, and national functions and resources were generously decentralised.[46] Besides departments and municipalities, three new territorial entities were created: regions, provinces and indigenous communities' territories.[47] Additionally, there was a complete revision of the system of separation of powers, first to re-establish an equilibrium among the three branches in a regime traditionally dominated by the presidential figure, and second, to further a more responsible government with the hope that accountability would promote both an efficient and a clean public administration.

Above all the judicial system was significantly reorganised and strengthened. Colombia moved towards an accusatory system which gives the state greater capacity to investigate and prosecute criminals, especially organised-crime bosses. A national judicial body was created to handle the administrative, financial and disciplinary aspects of the judicial system. The final power of the judicial review, which had been in the hands of the Supreme Court for almost four hundred years, was entrusted to a Constitutional Court with the mission of giving life to the new constitutional philosophy.[48] The new procedures to protect constitutional rights, foremost *tutela*, enhanced the power of every judge in the country.

The legislative branch, in turn, received more powers to control excesses in delegated legislation, make appointments, take initiatives in economic measures, and discuss the budget. Along with the strengthening of Congress there also came a change in the electoral rules to increase its representativeness as well as strict rules regarding conflicts of interests and accountability. More importantly, Congress now has the power of voting a non-confidence motion over individual ministers but without censuring the whole government.

The Constitution also reformulates the ends of the state. It expands them from the protection of persons and property to comprehend the promotion of general welfare, democratic participation, and the effective enjoyment of fundamental rights. The idea of *estado social de derecho* (social state plus rule of law) summarises this endeavour. That does not mean that privatisation or other policies to stimulate competition, productivity and market self-regulation are not envisaged. The Constitution explicitly authorises them, and protects freedom of enterprise and private property. State economic intervention is also authorised in order to rationalise the functioning of the economy and improve quality of life.[49] The explicit aim of supporting 'the proletariat', introduced in 1936, was not incorporated. The direction of monetary, foreign exchange and credit policies was taken from the executive responsibility and entrusted to an independent central bank. Other economic policies are the domain of the executive, usually within a general framework set up by Congress under the initiative of the Ministry of Economics and Finance.

The Court's decisions concerning the state can be grouped in four broad areas: state efficiency, separation of powers (horizontal and vertical), economic policies, and institutional strength against crime. As with the concept of participatory democracy, the Court has emphasised the idea of *estado social de derecho*, a concept which unites the ideal of the rule of law together with social concerns. Most of its considerations are pedagogical, that is, without specific juridical effects in any particular case. *Estado social de derecho* is a principle which none the less informs all interpretation of issues involving state powers, their functions and limitations. However, this principle has occasionally had important juridical effects.

How has the Court interpreted the Constitution regarding the promotion of state efficiency? A first daily source of state inefficiency is blunt negligence. The Court has expanded the use of *tutela* against omissions of state authorities, as can be seen from most of the cases summarised above, about the protection of the vulnerable. Usually, the Court orders a public entity to take a decision, to implement a law, or both. An also frequent kind of decision involves the enforcement of the right to petition: authorities must not only answer but try a solution, or even grant the person's demand, if it is legally well founded.[50] Judicial inefficiency has been tackled as well: a judge, for example, was ordered to deliver a sentence after a ten years' delay. Administratively cumbersome procedures, if not expressly ordered by law, have been successfully challenged by citizens as unconstitutional.[51] Other rulings by the Court regarding state efficiency have included issues of budgetary rationality and transparency, patterns of control and public personnel management.[52]

The Court has also served as an arbiter in the eventual conflicts of power among the different branches of government, and between the nation and the territorial entities.[53] The constitutional protection of the Central Bank's autonomy in the formulation of policies has been safeguarded by the Court as well. It eliminated the participation of the national economic and social council in the formulation of foreign exchange policies. It also stopped a congressional attempt to fix the criteria for the rescheduling and refinancing of the debt owed by coffee growers and businessmen. Meanwhile, Central Bank measures overlapping the executive function to represent the country in multilateral financial organisations were prevented.[54] The Court has not been as balanced in arbitrating conflicts of powers between the nation and the territorial entities. It has underlined that Colombia is still a unitary republic instead of elaborating on the new concept of territorial autonomy.[55] However, the Court has promoted the harmonisation of policies and collaboration among the national and territorial entities. It has also promoted the co-ordinating function of departments over municipalities.[56]

The judicial review of economic policies would not merit as many studies as the famous New Deal ('shift in time that saved nine') justices of the US Supreme Court. But in Colombia, as in the United States, the judicial review of economic measures has been characterised by the Court's self restraint and deference to the political branches of government. Similarly, in countries where the constitution has a chapter dealing with these matters, the courts have not been very active. The principle of neutrality in economic policy has been the guiding light, even in Germany.[57] The Colombian Constitutional Court has followed both lines of argument: less strict scrutiny of economic legislation and adherence to the principle of neutrality.[58]

The first practical test of this doctrine was the economic reform promoted by President Gaviria's government. A detailed analysis of this far-reaching reform concluded that 'in general terms, it can be said that it did not undergo significant modifications' when it came to be subject to judicial review. On the contrary, it concludes that the Court, by upholding tax, labour, foreign exchange, finance, agrarian and other reforms promoting competition, economic openness and internationalisation, gave additional legitimacy to these reforms.[59] Moreover, the Court, in a unanimous decision, upheld the privatisation of cellular phone services – challenged by labour activists on the grounds that it was against *estado social de derecho* and that foreign investment in this sector threatened sovereignty. The Court underlined that the Constitution expressly authorises the delivery of public services by private companies and recognised the right to free competition. Above all, participatory democracy was against privileges, including state privileges.[60] The freedom to establish radio and television stations, within the framework created by law, has also been protected by the Court, although the power of a newly created autonomous national agency to regulate access and use of the electromagnetic spectrum could not be bypassed.[61]

Perhaps the most far-reaching privatisation measure was implemented in the social security sector. Private pension funds were allowed to compete with public welfare agencies, while individuals were given the right to choose their own pension funds. The corresponding statute was upheld by the Court.[62] Nevertheless, the Court has enforced with rigour a constitutional provision stating that state employees do have the first option to buy shares in the privatisation process.[63]

The internationalisation of the Colombian economy has also been supported by the Court's decisions: the Uruguay Round Agreement was upheld; discriminatory restrictions on the importation of cars were ruled out. The Court also held that international co-operation agreements on customs do not need congressional approval. And it supported a legislative scheme intended to put an end to a public agency's monopoly for the importation of certain agrarian products.[64]

On the basis of these decisions one may be tempted to conclude that the Court has taken a neo-liberal stand. However, other cases do not fit this conclusion. The Court has also supported state interventions in the interest of social welfare and it has not declared unconstitutional some economic regulations.[65] It has given great weight to the promotion of social goals by the state. In a similar vein, the Court has taken very seriously the enforcement of social rights, although they have a programmatic nature.[66]

Individual economic rights have also been protected in their modern aspects, such as those concerning freedom of commercial speech, and in traditional controversies regarding the transparency of credit decisions.[67] Property rights merit special attention. Private property[68] is expressly protected but property without a public function is not. Three issues have gained public attention: extinction of property to fight corruption, which will be treated in the following section; confiscation ordered by administrative authorities not by a judge; and expropriation without compensation. The clauses concerning the last two issues have been interpreted in a way that restricts state powers, protects individual rights and expands judicial review of arbitrary dispossession.

A significant number of decisions taken by the Court during 1993 strengthen the capacity of the state to face the most pressing and threatening challenges against Colombian society: corruption, ordinary criminality and organised crime, from guerrillas to narco-terrorism. The Court has accepted the confiscation of property to prevent corrupt officials from enjoying money illegally earned. Moreover, it has not required a previous sentence of illicit enrichment as a precondition for the confiscation. Of course, the extinction of property requires that a law authorises it specifically; it also requires respect for due process.[69] In addition to strict measures to punish corruption, the Court also upheld legislation directed to prevent it, like extending prohibitions in procurement procedures.[70] The Court has also argued that formalities cannot be used as a shield to cover up irregular behaviour by public officials.[71]

Clientelism has been targeted by the Court. In various cases, the Court has argued against political appointments and supported the professionalisation of the civil service. In these cases, the Court has sided with public servants against the use of unjustified discretionary powers.[72]

Finally, the Court did not hesitate to strengthen the state when it came to review measures taken by the executive to fight violence resulting from guerrilla groups and drug traffickers. To guarantee public order, the 1991 Constitution provides for a state of exception, conferring on the executive three kinds of emergency powers. These have been used to strengthen the judicial system by enhancing the power of the public prosecutor. In the previous regime, the executive usually resorted to a state of siege to enhance the power of police authorities. Since 1991, the government has used emergency powers on various occasions: they seem to have worked better than the old state of siege without sacrificing rights to efficiency.

In 1994, a new statutory law regulated the use of emergency powers by the executive. This was approved after a long debate in Congress, with the vote of former guerrilla groups. It contains a precise description of presidential powers regarding fundamental citizen's rights. It also sets limits to those powers, while it creates judicial and congressional procedures to oversee and control the executive. More significantly it attempts to avoid the excesses incurred under the previous state of siege regime. The Court upheld the law with the exception of a few provisions.[73]

If one looks at the three key institutions for the maintenance of public order – the Public Prosecutor,[74] the police, and the army – it may be concluded that the Court has not imposed unreasonable limitations on their powers, while it has taken into consideration the problems of Colombian reality. It has opposed granting them additional powers when they manifestly violate a fundamental constitutional right.

However, some of the most controversial decisions of the Court have been related to measures taken to preserve public order. They have been perceived in certain circles as having a negative impact on the capacity of the state to face serious challenges. This was so in the case of the anti-kidnapping statute, which cancelled the freezing of the assets and the criminalisation of well-intentioned intermediaries. In another judgement, the Court repealed a 1987 law which penalised individuals carrying or using personal amounts of drugs, on the basis that the law was too broad and punished even consenting adults exerting their personal autonomy rights.[75]

One of the most recent polemics involved the state of military justice – widely criticised and currently under a process of reform. The Court ruled that active military personnel could not sit as judges in the verbal proceedings of a military court, arguing that this could affect their impartiality. This time the debate reverted against the Court: two congressmen, including a supporter of the anti-kidnapping law, and two national newspapers accused the Court of becoming a kind of constituent assembly and called for its abolition. The old system – it was argued – was better and judicial review should return to the Supreme Court. In June 1995, Congress almost approved a statute 'packing' the Court with six new appointees, establishing a two-thirds majority for the invalidation of statutory laws, treaties and amendments, among other possible limitations to the Court's actions. In fact, although the Court has shown restraint in all cases in which an expansion of its powers was at stake, it has systematically repealed all legislation which attempted to give it additional powers.[76]

Conclusions

The above considerations suggest that the Colombian state has been strengthened; it now has more efficient instruments to face the various threats against democratic institutions. The Constitutional Court has been instrumental in defending the state's interests. It has done so in a non-ideological fashion: the Court has been neither neo-liberal nor socialist in its interpretation of the role of the state. The Court has also stimulated the application of new instruments to fight corruption. However, compared with other aspects of the Constitution, those concerning the state have been the less well enforced, aside from those related to re-establishing and maintaining public order.

This study of the role of the Constitutional Court shows that the Constitution has not been a complete loss. It has been enforced, albeit partially, by both the Court and Congress. Judicial enforcement is dependent on either Congressional approval of a statute or a citizen's initiative. In this respect, society has been much more dynamic than Congress, although some significant statutory laws have been adopted and upheld. All in all, the new institutions have proved to be capable of producing concrete results. *Tutela*, for example, has been a very successful instrument for the redistribution of power, while showing that ordinary citizens, even the marginalised, are willing and capable of resorting to the Constitution as a tool to defend themselves. These innovations have not led to crisis. On the contrary, they have contributed to the spread of constitutional values.

It is clear from this chapter that the Constitutional Court has accelerated the implementation of the Constitution. Between 1991 and 1994 almost 2,000 judicial opinions were produced, in contrast to the yearly average of 100 constitutional decisions taken before 1991. More significantly, the contents of these decisions reveal a more balanced picture regarding the conflicts between liberty and order. They also reveal a philosophy that goes beyond the debate between new left and new right. They have preserved the original consensus that informed the Constitution. The Court has generally been on the side of those without access to power in the political process, reflecting the spirit of the Constitution. It has also been responsive to the protection of minorities. The Court has indeed been a leader of a revolution protecting fundamental rights: it has 'taken rights seriously'; it has conceived itself as a 'forum of principles'.

Almost all the key issues of modern constitutional law have been dealt with by the Court. In this respect, it could be said that Colombia has taken three years to travel the same distance that other democracies have taken half a century to cover. The very success of the Court has opened up questions regarding its future. In early 1994, there were already voices proposing a return to the old system of judicial review. But Colombian legal traditions may serve to prove these critics wrong.

Notes

1. The concept of participatory democracy in the Colombian context has nothing to do with the communist version. It is more similar to the analogue concept used by David Held. See Held (1987 and 1993). See also Macpherson (1977). The idea of spheres of democracy is similar to the one found in Bobbio (1985). For its linkage to the legitimacy of authority, see Pateman (1985).
2. The ballot on 27 May 1990 merely asked the voters to reply 'yes' or 'no' to the idea of strengthening participatory democracy through a Constituent Assembly which, with representation from all political and social forces, would reform the existing Constitution.
3. *Acción de tutela* is the writ for the protection of human rights. It is the judicial procedure which guarantees practical respect of the individual fundamental constitutional rights. It combines participatory philosophy (anyone can use it before any judge or tribunal without legal jargon or prerequisites) with a strict respect for human dignity (a decision must be given in ten days and the burden of proof is shifted to fall on the suspected violator of any particular constitutional right). In its first three years, *tutela* has been a key tool in the protection of ethnic and minority rights
4. Constitutional Court decision (hereafter quoted as CCD)/C-180 (mimeo, 1994).
5. CCD/ C-011 (mimeo, 1994).
6. CCD/ C-319 (mimeo, 1994).
7. CCD/ C-555 (mimeo, 1994).
8. CCD/ C-041 (mimeo, 1994).
9. CCD/ C-226 (mimeo, 1994).
10. Decree 2591 of 1991 regulated *Acción de tutela*. When it was first applied, criticism arose because the regulation was considered too generous. The Court made it even more generous when it came to review *tutela* decisions taken by judges. Moreover, it upheld it and struck out some of the few restrictions. See CCD/ C-543 (mimeo, 1994). In the following sections of this chapter, I highlight some of the most significant *tutela* decisions.
11. CCD/ C-448 (mimeo, 1993).
12. *Ibid.* See also CCD/ C-145 (mimeo, 1994).
13. Bill No.11 (1992), House of Representatives; and Bill No. 348 (1993), Senate (mimeo).
14. CCD/ C-089 (mimeo, 1994).
15. *Ibid.*
16. *Ibid.* In another case, the Court ruled unconstitutional that public finance be given exclusively to parties represented in Congress; see CCD/ C-020 (mimeo, 1993).

17. The statute against kidnapping was the first popular initiative introduced in Congress after 1991. More that one million citizens requested it. It was also the only popular initiative that became law. The Court ruled the articles of the law aimed at inhibiting and penalising the payment of ransom as unconstitutional. Not all magistrates agreed with the final decision; a few of them considered that the Court should have taken into consideration the fact that the law had resulted from a popular initiative. See CCD/ C-592 (Bogotá: mimeo, 1993). However, it is hard to find a Court's decision that has not been responsive to the principles of participatory democracy. For other relevant cases, see CCD/ C-145 (Bogotá: mimeo, 1994); CCD/ C-545 (Bogotá: mimeo, 1993); and CCD/ C-599 (Bogotá: mimeo, 1992).
18. See Article 103 of the 1991 Constitution, final paragraph.
19. See Article 20 of the 1991 Constitution, final paragraph.
20. In this case, the Court sided in favour of communal solidarity against the claims of the public institute in charge of child care. The full implications of this case are not at all clear. See CCD/ T-217 (Bogotá: mimeo, 1994). The Court has made it clear that the concept of 'solidarity' is tied to voluntary, individual or communitarian participation in attempting to solve social problems.
21. CCD/ C-027 (Bogotá: mimeo, 1993).
22. CCD/ C-350 (Bogotá: mimeo, 1994). The Court took seriously the principle of the multi-ethnic character of the Colombian nation. This had implications for the role of the President as a symbol of national unity: for example, the Court forbade the President to participate officially in Catholic religious ceremonies since not all Colombians were Catholics. For other cases of interest, see CCD/ C-224 and C-088 (Bogotá, mimeo, 1994).
23. See, for example, CCD/ C-146, T-199, and C-359 (Bogotá: mimeo, 1994).
24. See CCD/ C-359 and T-100 (Bogotá: mimeo, 1994).
25. For various cases regarding the rights of the handicapped upheld by the Court, see CCD/ T-298, 204, 067 and 068 (Bogotá: mimeo, 1994).
26. CCD/ T-097 (Bogotá: mimeo, 1994). See also CCD/ T-082 (Bogotá: mimeo, 1994).
27. CCD/ T-037 (Bogotá: mimeo, 1995).
28. CCD/ T-494 (Bogotá: mimeo, 1992).
29. CCD/ T-429 (Bogotá: mimeo, 1992); and CCD/ T-292 (Bogotá: mimeo, 1994).
30. CCD/ C-588 (Bogotá: mimeo, 1992).
31. CCD/ T-098 (Bogotá: mimeo, 1994).
32. CCD/ C-410 (Bogotá: mimeo, 1994).
33. *Ibid.*
34. CCD/ C-133 (Bogotá: mimeo, 1994).
35. See Article 86 of the 1991 Constitution.
36. Decree 2591, 1991, Article 42.
37. CCD/ C-134 (Bogotá: mimeo, 1994).
38. For these and other similar cases, see CCD/ T-125, 126, 293, 230, 233, 082, 028, 523, 219 (Bogotá: mimeo, 1994); CCD/ T-56 (Bogotá: mimeo, 1995); CCD/ T-487, 402, 593, 573, 604, 512, 444, 529 (Bogotá: mimeo, 1992); and CCD/ T-507 (Bogotá: mimeo, 1993).

39. CCD/ T-484 (Bogotá: mimeo, 1994).
40. CCD/ T-338, 512 (Bogotá: mimeo, 1993); and CCD/ T-111 (Bogotá: mimeo, 1995).
41. CCD/ T-428 (Bogotá: mimeo, 1992).
42. CCD/ T-180 (Bogotá: mimeo, 1993).
43. CCD/ T-380 (Bogotá: mimeo, 1993).
44. CCD/ C-530 (Bogotá: mimeo, 1993).
45. The opening address by President Gaviria to the Assembly is reproduced in Cepeda (1993), p. 313. Delegates' interventions can be followed through the pages of the Official Gazette of the Constituent Assembly.
46. A critical view of the experience with decentralisation is given in Chapter 4 of this book.
47. See Title XI of the 1991 Constitution.
48. *Ibid.*, Title VIII.
49. See the 1991 Constitution, Articles 1, 2, 333, 150, 151, and Title XII, chapter 6.
50. For example, CCD/ T-522, 499, and 613 (Bogotá: mimeo, 1992).
51. CCD/ C-606 (Bogotá: mimeo, 1992).
52. CCD/ C-337, 529 (Bogotá: mimeo, 1993); and C-070, 039, 357 (Bogotá: mimeo, 1994).
53. See, for example, CCD/ C-449, 510, 553, 560 (Bogotá: mimeo, 1992); CCD/ C-025, 151, 168 (Bogotá: mimeo, 1993); and CCD/ C-455, 545 (Bogotá: mimeo, 1994).
54. CCD/ C-485 (Bogotá: mimeo, 1993).
55. CCD/ C-517 (Bogotá: mimeo, 1992); and CCD/ C-479A (Bogotá: mimeo, 1994).
56. CCD/ C-04, 061 (Bogotá: mimeo, 1993); and C-423, 555 (Bogotá: mimeo, 1994).
57. See Kommers (1989).
58. CCD/ C-265 (Bogotá: mimeo, 1994).
59. Cepeda Ulloa (1994c), p. 223. A complete list of the Court's decisions can be found in pp. 224–27. See also Hommes and Montenegro (1994).
60. CCD/ C-138 (Bogotá: mimeo, 1994).
61. CCD/ C-189 (Bogotá: mimeo, 1994).
62. CCD/ C-337, 387, 408 (Bogotá: mimeo, 1994); and CCD/ C-072 (Bogotá: mimeo, 1995).
63. See CCD/ C-37, 013 (Bogotá: mimeo, 1994).
64. CCD/ C-511 and 590 (Bogotá: mimeo, 1992); and C-088 (Bogotá: mimeo, 1993).
65. CCD/ C-490 (Bogotá: mimeo, 1993),
66. CCD/ C-337 (Bogotá: mimeo, 1993); and T-290 (Bogotá: mimeo, 1994).
67. CCD/ C-355 (Bogotá: mimeo, 1994); and 053 (Bogotá: mimeo, 1995).
68. CCD/ C-37 (Bogotá: mimeo, 1994).
69. See CCD/ C-389 and 176 (Bogotá: mimeo, 1994).
70. CCD/ C-415 (Bogotá: mimeo, 1994).
71. See CCD/ C-046 (Bogotá: mimeo, 1994); and CCD/ T-101 and 144 (Bogotá: mimeo, 1994). These have been relevant to cases where Congressmen have been under investigation. NGOs devoted to fighting corruption have had successful access to the Court. See also CCD/ T-563 (Bogotá: mimeo, 1994).

72. CCD/ C-517 and 527 (Bogotá: mimeo, 1994); and C-040 (Bogotá: mimeo, 1995).
73. CCD/ C-179 (Bogotá: mimeo, 1994).
74. The Public Prosecutor has been granted strong powers. As a judicial authority, he does not need to ask for judicial authorisation for searches and seizures or any other investigative activities, unlike the United States where judicial warrants are currently required. The Public Prosecutor is independent of the executive. Most of the decrees issued under the constitutional instrument of 'state of commotion', strengthen the Public Prosecutor's powers. The Court upheld them with few exceptions: for example, the Public Prosecutor cannot suspend sentences already imposed by a judge in order to stimulate the collaboration of a witness, nor can he invade in any way the sphere of criminal judges; see CCD/ C-171 (Bogotá: mimeo, 1993).
75. CCD/ C-221 (Bogotá: mimeo, 1994).
76. See, for example, CCD/C-113 and 131 (Bogotá: mimeo, 1993).

CHAPTER 4

THE DECENTRALISED STATE:
AN ADMINISTRATIVE OR POLITICAL CHALLENGE?

Gustavo Bell Lemus

The process of decentralisation in Colombia, which has been developing since the mid-1980s, is probably one of the most dynamic amongst
the various processes of institutional change that the country has experienced in the last two decades. Initiated, without much debate, at the
end of the 1970s as a process against the concentration of power at the
centre, it originally served more as an answer to the evident loss of legitimacy of the state.[1] But today decentralisation has become politically
hard to reverse, mainly as a result of the consensus it provokes. It is
now the subject of intense local feelings; it raises hopes of change for a
large majority of Colombians.

Often presented as a state necessity to increase the efficiency and
effectiveness in the provision of services, decentralisation has deep historical roots in Colombia – roots that go back to the very first years of
independence. The country's civil struggles during the nineteenth century were often caused by anti-centralist motives, among many other
reasons. In addition, Colombians lived under an ultra-federalist regime
between 1863 and 1885.[2] Indeed, the longevity of the centralist 1886
Constitution encouraged the desire for decentralisation, as clearly
shown in the consensus that the subject commanded at the meetings of
the National Constitutional Assembly of 1991.[3]

Today decentralisation is a principle that governs the functioning of
the state. It has been adopted as a constitutional norm and, as such, it
has been accepted without much questioning. Moreover there are great
expectations that the principle will be developed to its full capacity, in
the belief that it will serve to raise living standards. From the perspective of the state, it has also been commonly accepted that
decentralisation will encourage a more rational distribution of public
resources.

Decentralisation has hitherto been studied, and widely discussed,
from administrative and financial viewpoints. However, it has not been
properly considered as a formidable challenge for political parties and
movements alike, today and in the immediate future. It is true that the
subject has been integrated into the wider analysis of the process of

democratisation. Nevertheless, little has been said on the demands that decentralisation poses to those actively responsible for its implementation at the departmental and municipal levels. In the last analysis, the failure or success of decentralisation depends on these actors in the democratic process: first and foremost the political parties.

This chapter will argue that the aims of decentralisation are constantly being obstructed by the lack of modernisation of political parties; while the state has been subject to great transformations, Colombian parties are lagging behind these institutional changes. While authors such as Luis Orjuela argue that technical problems are affecting the implementation of decentralisation, I believe that the major barriers are to be found in the realm of politics.[4] Deeply entrenched clientelistic practices and old patronage habits work against the high ideals of decentralisation. In the following pages, I have incorporated my own experience as a Governor of the Departamento del Atlántico during the period 1992–94, which may give valuable insights to a subject that otherwise runs the risk of being a source of national frustration. As decentralisation has also become fashionable in Latin American at large, these reflections may be relevant to the experiences of other countries as well.

Decentralisation in *La Revolución Pacífica*

The government of President César Gaviria (1990–94) led to a substantial change in the organisation of the state in Colombia. Under his administration, a new constitution was adopted. His government undertook some initiatives to develop the principle of decentralisation, which had been taking shape since the administration of Belisario Betancur.[5] Gaviria's *Plan de Desarrollo Económico y Social 1990–94* – known also as *La Revolución Pacífica* – incorporated the general principles that would serve as the basis for the reorganisation of the state, including decentralisation.[6]

In this plan, decentralisation was presented as a prerequisite for the functioning of *apertura* – as the model of economic development supported by the Gaviria administration came to be known. It was assumed that the state would operate better under a decentralised structure. Two reasons were given in support of this hypothesis by the authors of the plan: first, that some advantages would be derived from the scale of services provided by *departamentos* and *municipios*, and second that consumers, now closer to the providers, would exercise more control over the quality of services. In other words, the greater proximity of citizens to the state would result in more demands and therefore in higher quality of the final product. From this perspective, decentralisation is seen as part of a global strategy that seeks to adapt the state to the demands of the model of development adopted by the government: the *apertura económica*. To the extent that the central state could be relieved of the burdens of the provision of some services, it could then concentrate its efforts on other activities that facilitate the objectives of *apertura económica*.

The government designed a series of strategies to make decentralisation effective. These included the definition of the functions and powers distributed among the three basic levels of the state: the *nación,* the *departamento* and the *municipio*. They required an integral view of their activities and of the scope of services to be provided by each level. They also stipulated the resources allocated to the various *departamentos* and *municipios*, which would empower them to provide the respective services.[7] Regarding social development, for example, it was stated that basic services such as health, education, water supply and sanitation, housing and recreation, would be provided by the municipalities; the *departamentos* could also be in charge of them, but only temporarily.

Parallel to this redefinition of powers, resources, and functions of the state, the government encouraged a process of *apertura democrática* and a programme of institutional adjustment as a necessary complement to decentralisation. The *apertura democrática* sought to empower citizens with a series of political instruments which would guarantee their active and effective participation in institutional life. It also sought to give citizens some mechanisms of control over governments in *municipios* and *departamentos*. Besides the elections of city mayors, already adopted during the Betancur administration, these reforms included the popular election of governors, the *voto programático*, the recall of mandates, and the carrying out of plebiscites, referenda and public consultations to define local affairs.[8] These mechanisms would serve as the political basis for decentralisation. In addition, the reforms would give managerial support to *municipios* and *departamentos*, on the assumption that these entities had lost capacity to operate after so many decades of centralist rule.

The Challenges of Decentralisation

In theory decentralisation seems therefore well conceived, with a large degree of institutional coherence. At a first glance it should fulfil its aims without much trouble. The way decentralisation has been hitherto implemented by both the government and Congress would also suggest a firm commitment to the process: *municipios* and *departamentos* have assumed more functions; they are now more autonomous than in the past; they also have more responsibilities; and they have received a significant amount of new resources. Law 60 of 1993 is so far the major legal instrument summarising these efforts.

As suggested in the introduction to this chapter, the subject of decentralisation has attracted considerable attention from various circles. State agencies, such as the *Departamento Nacional de Planeación*, for example, have devoted time to study its fiscal implications. Discussion in Congress has been ample and enriching. Seminars and fora have served to enlarge an already extensive literature on the topic. However, there is a need to look more carefully into the political dimension of the process. The extent of the role played by politicians and their parties in the implementation of decentralised policies has not been sufficiently recognised. The parties themselves do not seem to be too aware of the challenges. The central government is probably too distant to appreciate all the implications of the problems. Above all decentralisation requires more technical expertise to deal with more complex organisations – an input of human resources, often difficult to find at the local level, where old habits prevail. It is here that the key to success or failure lies.

To what extent have political parties realised the magnitude of the changes brought about by the recent process of state modernisation? Whoever is in charge of a particular administration in Colombia soon faces the need to work in tandem with members of representative institutions – the *Concejo Municipal, Asamblea Departamental,* or Congress. My own experience indicates that, in general, these political actors are far from appreciating the pressing demands to update their practices. The challenges of decentralisation cannot be met in an environment dominated by clientelism. As the process has raised so many expectations, the problems of governability may become more acute. President Gaviria was aware of the threats posed by a resilient clientelism. As he pointed out when presenting the aims of the Revolución Pacífica: '*Para lograr que una verdadera apertura democrática apoye, legitime e impulse el proceso de descentralización fiscal y administrativa, es necesario adelantar acciones tendientes a disminuir, en la medida de lo posible, el clientelismo político . . .*[9] However, the government thought that this could be achieved through the new democratic tools introduced in 1991, such as the recall of the mandate and the like. With the benefit of hindsight, it has become obvious that something more was required to transform traditional political practices.

Within Colombian traditions and the existing constitutional regime, it is forbidden for the government to become actively involved in party politics – although arguably there is a fine line to be drawn here. But the state as such can do very little to renew political practices which directly affect the process of decentralisation. In the development of the PDI, for example, the central state designed the norms and regulations and provided for the training of civil servants. Once the legal framework for decentralisation was completed – Law 60 of 1993 mentioned above – and mayors and some other civil servants received some training, the final responsibility for the process was transferred from the centre to the periphery. And here the task of overcoming local political forces cannot be overestimated.

Thus, any evaluation of decentralisation has to appreciate that the process does not depend solely on the good will of the central state, nor even on that of local governments. The role of local political leaders and their parties is as crucial. Their lack of modernisation, their insistence on perceiving the state just as a major source of patronage, not only affects the provision of basic public services but also generates problems of public order. In the following sections, I further illustrate these problems, looking at two aspects of municipal administration that are fundamental to decentralisation: the management of aqueducts and urban planning.

Decentralisation and Human Capital: the Atlántico Experience

Perhaps there is no other sector that better illustrates the political and administrative challenges of decentralisation than that of water, that is to say, the administration of municipal aqueducts. Since 1986, the central government has embarked on various programmes aiming at the expansion of the provision of this basic service and the improvement of its general administration. In 1986, the Consejo Nacional de Política Económica y Social (Conpes) approved the Programa de Ajuste al Sector (PAS) whose objective was to increase the supply of water to reach 75 per cent of the population within the next six years. The different mechanisms to achieve this objective, included:

> ... el mejoramiento del desempeño operativo y financiero para las empresas mediante el diseño y puesta en marcha de programas nacionales orientados a la reducción de pérdidas, rehabilitación de sistemas, reducción de costos de operación y optimización de los sistemas operacional, comercial, financiero, administrativo, de apoyo y planificación.[10]

In developing the PAS, the central government liquidated the Instituto de Fomento Municipal (INSFOPAL) a national institute which had hitherto administered the municipal aqueducts, and then passed their administration over to the *departamentos* and *municipios*. The Gaviria government, in its *Plan de Desarrollo 1990–94*, defined four principal objectives regarding water supply, the first one being '*reestructurar las instituciones del sector en línea con la política de descentralización, definiendo además las responsabilidades de los niveles nacional y regional*'.[11] In April 1991, the Atlántico department entered into an agreement with the Consejo Regional de Planeación Económica y Social de la Costa Atlántica (CORPES) within the PAS – known as the *Plan de acción para el sector de agua potable del Departamento del Atlántico*. The aim of the plan was to push ahead with the basic objectives of the PAS. The plan was designed with a broad vision: not only did it hope to tackle the technical aspects of water supply, but it was to have a solid administrative and institutional base, which would guarantee the efficiency and continuity of the provision of the service. The *departamento* was equipped with a new administrative unit – the Unidad Administrativa Especial para el Sector de Aguas (UESA) – directly in charge of the plan. This unit was to be responsible for co-ordination with other national and regional entities in the development of the plan. That same year, 1991, civil servants from all towns within the *departamento*, with the exception of one – Malambo – were trained in the areas of management, accounting methods, technical operations, marketing, computing systems and finances.

In Atlántico the plan consisted of four parts, three of which concentrated on rebuilding and improving existing aqueducts, and the construction of new aqueducts in rural areas. The fourth was devoted to '... *el estudio e implementación del desarrollo institucional buscando dotar a los municipios de un ente administrador de los servicios con capacidad técnica, financiera y administrativa*'.[12] This latter point was developed through an agreement signed with Universidad del Norte – a private university – to carry out research on 21 *municipios* of the *departamento.* This research was to identify key areas to improve the management of local aqueducts; it also aimed to *'crear conciencia sobre la importancia del desarrollo institucional para poder implantarlo dentro de un ambiente de recurso humano dispuesto al cambio, que le permita mediante un buen manejo la autocosteabilidad del servicio'*.[13]

The study carried out by the university recommended that three *Asociaciones de Municipios* be created – each of them comprising seven *municipios*. The establishment of four private companies with minor public participation, and of nine governing bodies was also recommended. In March 1992 nine new mayors were popularly elected; they started their terms on 1 June that year. In the first formal meeting held with the recently elected mayors, I asked them to support the plan under execution. This involved, among other aspects, the continuity of the personnel already trained in aqueduct management.

In the second semester of 1993, we carried out an evaluation of the suggestions made by the Universidad del Norte. The results were frustrating. Of the three *Asociaciones de Municipios* recommended by the university, only two had been created; of the four private companies with public participation, two had been established; and of the nine governing bodies just three had been created. The evaluation also stated that:

. . . sin embargo muchas de estas entidades aún no funcionan de forma independiente de la administración municipal, por falta de voluntad política de los alcaldes, quienes ven en los servicios públicos una fuente de burocracia y de manejo de situaciones de carácter político afectando con esta actitud, la buena marcha de los servicios.[14]

Moreover, by the end of 1993, a large proportion of the personnel trained in 1991 were no longer in their posts, thus forcing the Unidad de Aguas and the CORPES to reinitiate the training of some 96 new employees. In August 1994, the Unidad de Aguas and the Ministerio de Desarrollo entered into an agreement to train additional personnel from the two *Asociaciones de Municipios* and from four other *municipios*. Only a few civil servants who received training in 1994 kept their posts in 1995, when yet again new elected mayors took office. Indeed, in a large proportion of towns, particularly those outside the *Asociaciones de Municipios,* no trained personnel could be found. These were typically *municipios* where the aqueduct depended directly on the mayors. In these towns where a trained human resource is so scarce, the situation is critical: the lack of knowledge to perform the most simple task has meant that the service has not been provided. The experience with the administration of water supply in Atlántico gives evidence of the political limitations on implementing a programme of decentralisation. In a significant number of cases, elected city mayors were more interested in party politics, particularly in attending to the demands of their own supporters, than in the provision of public services, now under their responsibility. Resources invested in human capital were wasted. Entire communities could not have access to water supply. After I left the administration, the new governor was yet again under pressure to start another training programme whose results may prove equally frustrating.

As suggested above, problems related to the provision of public services can led to disturbances of public order. As Governor, I had to intervene on two occasions in the affairs of *municipios,* whose autonomous nature did not serve to overcome their lack of capacity in providing water supply to their communities. In both cases their incapability led to public outcry; and in one of them to serious rioting. This occurred in two towns which are part of the so-called Area Metropolitana de Barranquilla – an area inhabited by a large number of middle-class professionals. It must be pointed out that the best managed aqueducts have been those administered by companies set up away from political influence.

The second experience that further illustrates the problems faced by decentralisation refers to the training of personnel in urban planning. Under the previous regime, in addition to patronage from the central state, local finances – particularly in the poorest *municipios* – largely depended on the arbitrary action of congressmen who had access to pork-barrel money. Under the new system, decentralisation attempts to provide resources following more rational criteria. These criteria are set up by the constitution itself and also by the law. They provide a general framework for the distribution of resources among the three levels of the state: the nation, the *departamentos* and the *municipios*. Some of those resources are directed to the so-called *Fondos de Cofinanciación* – which are funds assigned to *municipios* and *departamentos* to develop particular projects at their request, but with the condition that they be prepared to serve as co-financers. All projects should be presented before the Banco de Proyectos, following a standard procedure for application of funds designed by the Departamento Nacional de Planeación.

Cofinanciación has become an alternative of paramount significance as a means of financing projects of infrastructure, particularly for those *departamentos* and *municipios* with scant resources. However, to take full advantage of its benefits, these entities have to fulfil the official requirements properly. These include the establishment of their own Banco de Proyectos, the standard procedure to apply for the funds mentioned above, and of course a bureaucracy with sufficient skills to gain access to the funds – usually trained local planning officers.

Atlántico was the first *departamento* to set up its own Banco de Proyectos. We also provided the appropriate training courses: between 1993 and 1994 some 264 civil servants from the *departamento* and various *municipios* enrolled in training sessions to become acquainted with the new system. This expediency bore little fruit. As with the experience of training personnel in the operation of aqueducts, the results were similarly frustrating. A year later, 148 of those taking the courses had been sacked from their jobs.[15] These redundancies mostly took place in the *municipios*, whose structure is autonomous from the governorship.

This lack of continuity of civil servants in municipal offices affected the capacity of *municipios* to bid for funds. The number of projects presented before the Banco de Datos, after an initial upsurge following the training courses, decreased significantly: 211 projects in 1993; 347 projects in 1994; 22 in 1995. In fact seven projects out of the 22 presented in 1995 were the initiative of one single *municipio,* Luruaco, whose planning office continued to be in the hands of the same person. In contrast, the respective Heads of Planning of other municipalities such as Sabanagrande, Sabanalarga and Santo Tomás were removed from their posts. Not surprisingly, these municipalities had not submitted any bids for funding.

The picture should be familiar to those studying clientelism. Partisan politics and personal relations become a barrier to state modernisation. Jobs in public administration tend to be used as a commodity in the traditional exchange of favours between politicians and their followers. While a centralist system is in no way a guarantee against patronage, one should be aware that a process of decentralisation is bound to encourage new clientelistic practices. In the Colombian context, popular elections of city mayors and governors, as the recent experience in Atlántico show, have often led to job instability in areas where continuity was crucial to the interest of the community. Once in a position of power, be it an *Alcaldía*, a seat in a *Concejo* or in the *Asamblea,* the elected official seeks to enlarge the participation of his/her political faction in the bureaucracy. Jobs are therefore filled with complete disregard for any technical qualifications. Previously trained personnel become redundant overnight. The waste of human capital is obviously high, particularly in small municipalities where this is so scarce.

These two examples from the Atlántico experience – in the management of aqueducts and in the offices of urban planning – show some of the difficulties faced by the process of decentralisation. Above all, they serve to reinforce my argument: traditional political practices contradict the aims of decentralisation. Far from encouraging efficiency or a more rational distribution of resources, in some cases decentralisation, accompanied by rampant clientelism, has produced the opposite. Indeed a lack of awareness of these, often unintended, consequences of decentralisation may lead to further problems of governability and public order.

These challenges should not detract from the significant steps taken in the process of *apertura*. The democratic reforms of the last two decades have had an impact on the political culture of Colombians. They have transformed the management of some *municipios*, although these cases are still probably exceptional. But in these cases the challenges of decentralisation have been met by the emergence of new political forces with an alternative vision of public administration, more in tune with the requirements of the constitution. They have also shown success. Yet this has been limited success. The real test for decentralisation will take place in the areas of education[16] and health, where the process was about to start at the time of writing these pages.

Conclusions

In March 1992, Eduardo Wiesner presented the government the results of the *Informe final de la misión para la descentralización* – a commission set up by the Departamento Nacional de Planeación to follow up the development of the process of decentralisation. The report of the commission, presided over by Wiesner, made some interesting observations regarding the politics of decentralisation.[17]

To start with, the report expresses that the final goal of decentralisation and fiscal federalism is to ensure the conditions of governability at the local level which, in turn, would guarantee governability in the nation at large. In this context, governability is understood in terms of the state capacity to provide services efficiently, improving therefore the living standards of citizens. The achievements of these aims, the report points out, will not be free of obstacles and difficulties. Among the many forces identified as major barriers to the success of decentralisation, the report highlights *'el papel de intereses políticos muy concretos que tienen algo importante que ganar o perder según sea la dinámica de cambio que surja de una u otras políticas'*.[18]

In the last analysis, decentralisation is a real challenge for the citizens themselves, now empowered with various constitutional tools to control the actions of elected officials. The final responsibility must of course be laid on them, and on the parties that supported their election. Given the nature of Colombian politics, and the lack of professional civil servants – a serious problem at the local level, precisely where the process of decentralisation is most strongly felt – political parties have a fundamental role to play in implementing the policies of decentralisation. This is why the challenges of decentralisation are naturally more political than administrative. Indeed, there has been undeniable progress regarding the latter: the appropriate institutions to oversee the process have been established; a legal framework has been designed; the country has agreed on a formula to distribute and transfer resources; functions have been redefined among the various levels of the state. What is lacking is a strong political will to put this administrative design into practice.

The challenges faced by decentralisation may not be felt so acutely in Bogotá or in other major capital cities. But my experience as Governor in Atlántico suggests that the problems are very serious in the *municipios*. These are best illustrated when looking at the scarcity of human capital, and by appreciating how the few efforts to train a civil service at the local level have been quickly frustrated by clientelistic practices. These problems are aggravated by a recent avalanche of new legislation and official procedures, imposing new demands on jobs that few are willing to take.[19] The dimension of the challenges faced by decentralisation should not be underestimated. They are inextricably tied to the fate of state reforms in Colombia. As President Gaviria observed in the introduction to his Revolución Pacífica '. . . *el reto de la descentralización será la vara con la cual será medido el desempeño del Estado en los últimos años del siglo y no debemos desestimar la tarea que tenemos por delante'*.[20]

Notes

1. See Orjuela's chapter in Dugas et al. (1992), p. 35.
2. The most comprehensive study of Colombian federalist tendencies from independence to the mid-nineteenth century is Gilmore (1995). For the radical period (1863–85), see Rodríguez Piñeres (1965).
3. On various aspects of the reforms adopted by this Assembly, see the chapters by Hoskin and Cepeda in this volume (Chapter 2, and Chapter 3).
4. See Orjuela's chapter in Ungar (1993), p. 114.
5. Orjuela, in Dugas et al. (1992), p. 44.
6. See Departamento Nacional de Planeación (1991).
7. See Vélez (1994).
8. See Chapter 3 in this volume.
9. Departamento Nacional de Planeación (1991), p. 47.
10. Departamento Nacional de Planeación, Documento 2241, UNIF DIS (Bogotá: mimeo, 27 Feb. 1986).
11. Departamento Nacional de Planeación (1991), p. 281.
12. Gobernación del Atlántico, 'Programa de ajuste al sector de agua potable' (Barranquilla: mimeo, Nov. 1994).
13. Gobernación del Atlántico, 'Programa de ajuste al sector de agua potable. Programa de saneamiento básico. Ejecuciones' (Barranquilla, 1994), p. 10.
14. *Ibid.*, p. 12.
15. Gobernación del Atlántico, 'Evolución del grupo de funcionarios en formulación y evaluación de proyectos y metodología del banco de proyectos' (Barranquilla: mimeo, 1995).
16. See Jesús Duarte's chapter in this volume (Chapter 6).
17. Departamento Nacional de Planeación, 'Descentralización y federalismo fiscal' (Bogotá: 1992).
18. *Ibid.*, pp. 23–4.
19. Well-trained professionals are generally reluctant to take on jobs in the public sector. Among other things, they fear to be sanctioned as a result of wrongly applying procedures that very few understand. A magistrate from the Consejo de Estado has referred recently to a civil servant's 'paranoia', regarding these fears; see Montes Hernández (1994), p. 29.
20. Departamento Nacional de Planeación (1991), p. 24.

PART II

THE STATE AND SOCIETY

CHAPTER 5

VIOLENCE AND THE STATE IN COLOMBIA

Alvaro Tirado Mejía

Colombia, the historian Malcolm Deas points out, has not always been a violent country.[1] In the past, it has enjoyed periods of relative tranquillity, during which the levels of violence were lower than in many European and American countries, involved as they were in international, religious, colonial or revolutionary wars. As Colombia has increasingly become identified with violence, it is important to stress from the beginning what otherwise may seem obvious: that violence is not the national character of Colombians; hence the relevance of Deas's observation. The history of the country, as of many other complex societies, is full of paradoxes. In the Latin American context, Colombia is unique in its traditions of prudent economic management and institutional stability. Nevertheless, for the outside world the country has gained international fame as the paradise of drug trafficking and the native land of some of the most notorious criminals of the twentieth century.

Perceptions – national and international alike – of Colombia as a violent country reflect of course a crude reality. The figures speak for themselves. While homicide was the seventh highest cause of death in 1973, it has become the first since 1990. It is estimated that some 165,000 people met a violent death between 1980 and 1990.[2] Available homicide statistics indicate that Colombia has by far the highest rate in that decade: 77.5 per 100 thousand inhabitants.[3] It is followed by Brazil, with a rate more than three times lower: 24.6, Panama: 22.9, Bahamas: 22.7, and Mexico: 20.6. The United States, widely regarded as a violent country, has a homicide rate of 8.0.[4] The widespread possession of firearms in the hands of private individuals in Colombia – more than three million firearms; and almost half of them illegally held – adds to the picture of a violent country.[5]

For most students of Colombia, violence was not their primary field of research until recent decades. However, there has been a growing interest in the subject, reflected in the proliferation of conferences and publications.[6] Indeed this interest has developed into a new discipline, whose practitioners are referred to as the *violentólogos*, to include not only those who devote their time to its study in research institutes, but also a wide range of specialists in areas such as history, political science, anthropology, sociology, economics, the clergy, the army and the police. As a result of this interest, there is a significant body of literature looking at various aspects of violence from different angles. There emerged distinct forms of violence: from the guerrilla groups, the paramilitary, the *sicarios* (hired killers), the gangs from the inner cities; or violence in the frontier, areas of recent settlement, such as Quindío in mid-twentieth century or Urabá in recent decades, or the emerald zone in Boyacá.

The causes of violence and its degree of intensity vary according to the different interpretations, as do the angles from which the problem is examined: historical, political, or regional. Nonetheless some generalisations are plausible. The literature does not refer now to a single phenomenon – *la violencia* – as in the past, but to *violencias*, to highlight its multiple manifestations. Violence often has distinct regional characteristics. Political violence does not account today for the largest number of casualties – only 10 per cent of violent deaths are related to politics. The breakdown of the judiciary and the subsequent rise in impunity are increasingly perceived as a major, even determinant factor, in the aetiology of Colombian violence. In this chapter I attempt to review some of the most significant factors that have contributed to the development of one of Colombia's major problems. In the first section, I examine some of the historical factors underpinning current manifestations of violence. In the second section I analyse how violence from guerrillas and drug trafficking has affected Colombia in recent decades. This is followed by some reflections on the state and the judiciary in an attempt to identify some of the major causes of a complex problem.

The Multiple Dimensions of Violence

The change of government in 1946, and the transition from a Liberal to a Conservative hegemony, unleashed a period of civil conflict which exploded with the events of 9 April 1948 and continued through the 1950s and 1960s. This period of Colombian history is known as *La Violencia*. The Liberal guerrillas, initially organised to oppose the Conservative regime, died out during the 1960s. But in some areas they were replaced by groups of bandits and by a new breed of guerrillas, with revolutionary aims inspired by the various tendencies of communism.

The expansion of guerrilla groups in Colombia led to an explosion of new organisations: pro-Soviet guerrillas (Fuerzas Armadas Revolucionarias de Colombia, FARC); pro-Chinese guerrillas (Ejército Popular de Liberación, EPL); Cuban style *foquista* guerrillas (Ejército de Liberación Nacional, ELN); nationalist pro-Cuban guerrilla (Movimiento 19 de Abril, M-19); *indigenista* guerrillas (Quintín Lame); and Trotskyist guerrillas (Partido Revolucionario de los Trabajadores, PRT). There was nothing unique in the emergence of guerrillas in Colombia, as they spread practically all over the continent following the Cuban revolution. What seems unique to Colombia is their long survival. The FARC, still active today, is the oldest guerrilla movement in the continent – some of its leaders are over 70 years old. The ELN, after being almost extinguished in the 1960s, has re-emerged with strength. Other groups, like the M-19, Quintín Lame, EPL, and PRT have now joined the political system through peace agreements and amnesties, but by the 1990s they had outlived most of their counterparts elsewhere in the continent.

While guerrilla groups developed, drug trafficking made its appearance.[7] The country witnessed first the *bonanza marimbera* – the marihuana boom which left a spiral of violence in the Atlantic Coast. Then came cocaine, which strengthened drug trafficking and led to further violence – intrinsic now to the nature of the trade. Drug barons – particularly members of the so-called 'Medellín cartel' – posed serious challenges to the state, through the use of political assassinations and an army of terror, soon labelled 'narco-terrorism'.

In addition to the emergence and consolidation of criminal organisations, there were other structural factors which help to explain the explosion of violence in recent decades. Traditionally, Colombia has experienced an almost constant process of internal migration and colonisation in the last two centuries. In the last 40 years, this process was most evident in regions such as the *pie de monte llanero* in the eastern plains, Urabá, the Upper Magdalena, Caquetá, and Putumayo. In these regions, population settlement and violence run hand in hand, and it is not difficult to establish the relationship between them, although some people deny it. In these areas of colonisation, the state does not exist, and therefore there is no governmental power to arbitrate eventual conflicts. The process may be simply described in various stages. The settler arrives first, clears it and acquires very precarious rights of possession *(mejoras),* which are often sold to someone else, who may or may not have more means, but who nevertheless still takes a long time to consolidate his hold on the property. The absence of the state is evident in the lack of roads, of schools, of public services, and, above all, in the lack of authority. State authority arrives late and usually in an arbitrary fashion. Much later, if at all, the law appears in the form of a judge. Thus, in the absence of the state in what are immense territories, it is no coincidence that the guerrilla has often taken over by force the role of mediator, usually well accepted by a large percentage of these populations. In the absence of the state, these regions, geographically in the periphery, are also attractive to drug traffickers. There prospers that ambiguous alliance between guerrillas and drug traffickers that the country has witnessed over the last few years.[8]

This pattern of settlement and conflict is also present in urban areas. In the last four decades, Colombia has transformed from being a rural to an urban country, a process also experienced elsewhere in Latin America. The growth of shanty towns such as the *favelas* of Brazil and the *barriadas* of Caracas are good examples of how violence breeds in these recent urban settlements where there are no public services and unemployment is rampant. In Colombia these problems are exacerbated by the fact that, as a country of cities, migration spread in many different directions. Other factors also conditioned the rise of violence in newly established urban settlements. Rural migration to the cities has mostly been determined by economic considerations. However, since the 1940s there has also been a constant flux of migrants expelled from rural areas where violence took place. These migrants brought with them some of the attitudes that prevailed in their rural surroundings. As can be clearly observed in superb testimonial books with vivid recollection of their experiences, the vast majority of migrants remember *La Violencia* in their native towns, either because they lived through it or because they heard the story from their elders. On arriving in the cities, many of them settled as squatters, following a similar pattern of colonisation that has gone hand in hand with violence.[9] In these new *barriadas* – neighbourhoods – where the migrant peasants settled, once again there was no state to provide public service or to enforce law and order. In the absence of the state, they resorted to organising themselves as they had in the countryside, to defend themselves from bandits and thugs. This was the origin of many gangs, *brigadas populares*, which spread in the *barrios* of the large cities. Additionally, as it becomes clear from the testimonial literature quoted above, the move to these new forms of violent organisations was eased as in some cases they received training from guerrilla groups, while some of them were recruited and financed by drug traffickers as *sicarios* – hired assassins.

Thus by the mid-1960s violence, which had hitherto been mostly rural, also became urban. As time went on urban violence increased. In 1965, the homicide rate of the 20 largest cities accounted for half of the nation's total, but by 1980 this proportion had increased to three quarters.[10] Up to 1978, guerrilla groups had grown slowly, but since then they have intensified their activities and some groups, like the M-19, even began to operate in the cities. As can be seen from this summary, violence as experienced by Colombian society is an extremely complex phenomena: to some extent it is politically motivated, but it is also related to common crime. Although of different origins, these expressions of violence are often inter-linked, making the task of identifying the roots of the problem and its treatment more difficult.

From Political Violence to Narco-Terrorism

Political violence today fundamentally refers to that produced by guerrillas and the forces combating them. Political violence between Liberals and Conservatives as in the past, is no longer central to recent conflicts, although it is occasionally present in some places. The emergence of guerrillas in the 1960s coincided with the National Front regime, a system of coalition rule, where power was exclusively shared between Liberals and Conservatives.[11] As these two parties equally distributed all public posts (including of course parliamentary seats) between themselves, there was no room for opposition from other groups. The rigidity of the system encouraged armed insurrection: since the legal channels for protest and representation were closed to the opposition, sectors in the unions, the universities and in the peasantry decided to radicalise their actions, taking up arms as was then the trend in Latin America.

After 1974 the National Front agreement came gradually to an end. Nevertheless, in broad areas of the population, there was a perception that the system remained closed, without any desire to reform itself. Simultaneously, while the armed movement grew, sectors in the opposition and within the establishment began to discuss the need for a political opening, *apertura,* as an answer to and remedy for violence. The first serious attempt was made under the presidency of Belisario Betancur (1982–86), who proposed to deal with the guerrillas in political not just military terms. Amidst the so-called national dialogue, conversations were initiated with the different armed groups. In the final analysis, they were never satisfactorily concluded. On the contrary, the national dialogue was followed by further violence. Groups such as the M-19 grew more radical, to the point of committing lunatic actions like the seizure of the Supreme Court, on the pretext of forcing the magistrates, held as hostages, to pass judgement on the President of the republic.

Belisario Betancur's project, indeed a precursor of later initiatives, was nevertheless doomed to failure for various reasons. The political parties, in general, did not support it. The army felt alienated from a project perceived as hostile to the institution. It therefore did not collaborate with the peace process; it even torpedoed it. In turn, the guerrillas tried to take advantage of the circumstances: rather than seeking peace, they aimed at gaining military strength and territorial and social space. Faced with the resurgence of guerrillas, and hounded by their attacks and kidnappings, some social sectors, occasionally in tandem with drug traffickers, decided to take the law into their own hands and created the so-called *ligas de autodefensa* (self protection groups).

In spite of the frustrations, the search for a political solution – and not simply a military and repressive answer to the guerrillas – was continued by the following governments, Virgilio Barco (1986–90) and César Gaviria (1990–94), with partial success. Indeed, at the beginning of the Gaviria administration, a peace agreement was negotiated with the M-19, EPL, PRT and Quintín Lame – a significant second wind for peace, particularly for a group such as the M-19 which found itself isolated from public opinion after the disaster of the Palace of Justice, but which now took a more realistic approach at the negotiating table. As a result of these agreements, several thousands of guerrillas were demobilised. However, the FARC and the ELN remained in arms.

As the process of negotiations with the guerrillas developed, the political system was profoundly transformed. To the opposition's complaints that the system was closed, exclusive and incapable of self-reform, the answer was to convene a National Constitutional Assembly, where all social and political sectors were represented, including ethnic and religious minorities, traditionally alienated from the public debate, and of course the guerrilla groups that took part in the peace accords. The result was a new constitution, which gives protection to a wide range of human rights, and encourages political participation. The new constitution has also modified the regional conformation of the country and strengthened the judiciary.[12] In addition, Gaviria gave political representation to the guerrillas who participated in the peace agreement, including a top cabinet job, the ministry of health, to a leader of the M-19, setting a new precedent: here was a guerrilla chief turned cabinet minister, and no government had been overturned.

In the face of these significant changes, it has become difficult for those still in arms to justify their actions on the supposedly exclusive and rigid character of the system. Thus political reform has ceased to be the banner of the remaining guerrilla groups, which seem to be more interested in securing regional power in those areas where they operate, than in the takeover of central power to transform the whole of society. This can be seen through their persistent armed rebellion in rural areas in the periphery, in a country which is now mostly urban. Other factors also help to explain their increasing isolation from public opinion, both national and international: the lack of ideological clarity following the downfall of international communism, the insistence of financing their operations through kidnappings and extortion – which no doubt has led them to amass large amounts of money, their contact with drug traffickers, and indeed their own involvement in the drugs trade. Furthermore, because of their methods and their alliances, and because of the dynamics of the Colombian situation, it has become increasingly difficult to distinguish political from common violence.

Drug trafficking was a major factor in contributing to the extraordinary growth of violence in recent decades. As an illicit activity, drug trafficking is intrinsically violent. Developed outside the law around immense sums of money, drug trafficking has had a vastly corrupting effect on society and on state agents – particularly judges and policemen. Because of the illegal but overwhelmingly lucrative aspect of this activity, business is carried out under a code that overlooks violence and death. Whoever fails to fulfil his/her side of the bargain in a business deal is not taken to court: they or their family pay with their life. State agents or any other person who decides to oppose their activities face a dilemma: to become an accomplice or a victim, to accept bribery or death.

In the 1970s, newspaper reports and official statistics began to register the appearance of corpses in the cities, many of them with signs of torture, often the product of settling accounts among drug traffickers. Drug traffickers expanded their interests. As they became richer, they invested in other areas of the economy, particularly in real estate to become important landowners. They applied the violent methods with which they were acquainted in their new businesses. In the countryside they also decided to respond with violence to the attacks of the guerrillas: to some extent this was the origin of the *paramilitares*. In the face of guerrilla threats – extortion and, above all, kidnappings – the drug-traffickers-turned-landowners, occasionally with the cooperation of members of the army and the police, fought the guerrillas outside the law and with ferocious violence. By the end of the 1980s, the country was suffering a horrendous wave of massacres. These criminal organisations did not limit their violent actions to attacking the guerrillas. They launched a direct challenge to the state: soon they also targeted prominent politicians and state agents, particularly members of the judiciary. 'Narco-terrorism', as it was labelled in the early 1990s when it escalated to dramatic proportions, was geared both at intimidating the population and at forcing the state to give way.

In this complex picture of Colombian violence, some of the actors have taken on different and often simultaneous roles which are worth noticing. Drug traffickers as such, for example, are enemies of the state. So are the guerrillas, whose preaching against private property and in favour of expropriation also threatens drug traffickers. As landowners, drug traffickers tend to take the role of keepers of 'law and order' against the guerrillas, therefore becoming allies of the army and the police. However, the guerrillas, while fighting drug traffickers and their much feared *autodefensas*, also make alliances with them, protecting their plantations and laboratories against the actions of the army and the police. The two latter institutions are obvious enemies of drug traffickers. Some of their members, however, occasionally contribute to the *autodefensas* to combat the guerrillas.

Law enforcement agents, in turn, are also victims of attacks from both guerrillas and drug traffickers. It has been estimated that more than 230 policemen were shot dead by drug traffickers in Medellín in 1990, when the cartels offered to pay 2 million pesos for each dead policeman. But police officers also succumbed to corruption, playing therefore the role of allies of drug traffickers. The state has made significant efforts to combat corruption. In 1993–94, for example, 'about 6,000 policemen were sanctioned, that is to say seven per cent (approx) of the institution's members had been under investigation, judged and punished'.[13] However, the results have been short of any major success against the corrupting influence of drug trafficking since, as a well-known general during the Mexican revolution used to say, 'no army can resist a million dollar cannon shot'. Corruption within the army and the police also has direct consequences for the abuse of human rights, in so far as these state agents with links to drug traffickers and other criminal organisations have tended to be involved in some of the most atrocious assassinations and massacres. This can be seen through the investigations into the massacres of Trujillo, El Nilo, Remedios and Urabá.

One of the major paradoxes of the Colombian experience is how it has been possible to sustain a democratic, civilian regime and economic growth in the middle of extraordinary levels of violence. Regarding the first point, I have already mentioned some of the main efforts to encourage further democratic developments in order to tackle violence of political origins. I will now highlight some relevant points on the impact of violence on the economy.

The Colombian economy has been, next to the Chilean, the most solid Latin American economy in recent decades. Since the 1950s, the country has experienced unique uninterrupted growth. Colombia escaped the worst of the Latin American debt crisis. In recent years, the country has also experienced important gains in social development. For the casual observer, it would seem that violence has not affected economic performance. On the contrary, there are some suggestions that correlate economic growth with violence. Recent research, however, indicates otherwise. Armando Montenegro and Carlos E. Posada have observed that beyond a certain level of criminality (referred to as the level compatible with the maximum rate of economic growth), violence begins to affect the process of production through its impact on savings and investments.[14] After a thorough examination of economic and social indicators, Montenegro and Posada conclude that violence is seriously damaging the process of economic growth in some departments. Mauricio Rubio's research also points in a similar direction.[15]

The international aspects of Colombian violence also deserve further examination. Drug trafficking, as the fundamental cause of recent violence, is in this respect particularly relevant, given the international dimensions of this criminal activity and its impact on Colombian foreign relations. The issue of extradition is at the front line of Colombian foreign policy. Linked to extradition was the problem of narco-terrorism that the country faced in the late 1980s and early 1990s – a wave of assassinations against politicians, policemen and members of civil society. International mercenaries – of Israeli and British origins, among other nationalities – became involved with the paramilitary, training the forces employed by drug-traffickers-turned-landowners in the Magdalena Medio, where some of the most horrendous massacres have taken place. In addition, drug trafficking is to some extent linked to the arms trade – and the use of sophisticated weaponry by criminal organisations has been a determining factor in recent Colombian violence.[16] Other international crimes are linked to the drugs trade, such as money laundering. Finally, drug trafficking affects Colombia's international position since in the attempt to curb the trade, some countries violate Colombia's sovereignty by taking actions beyond their own territories.

Violence originating in guerrilla activities has significant international dimensions as well. Of course, during the Cold War references to the international affiliation and support given to the guerrillas were common. Following the fall of the Berlin Wall, the dismantling of the Soviet empire, and Cuba's own position, this is no longer the case. Guerrilla activities are now financed internally through the *vacuna* ('vaccination') – protection payments, kidnapping and extortion. But the frequent kidnapping of foreigners and the ransom demanded for their liberation, as well as the constant threats of extortion against multinationals, especially oil companies, are seriously affecting Colombia's international relations. Additionally, the guerrillas have resorted to attacks against the armies of neighbouring countries, as has happened on the borders of Ecuador and, more recently, Venezuela. This has created a most conflictive scenario. Indeed, the most pressing problems of foreign relations that Colombia is currently facing are linked to violence-related activities: drug trafficking with the United States, and guerrilla attacks in the case of Venezuela.

Violence, the State and the Judiciary

Although an aetiology of violence might suggest an eclectic position, given the multiple origins of the problem, there are in my view some major and determinant causes worthy of consideration. Above all the absence of the state, particularly the lack of a proper judiciary, stands out. Of course magistrates and judges do exist, most of them honest and enlightened. Furthermore, in the face of threats from drug traffickers, for example, some of them have proved to be courageous, even heroic. The number of officers employed by the judiciary has grown significantly in recent years: from 13,589 in 1973 to 32,196 in 1992. Their salaries have also improved: in 1993 some of them enjoyed wage increases of up to 132 per cent. Nevertheless, the incapacity of the state to provide justice has become a major problem; indeed, justice is practically non-existent. According to Armando Montenegro, only twenty out of every 100 criminal offences lead to a charge; fourteen out of those twenty lapse. Of the remaining six, in only three cases will a sentence be passed. In other words there is a 97 per cent probability that a criminal will escape sentence.[17] In addition, a typical criminal trial takes ten years, while a civil suit lasts about five. In 1992 there were 2,000,000 unresolved cases in the criminal courts and 1,800,000 in the civil courts.

As impunity reached such dramatic proportions, the issue of the efficiency of the judiciary became the focus of national debate. As already mentioned in previous chapters, a major aim of the new constitution was to strengthen the judiciary through the creation of new institutions such as the Fiscalía General and the Defensor del Pueblo. The government has tried to make procedures more agile. In the search for greater efficiency, and in the face of the extraordinary assault that delinquents launched against the judiciary, some new figures hitherto alien to Colombian traditions have now been incorporated into the legal system – such as anonymous judges and negotiated sentences.

Many reasons have been given to explain the breakdown of the judiciary: an excessive formalism; the difficulties of reaching settlements through conciliation outside the courts, the criminalisation of too many activities, the lack of state resources. However, the breakdown of the judiciary has been accompanied by some major problems. As already suggested, magistrates have been the object of violent attacks by criminal organisations with an intensity with few parallels elsewhere. Drug traffickers in particular, but also guerrilla organisations, have resorted to threatening, and indeed assassinating, people involved in relevant cases – be they policemen, judges, lawyers or witnesses. The Colombian record is unique. In 1984, Rodrigo Lara Bonilla, Minister of Justice, was assassinated while in office. Only a few years later, another Minister of Justice, Enrique Low Mutra, was killed shortly after leaving his post. Enrique Parejo, also in charge of Justice, had escaped death in 1987 from a criminal attempt in Budapest, where he was serving as Ambassador after leaving the cabinet. All of them were victims of drug traffickers, who also ordered the assassination of the Procurador General de la Nación (Attorney General), Mauro Hoyos. The assault on the Palace of Justice by the M-19 in 1985, and the counter attack by the army, left half the members of the Supreme Court and the Consejo de Estado either dead or wounded. Between 1979 and 1991, a report from the Comisión Andina de Juristas recorded 515 cases of violence against judges and lawyers; 329 of those were either homicides or assassination attempts. In other words, every year 40 judges and lawyers were victims of violence, and 25 suffered direct attempts against their lives and death.[18]

This assault on the judiciary went hand in hand with the rise of criminal activities from various sources, including guerrilla activities in wide areas of the national territory, drug traffickers, and various forms of economic crime linked to sudden economic growth. All this happened amidst an atmosphere of tolerance and permissiveness, and rapid changes in social values (of which more later). The inefficiency of the judiciary encouraged the rise of so-called 'private justice' – another form of delinquency. The problem is therefore exacerbated by a vicious circle, where the generalisation of crime, the breakdown of the judiciary and high rates of impunity are closely interrelated. As C. V. de Roux, Consejero Presidencial para los Derechos Humanos in Colombia, observed:

> no judicial system can work properly without meeting the condition that criminal behaviour be a statistically exceptional form of conduct. This condition is not met in Colombia. Here crime is a generalised behaviour. Consequently there will never be enough officers or efficient procedures or enough facilities to stop the debacle of the administration of justice.[19]

What is to be done in the face of such an overwhelming problem? Let me venture my opinion. Remedies ought to be multiple, as diverse as the manifestations of violence in Colombia. Moreover, different solutions should not be perceived as contradictory; they could complement each other. For example, a negotiated settlement with the guerrillas is a healthy option; society of course is better served by a former guerrilla working in the bureaucracy or participating from the legal opposition than by the on-going fighting in the jungle. In this sense the country has to some extent advanced. There is no doubt that the incorporation of thousands of guerrillas into civilian life during the Gaviria administration has been a positive development. But it ought to be remembered that political violence – which has captured the state's attention – is not the only nor the greatest source of violence. It has been estimated that 90 per cent of Colombian crime is non-political; and here the rule of law becomes an imperative. This is not to suggest that the enforcement of the law should not also be a proper answer for political crimes.

However, an attitude of tolerance towards crime has taken root in Colombia, conditioning a weak response from the state and civil society. In the face of a criminal onslaught, it seems that the answer has been to surrender, to grant all sorts of amnesties, from political amnesties to tax amnesties, to bend the law when dealing with the police or even in academic circles. To accommodate the laws to the wishes of those who break them has become acceptable. As the state does not play its proper role, to save face the best possible solutions appear to be negotiated, but from a disadvantageous position: the strong party here is the criminal, who imposes the conditions regardless of the rule of law or of any ethics of the state.

The problem of confronting violence is not strictly a legal one, nor is it only the responsibility of the judicial system. It should also be a concern of civil society, which seems to behave as if this was not its own problem, whose solution depends on alien forces. For example, those involved in dealing with guerrilla problems only include the government, the army and the guerrillas themselves. The dominant mentality is under pressure to change: there are at work the profound transformations of the last three decades, rapid economic growth and the sudden abundance of material wealth, and the internationalisation of the country at all levels. There emerges, above all, a society whose recent generations have been educated in an atmosphere of extreme violence, under which social values have to be accommodated to conditions where force prevails.

In these circumstances, the ethical differences between right and wrong have been blurred, while the border between what is legal and what is illegal vanishes. In November 1994, the weekly *Cambio16* carried on its front cover a picture of a suspect accused of various crimes, including murder. The headlines of this cover, echoing an interview with the suspect read: 'I am "narco" but decent'.[20] Salazar and Jaramillo further illustrate this point by quoting the testimony of a drug trafficker: 'I never felt that I was a delinquent nor have I anything to repent, because I do not think I committed a crime or sinned, as my actions were not included in the ten commandments issued by the law of God.'[21] The trivialisation of crime, including the most atrocious, has reached extraordinary dimensions, as proved by the accounts of the massacre in Trujillo, where more than 100 people were assassinated. Judicial records establish that the assassins mutilated some of their victims with an electric saw. The macabre features of this conduct are also highlighted by the words of one of the killers before they faced their victims: 'let's have breakfast first, otherwise we will not be able to digest it'.

Given the seriousness and gravity of the problem, it is obviously difficult to find a proper, simple remedy. But if, as shown in this chapter, violence springs from multiple reasons, it must be underlined that the solutions should also be multiple. Although the distinction between political violence and common crime has tended to disappear, it is still arguable that political violence should be tackled politically and not exclusively through military actions. Nevertheless, it should be realised that there is limit, beyond which the state cannot negotiate its *raison d'être*. Common crime, which accounts for the bulk of violence in Colombia, has probably not been at the centre of state concerns. Its extraordinary dimensions suggest that here there cannot be other appropriate policies excepting that of enforcing the rule of law. And this is only possible through the strengthening of the judiciary. Judges, however, do not work in isolation. Their budgets may be improved. Laws may be changed. But in the final analysis, their actions are only effective through the participation of civil society, whose values need to be reconsidered.

Notes

1. Deas and Gaitán (1995), p. 7.
2. Bushnell (1993), p. 252.
3. Deas and Gaitán (1995), p. 14.
4. Deas and Gaitán (1995), p. 268.
5. Vargas Velásquez (1993), p. 153.
6. The literature is vast. The reader is best advised to consult the following bibliographical essays: Ortiz Sarmiento (1994), Russell (1973), Sánchez (1985), and Peñaranda (1992).
7. An introduction to a social history of the Colombian mafia is Betancourt and García (1994).
8. For a description of this ambiguous encounter, see Molano (1992).
9. See, for example, Salazar (1990) and (1993).
10. Deas and Gaitán (1995), p. 214.
11. See observations about this regime in the chapter by Hoskin in this volume (Chapter 2).
12. See Chapters 2 and 3 of this volume.
13. Deas and Gaitán Daza (1995), p. 332.
14. Montenegro and Posada (1994), p. 8.
15. Rubio (1994).
16. The links between drugs and the arms trade worldwide are examined in Labrouse (1993).
17. Montenegro (1994a), p. 38. A more recent study by the former Minister of Justice, Néstor H. Martínez, refers to a rate of impunity of 99.5%. Martínez (1996).
18. Bonilla and Valencia Villa (1992), p.1.
19. C. V. De Roux, 'Notas sobre la campaña SOS Colombia', quoted in Salazar and Jaramillo (1992), p. 59.
20. *Cambio16,* Colombia, 21–8 Nov. 1994.
21. Salazar and Jaramillo (1992), p. 99.

CHAPTER 6

STATE WEAKNESS AND CLIENTELISM IN COLOMBIAN EDUCATION

Jesús Duarte

The 1991 Constitution introduced nine years of compulsory education for all Colombian children. Although the country is far from this level of schooling, the government of President Ernesto Samper decided to take up the challenge of making this constitutional mandate a reality. This chapter examines some of the structural obstacles the government faces in achieving this goal. In the first part, it will summarise the present situation of Colombian education, and compare its position with other Latin American countries. The second part will present briefly the main proposals of the *Salto Educativo* – as the government's plan is called. The third part will examine the historical weakness of the central government in educational matters. The last part will discuss the politicisation of the administration of public education.

Colombian Education in the 1990s: An Overview

The present Colombian education system comprises one year of pre-primary education, five years of primary education, and six years of secondary education. Graduates from secondary schools can go either to the higher education institutions which offer technical, technological or university programmes, or, outside the formal education sector, to the vocational training system. The five years of primary and first four years of secondary education, together with one year of pre-primary education, comprise the basic education cycle which is mandatory for all Colombian children in the Constitution. (The main indicators of Colombian education are presented in Table 1.)

Pre-primary education enrols half a million pupils. A recent study by the Departamento Nacional de Planeación (DNP) indicates that about 37 per cent of children aged three to five are currently enrolled at this level.[1] Over 90 per cent of them are from urban areas, and 60 per cent are catered for by private institutions.

Primary education enrols over 4.5 million pupils, almost equally divided between boys and girls. Most of them are looked after by state

Table 1. Colombia: Basic Indicators in Education, 1993

Enrolment and Coverage

% Illiteracy (over 15 years old, 1985) (1)	12.2
Total Enrolment 1993 (2)	
pre-primary	506,080
primary	4,599,132
secondary	2,796,007
higher education	525,969
% of Private Enrolment/ Total Enrolment (2)	
pre-primary	56.6
primary	17.2
secondary	37.4
higher education	61.4
Net Coverage by Levels (3)	
pre-primary (3–5 years old)	36.9
primary (6–11 years old)	79.1
secondary (12–17 years old)	54.1
higher education (4)	11.5

Finance

Central Government Spending on Education as % of GDP (4)	3.1
Central Government Spending on Educ. as % of Central Gov. Spend. (5)	15.0
Central Government Spending *per capita* on Education in 1990 (in US$)(5)	28.4
Public Spending Per Pupil by level in 1990 (in US$) (4)	
primary	92
secondary	183
higher education	1,086
Central Government Spending Per Pupil as % of GDP *per capita* (5)	
primary	8.3
secondary	15.7
higher education	86.0

Sources
(1) DANE, La Pobreza en Colombia, Bogotá, 1989.
(2) MEN, 1995.
(3) DNP-UDS-Mision Social, Encuesta de Caracterización Socioeconómica, 1993.
(4) DNP-MEN, El Salto Educativo, 1994.
(5) My own calculations using data from DNP-UDS.

schools. Despite the gains made in the expansion of schooling in the last four decades the net coverage of primary education is far from being universal and twenty out of 100 children aged six to eleven remain outside the school system. The efficiency of primary schools continues to be low throughout the country: on average, only 56 per cent of children who enter the first grade finish the primary cycle, and only 40 per cent of them do it within five years. National-level figures conceal enormous differences across and within regions, and across income groups. In some departments, such as those of the Atlantic and Pacific coasts, or in rural areas, both the net coverage and the completion rate of primary education are far below the national average. Similarly, the difference in primary school attendance between children from the poorest and richest quintile households is about 20 per cent.[2]

Secondary education has nearly 2.8 million pupils. Most of them, 94 per cent, are from urban areas. Private schools cover 37 per cent of all enrolments at this level, though their share has decreased since 1960 when they represented 60 per cent. The net coverage of secondary education for children aged twelve to seventeen is 54 per cent, and only 60 per cent of children who enter secondary schools finish the whole cycle. School attendance in secondary education varies by income level. Children from the bottom quintile have an attendance rate a quarter lower than those from the top quintile.

Higher education serves some 525,000 students, 40 per cent of them in public universities. The coverage of higher education remains modest, 11.5 per cent, and enrolments in this level are highly concentrated among the 40 per cent richest households.[3]

Central government expenditure on education as a percentage of GDP was 3.1 per cent in 1993, and the share of education in the central government budget was 15 per cent (see Table 1). Despite the fact that Colombia has still not achieved universal coverage in primary education, the share of this level in central spending on education has decreased from 50 per cent in 1975 to 38 per cent in 1990–93. The share of secondary education is around 30 per cent, and for higher education around 21 per cent. The remaining 12 per cent is devoted to non-formal education, cultural and sports activities.[4]

As can be seen in Table 2 (overleaf), Colombian education performs poorly when compared with other Latin American countries or international standards. In primary education Colombia's most important neighbours have attained net coverage near to the universal level, while we have just 80 per cent; with the exception of Venezuela, all of them have a greater proportion of children completing this educational level. Colombian secondary education coverage is similar to that in Mexico and Venezuela, and higher than in Costa Rica, but far below that in Chile, Peru and Argentina. The coverage of higher education in Colombia is the lowest among the selected countries.

Similarly, central government spending on education as a share of GDP in Colombia at 3.1 per cent is far lower than in our selected Latin

Table 2. Comparing Colombian Education with Selected Latin American Countries c. 1993

Country	% adult literacy rate (+15) (1)	net primary enrolment ratio (6-11 yrs) (2)	gross secondary enrolment ratio (1)	gross tertiary enrolment ratio (1)	completion rate for primary education (1)	public expenditure in education as % of GDP (1)	women per 100 males in primary (3)	women per 100 males in secondary (3)
Argentina	96.0	97.2	71.0	39.9				
Chile	94.0	90.5	72.0	20.6	77.0	3.7	95.0	115.0
Colombia(4)	88.0	79.1	54.1	11.5	56.0	3.1	98.0	100.0
Costa Rica	93.0	87.1	42.0	26.3	79.0	4.6	94.0	103.0
Mexico	89.0	100.0	55.0	14.0	72.0	4.1	94.0	92.0
Peru	86.0	98.9	67.0	33.1		3.5		
Venezuela(5)	89.0	91.0	54.0	26.6	48.0	4.1	99.0	104.0
Developing	69.0	86.0	41.0	6.8	71.0	3.9		
Developed(6)	97.0	100.0	90.3	37.9		4.9	108.3	100.0
World (6)	75.0		50.4	12.7		4.8	85.2	78.6

Sources
(1) UNDP, Human Development Report, 1994.
(2) ECLAC, Statistical Yearbook for Latin American and the Caribbean, 1993.
(3) World Bank, World Development Report 1994.
(4) Table 1.
(5) The figure for secondary education is from A. Fiszbein and G. Psacharopoulos, 'A Cost-Benefit Analysis of Education in Venezuela', *Economics of Education Review*, vol. 12, no. 4 (1993), pp. 293-298.
(6) UNESCO, World Education Report 1993, data for 1990.

American neighbours: in Mexico it is 4.1 per cent, in Chile 3.7 per cent, in Peru 3.5 per cent, and in Costa Rica 4.6 per cent. As a result, compared to other Latin American countries, Colombia shows low spending per pupil in primary and secondary education. As a recent document from the World Bank claims, only Bolivia, El Salvador and Paraguay spend less than Colombia on these basic levels of schooling. In contrast, the absolute level of public spending on higher education in Colombia is similar to the average for the region. However, in relative terms, Colombia is spending twelve times more on higher than on primary education, the highest ratio in the region with the exception of Brazil and Paraguay according to the World Bank.[5]

The *Salto Educativo* of the Samper Government.

The government of President Samper, which took office in August 1994, seems to be committed to putting education high on its list of priorities. In October 1994, the government launched its educational development plan for 1994–98, called *El Salto Educativo,* and subtitled *'Educación, Eje del Desarrollo del País'.* This plan takes into account the mandates of the 1991 Constitution on basic education, and the recommendations of the *Misión de Ciencia y Educación* led by the writer Gabriel García Márquez.

The priorities of the *Salto Educativo* are concerned with the expansion of the coverage of basic education, improving the quality of public education, and improving equity in the access to all levels of schooling. To achieve this, the government plans to increase central government expenditure in education from 3.1 to 4.9 per cent in 1988.

Regarding the expansion of basic education, the *Salto Educativo* proposes guaranteeing access to the school system for all children and providing them with one year of pre-primary school and nine years of the basic cycle of education. It means the creation of 300,000 new places in pre-primary education, and 600,000 new places in basic education, especially in the first four years of secondary schooling.

To enhance the quality of basic education, the government aims to gradually increase the length of the school day from 3.5 to six hours, and provide schools with textbooks, instructional materials and libraries. The government also proposes to improve teachers' salaries progressively, provide them with in-training courses to improve their qualifications, and raise the educational requirements of new teachers.

To guarantee access to education to children from low-income households, the government will subsidise more than 300,000 pupils in pre-primary and primary schools, and will distribute 350,000 vouchers, which cover the direct cost of schooling, among children from poor families to attend private secondary schools. In addition, the government will create 180,000 new loans for students enrolled in higher education institutions.

The plan also proposes the reorganisation of the administrative structure of state schools, and develops the framework for the implementation of both a 1993 law regulating the transfer of financial resources for public schooling to departments and municipalities, and the newly adopted *Ley General de Educación* of 1994.

There has recently been much discussion about the total cost of President Samper's social programme, in which the education plan is included.[6] It is likely that some of the goals proposed by the plan will be only partially achieved. However, in contrast to the educational plans of the previous two governments, which proposed similar goals but did not forecast important increases in central public spending on the sector, the Samper plan proposes to increase the central budget devoted to education by 1.8 per cent of GDP during the period 1994–98. The present good performance of the Colombian economy, and the increasing government revenues from the oil sector anticipated for the rest of the decade, could give a firm basis to the proposed financial scheme of the *Salto Educativo*.

In this chapter, I will not discuss the financial constraints of the plan. Rather, I will concentrate on two obstacles that the government may have to face in the implementation of the educational programmes: the weakness of the Ministry of Education, and the clientelistic structure of the administration of public education, especially at regional level. These two issues concern not only the implementation of the education plan of President Samper, but also the implementation of any programme directed at improving Colombian education.

The Weakness of the Central Government

A review of education in Colombian history would show that the central government has never managed to impose clear authority and influence over the regional education systems. This is not the place for such a review, but it is worth pointing to some historical developments to illustrate this argument.[7]

During the nineteenth century, most of the legislation and policies concerning education approved by the central government remained unfulfilled. The whole period from Independence to 1886 is characterised by attempts by the central government to expand primary instruction, to introduce technical education, and to build a national system of education. Whatever the contents and the scope of the proposals, none of them ensured the funds needed to carry them out. For example, the various governments of the 1850s and 1860s claimed that 'Peace, Roads and Schools' were the way towards national economic progress, but the available figures for this period show a decline in enrolments, and the central governments neglected public education almost totally to the point that, in some years, it included no item for education in the national budget.[8] The education reform of President Eustorgio Salgar proposed compulsory elementary schooling, neutrality in religious education, and a national system of education uniformly organised, directed and supervised by the central government. It is claimed that the reform was one of the causes of the 1876–77 civil war. The radical government won the war, but it was disastrous for education: classes were suspended, textbooks were destroyed, and classrooms were used as barracks.[9] Economic stagnation, civil wars, and political instability weakened the possibility of the plans becoming reality. Regional and local governments paid and managed the largest part of the education system.

The various governments of the *Regeneración* period dismantled the controversial points of the Salgar reform: the 1886 Constitution ended compulsory elementary instruction and established that public education would be organised and controlled in agreement with the Catholic Church. The *Concordato* between Colombia and the Vatican, signed in 1887, assigned to the Catholic Church both the control of the content of education, and the moral and political control of teachers and public instruction staff. On transferring these functions to the Church, the government was tacitly admitting the weakness of the central state in educational matters.

Rafael Núñez acknowledged the deficiencies in the institutional framework of public education, and elevated the unit responsible for education to the Ministry of Public Instruction. From Independence to 1886, public instruction had been an office attached and subordinated to the Ministry of Government. In the States of the Union, during the federal period (1863–86), the situation was similar. Public instruction authorities, both at national and state level, lacked autonomy and independence, and educational matters obviously remained secondary in relation to other political business. They did not have the authority to appoint or dismiss administrative staff and teachers. They did not directly manage public funds for education. They had few and inadequate instruments for implementing educational policies. Teachers and school directors were not accountable to the public instruction authorities, but to the secretaries of government in Bogotá or in the state capitals.[10]

During the first thirty years of the twentieth century, as Helg points out, the Ministry of Public Instruction continued to be unable to maintain much of an active presence in the provinces:

[el Ministerio] . . . no tiene ningún poder de nombramiento sobre los niveles inferiores de la jerarquía educativa. El aislamiento y la impotencia del Ministerio de Instrucción Pública, tanto como la independencia de los departamentos, son sorprendentes. La instrucción pública es en efecto un deber de los departamentos, mas no de la Nación.[11]

During the Liberal administrations of the 1930s and 1940s the central government took some steps to intervene more actively in public education. The constitutional reform of 1936 established the 'supreme inspection' of the state in education, deleted any mention of Church control over educational content and teachers, and established that elementary education would be compulsory.

It is true that during the Liberal Republic (1930–46) there was a shift towards more central state intervention, and that the Liberal governments introduced new conceptions and ideas into education. However, looking at both the figures for enrolment and public expenditure on education, I would argue that most of the 'transformations' in education were rhetoric rather than reality.[12] As can be seen in Figures 1 and 2, all general indicators for education remained stagnated. Public expenditure on education as a proportion of GDP did not increase but decreased from 1.4 per cent in 1938 to 1 per cent in 1946. Similarly, enrolment rates did not reveal much progress during this period, though the number of students increased at all levels. In primary education the gross enrolment rate remained at 42 per cent, which meant that the opportunity for access to primary education did not improve. Higher education was the only level that experienced important increases, though from a very low base.

In 1940, despite the legislation introduced by the Liberal administrations, the minister, Jorge Eliécer Gaitán, had to acknowledge the minimal role of the central government in education:

Fig. 1 Public Spending on Education as a Percentage of GDP

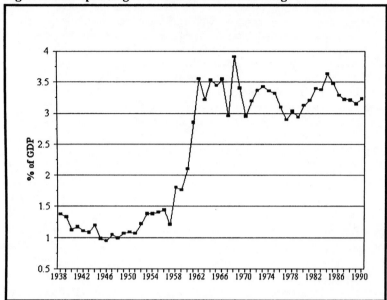

Fig. 2 Gross Coverage in Education by Levels

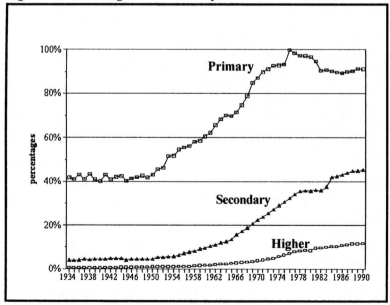

En el funcionamiento de la escuela pública colombiana hay una verdadera sociedad anónima formada por la Nación, el Departamento y los Municipios, que se debate en medio de la incongruencia. Allí todos son responsables y ninguno tiene la responsabilidad. Su desarmonía, que va desde la dirección administrativa hasta lo económico como lo pedagógico, se traduce en pugnas, formulismos, litigios y abandono de lo que debería ser el central objetivo de las actividades. Enfrente de todo lo cual, al Ministerio de Educación, que debería contar entre lo primordial la educación primaria, le corresponde el triste papel inoperante de convidado de piedra.[13]

The 1950s were the beginning of the great expansion of Colombian education, which lasted until the end of the 1970s. The gross coverage of primary schooling increased from 45 per cent in 1950 to 90 per cent in 1970, and to 100 per cent in 1978. The gross coverage for secondary education increased from five per cent in 1950 to 38 per cent in 1976, and in higher education from 0.1 per cent to seven per cent in the same period (see Figure 2, p. 133). This expansion was associated with the rise in public spending on education, with a greater involvement of the central government, and with the acceleration of economic growth:[14] national expenditure in education[15] as a proportion of GDP increased from one per cent in 1950 to three per cent in 1978, and public spending devoted to education grew from about 9 per cent at the beginning of the 50s to 20 per cent in 1978 (see Figure 1, p. 133).

The educational expansion coincided with an increasing centralisation of the finance and administration of public education. In 1960 the Lleras Camargo government (1958–62) decided to take responsibility for financing primary public education. During the 1960s a great number of secondary schools were also created, and some of them were financed and administered directly by the ministry. During the Carlos Lleras Restrepo administration (1964–70), the government adopted an educational reform to reorganise the administrative structure of the Ministry of Education, and to establish a number of new independent institutions ascribed to the ministry, responsible for some of its functions, such as higher education, science and technology, culture and sports. The reform also had the intention of enhancing the control of the central government over the spending of public funds for education in the departments through the FERs (Fondos Educativos Regionales), established in 1968. In 1975 the López Michelsen government (1974–78) nationalised public spending on secondary education.

The FERs have so far been the central government's most successful strategy for gaining control over the regions in educational matters.

Thus it is worth having a look at their development. Before 1968, though the central government paid primary education costs and a great proportion of the costs in secondary education, it did not control expenditure at the local levels. On the contrary, as Hanson claims, 'once the money entered the account of the state [departmental] treasury, the ministry lost control of the funds'. The departmental secretaries of education commonly ignored central policies. The funds earmarked for education were often diverted to more political projects. It was not uncommon for teachers to be hired when there were no funds to pay their salaries, or for governors to hire teachers during electoral campaigns in exchange for political support.[16]

The FERs were designed to take away the power that departmental authorities had over the management of the educational funds transferred from the centre, and to force them to follow central government policies. The FERs were basically contracts between each governor and the ministry, in which the former committed the departmental educational authorities to reorganising their offices, to appointing only qualified teachers, and to appointing teachers exclusively with money budgeted to that end. The contracts also forced the departments to receive a representative of the ministry who would evaluate, and even veto, all administrative aspects involving central educational funds.[17]

With the FERs, the central government, after many failed attempts throughout republican history, would have an instrument to intervene in public education at departmental level. By 1971, Luis Carlos Galán, the Minister of Education, could affirm that the only 'real link' between the central ministry and the departments were the FERs. However, Galán also pointed to the relative feebleness of this link:

> A los FER se acude muchas veces en busca de que el Ministerio solucione problemas de orden financiero, pero se les da poca o nula participación en la toma de decisiones administrativas, muchas de las cuales originan esos mismos problemas.[18]

The FER strategy met many problems in its implementation, especially in the first stages, caused by the opposition of the departmental authorities. There were many violations of the contracts by some of the departments, and frequently the central government had little power to punish transgressors.[19] Nevertheless, in the 1970s they proved to be a useful instrument for improving the administration of central expenditure on education.

However, as the FERs became powerful and expanded their functions

in the late 1970s, they began to be seen as another political and
'bureaucratic quota' by regional political forces. The FERs then experienced a change; from technical entities they were transformed into
increasingly politicised and bureaucratic institutions. The appointment
of their directors, which was initially made autonomously by the Minister of Education, started to be negotiated between the Minister and the
regional political leaders. Since then, the director of the FER has been
formally appointed by the Minister from a trio of candidates presented
by the governor, but the former usually appoints the latter's favourite.
Since 1978 the FERs have become politicised and controlled by regional politicians.

The 1980s would show a reverse in some of the trends experienced
in Colombian education during the previous three decades. The rapid
enrolment expansion of the sixties and seventies slowed down at all
educational levels. Gross coverage rate in primary education decreased
from 1976 to 1986 and then, during the final part of the decade, it increased slightly. Enrolments in secondary and higher education
continued their upward trend, though slower than in the previous decade
(see Figure 2, p. 133). Total public spending on education as a percentage of GDP rose from 3.1 per cent in 1980 to 3.6 per cent in 1984,
before declining to 3.2 per cent in 1990 (Figure 1, p. 133).

The 1980s saw a clear trend towards the decentralisation of the administrative functions that the central ministry had concentrated in the
previous decade. In 1986 the government decentralised the construction
and maintenance of schools and sports buildings, as well as the financing of their activities, to municipalities. In 1988 a law reorganised the
ministry and decentralised the administration of all public schools and
teachers to the departments. In 1989 the administration of all teachers
paid by the central government was transferred to the municipal mayors.

In the 1990s, as a complement to the decentralisation of the administration of public education, there have been a number of measures
empowering departments and municipalities with the autonomous use
of educational funds transferred by the central government to these levels. Law 60 of 1993 regulated the transfer of central funds for education
and health to departments and municipalities. The *Ley General de
Educación* of 1994 assigned a greater role to the departments in the administration of the central funds transferred for public education. In the
latter, the FERs were placed directly under the departmental authorities
and were to be part of the organisational structure of the Departmental
Secretariats of Education (SEDs) in the future. Their directors will be
appointed not by the Minister but by the departmental authorities.

We have seen, therefore, that the central government's influence and control over what actually happens in public education in the regions has been, and still is, minor. We have also seen that the links between the ministry and the lower levels of government have always been weak. Although, according to national legislation, educational policy is to be set by the ministry and should be implemented by the SEDs, the latter enjoy a great deal of autonomy. The SEDs are meant to parallel the former in terms of organisation, but the departments are entitled to establish whatever institutional structure they like. SEDs' directors and staff are appointed by departmental governors, and are accountable only to them, not to the ministry. As a result, there is no direct chain of control between the ministry and the SEDs, and, therefore, there is no national and unitary structure for the administration of public education in Colombia. There is a structural separation between the national and departmental systems of educational administration. Departmental authorities are not accountable to the ministry, and the latter has little influence on the former. As Hanson points out, the ministry plays the role of an adviser rather than a superior to the SEDs, and the latter routinely ignore ministry policy whenever it proves convenient.[20] The FERs have been the only successful link between the ministry and the departments. However, the FERs limited their action to the reduction of departmental mismanagement of central funds for education, and did little to enforce the observance of other national educational policies.

The inability of the central government to penetrate the regions has also been aggravated by the weak institutional capacity of the ministry, which prevents it from performing its functions of policy guidance, overall evaluation of the system, and technical support for the regions. The ministry lacks an effective information system that allows the centre to know what is going on in the regions. For example, it was only in 1992 that the ministry was able to have, for the first time in Colombian history, reliable figures about how many public teachers there were, where they were located, and which level of government was paying them. There is no effective system of national inspection that allows the ministry to know how the administration of public teachers and schools is working. The ministry has no reliable mechanisms of control over and evaluation of the use of revenue transfers to the municipalities and departments, nor of the use of central funds for national educational projects. Finally, there is no system of monitoring and impact evaluation of the national programmes in education that helps the ministry to adjust the policies being implemented.[21]

In recent years there has been a certain degree of agreement that at the end of the process of decentralisation, the municipalities should have greater autonomy for the management of teachers, schools and public funds for education. But there has been less agreement about both the steps and the pace of the process and the role of the departments. In February 1995, for example, a national strike of state teachers, which delayed the beginning of the academic year for a week, asked the government to reform a decree that regulated the steps for the municipalisation of public education.[22] The decentralisation of education might facilitate the achievement of the goals of the *Salto Educativo*, since decision-making at municipal level can reflect local needs more accurately, and local authorities can be more responsive to the demands of their constituencies. However, the implementation of decentralisation has been slow, and most departments and municipalities are not fully responsible for their new functions. On the other hand, the weak technical capacity of the ministry, which is mirrored in the SEDs and municipalities, is in itself a restraint on building a decentralised system. If the government is serious about attaining the goals of the *Salto Educativo*, the ministry has both to overcome its institutional weaknesses and design credible instruments which link the centre with the departments and municipalities. These instruments have to face a double and difficult task: to enhance the ministry's capacity to enforce the national policies in the regions, and to support the process of decentralisation.

Beside this, the central government would have to face another obstacle which in my view, has impeded faster progress in Colombian education: the politicisation of the administration of public schooling at departmental and municipal level. This is the subject of the next section.

Clientelism and the Administration of Public Education

The analysis presented here is based on the education systems of two Colombian departments in two different regions. However, there is some evidence that they can also be applied to other regions of Colombia. Previous research and a number of articles in newspapers and weekly magazines indicate that the phenomena described in this section are not unknown in other regions.[23]

The Colombian education system has a set of clear national norms for the selection, appointment, transfer and promotion of public teachers, a national teachers' salary scale and procedures for payment of their pensions and other social benefits. The law states that public primary school teachers must have as a minimum qualification a degree in pedagogical secondary education; for secondary schools teachers must have as a minimum a degree in higher education. The law also states that the selection and appointment of public teachers must be by merit. To achieve that, the SEDs or the municipal authorities must hold public competitions (*concursos*).[24]

Teachers' transfers are administered by the SEDs and municipalities, and they must not affect the normal studies of children in public schools.[25] Public teachers are promoted according to their length of service, their qualifications, and their in-service training courses. Special offices in the SEDs are in charge of the promotions of national and departmental teachers.[26] The SEDs are also responsible for the administration of the disciplinary regime of public teachers according to national norms.

These norms form the basis for what might be called a universalistic model of interaction between public teachers and the state, in which access to the system is open to all who attain the aforementioned requirements; the system is regulated by universal norms which are applied in principle to all individuals without regard to any distinction.[27]

However, the evidence from field work indicates that in the departments studied, and in other parts of Colombia, most of the interaction between public teachers and the departmental and municipal educational agencies is quite different from the universalistic model. It can be better described, using Valenzuela's concepts, as a system where the goals of the transactions are particularistic, while the nature of the transactions are individualistic. 'Particularistic goals are those which are sought to satisfy the needs of an individual or his immediate family.' Categorical goals, as opposed to particularistic ones, are designed to meet the needs of groups. On the other hand, individualistic transactions involve face-to-face contact between a client and a broker or patron, while collective transactions involve bargaining and accommodation between functional organisation, or interest groups, and political parties.[28] Particularistic goals obtained through individualistic transactions are typical of patron-client systems.[29] A look at how teachers are recruited, transferred or promoted will serve to illustrate these points. In addition, one should also pay further attention to the phenomenon of corruption in state education.

There has been no public competition for the recruitment of national and departmental teachers in the departments studied in the last twelve years. With only one exception, in the case of the first group of district school directors in 1983 in one of the departments, school principals and educational staff have also been appointed without public competitions, despite the fact that these became obligatory in 1979. The system of *concursos* seems to be almost unknown by the municipal educational authorities, and municipal teachers have always been directly hired by the mayors.

Most teachers seem to be appointed not because of their academic qualifications but for their political recommendations. Letters of political recommendation are an unofficial but necessary condition of appointment. The odds on being appointed in the education sector increase with the strength of the applicant's *palanca* (political patron) within the departmental or municipal administration. In addition, political contacts seem to be very important for advancement in the education sector, for posts such as headmaster, school district director and supervisor. This situation seems widespread not only in the two departments studied but across the country. In 1985 a Minister of Education, Doris Eder, caused controversy by stating that '*el cien por ciento de los educadores en Colombia han sido nombrados por recomendaciones políticas y es raro que un funcionario no nombre a un maestro con una carta de un dirigente*'.[30]

The political pressures on the educational authorities, both departmental and municipal, to satisfy the demands for jobs in the education sector, together with the clientelistic origins of the directors and staff of these authorities, result in unfair dismissals of teachers, a high turnover of teachers, and in the recruitment of teachers and non-teaching personnel who do not possess the minimum qualifications required by the law. It seems that most teaching and administrative-staff positions in the education sector in the two departments studied were at the mercy of clientelistic exchanges. However, some positions were more vulnerable than others. National teachers and departmental teachers with permanent status were less likely to be removed from their positions because the Teachers' Statute guarantees them some stability, and specifies causes and procedures for dismissal. The highest turn-over of teachers was experienced among departmental and municipal teachers hired on short-term contracts, together with those working on an hourly basis. Very often when the SED director (*Secretario*) and the top staff of the SED were changed, most temporary departmental teachers were replaced. Similarly, with a change of mayor, most municipal teachers were replaced.

Political pressure on the educational authorities also led, as mentioned above, to the recruitment of teachers and non-teaching personnel without the minimum qualifications required by law. An additional practice is the appointment of departmental and municipal teachers without funds to pay them. Despite the existing norms on the appointment of public employees, departmental and municipal authorities continued, especially around elections, to hire public teachers often with little regard to whether funds were available for their salaries. When teachers' protests arise because the departments cannot pay their salaries, the central government is forced to take on the financial burden if it is to avoid school disruptions.[31]

The system of transfer of public teachers also seems to work on clientelistic criteria. Most transfers of public teachers are made with the help of a political intermediary, regardless of the consequences to school life. Teachers contact political brokers to ask leading regional politicians to put pressure on the SED's authorities to transfer them from rural to urban areas, or from small towns to bigger cities.[32]

Clientelism is also essential for other aspects of the life of teachers and non-teaching staff, such as the managing of promotions, pensions and other social security benefits. For instance, all teachers with permanent contracts are automatically entitled to promotion according to years of service, additional academic degrees or in-service training. However, procedures are complex and funds are often insufficient. To obtain the increase to which one is entitled is therefore a lengthy process, and teachers need political *palancas* to speed it up. Scarce funds lead educational authorities to select the few teachers who will receive their promotion entitlements according to partisan politics.

A phenomenon hitherto almost unknown in the literature on public education in Colombia, though apparently widespread in the two departments studied, is that of corruption in the appointments and transfers of teachers.[33]

Corruption in the appointments of public teachers seems to operate in a simpler way. Brokers inside the SED, FER, or the municipal education secretariats, or outside them but possessing good contacts there, know the number and location of upcoming teaching vacancies, and put them up for sale. When a client for the vacancy is found, these brokers make use of their contacts. These are high-ranking members of the departmental bureaucracy or persons able to exert pressure on the *Secretario* or the FER director or the governor. In this way the appointment is obtained. Money from the transaction is distributed among the members of the brokerage chain.

The 'selling' of transfers works in a similar way. The brokers get in

Fig. 3 Department 1: Distribution of National Teachers, Quality of Teaching and Subsidies on Education by Municipality

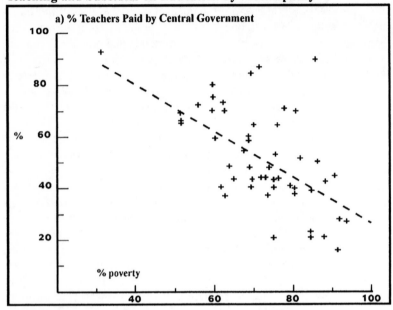

a) % Teachers Paid by Central Government

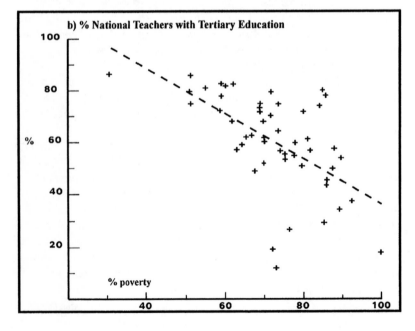

b) % National Teachers with Tertiary Education

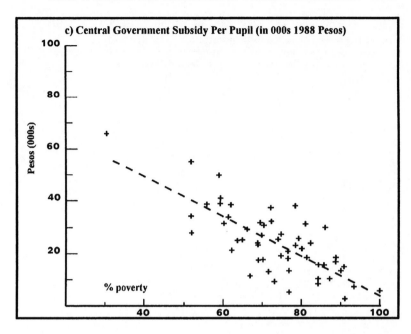

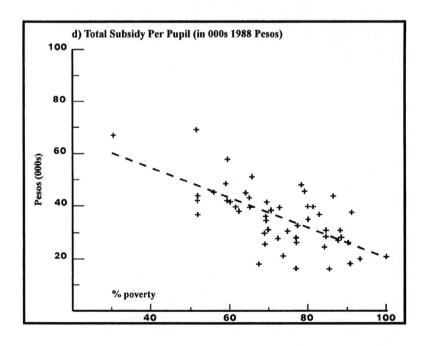

Fig. 4 Department 2: Distribution of National Teachers, Quality of Teaching and Subsidies on Education by Municipality.

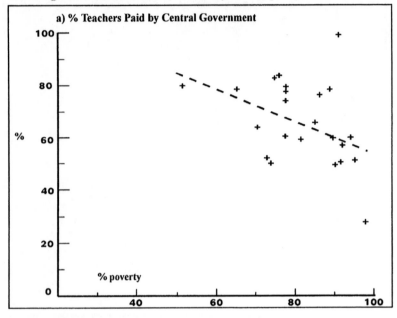

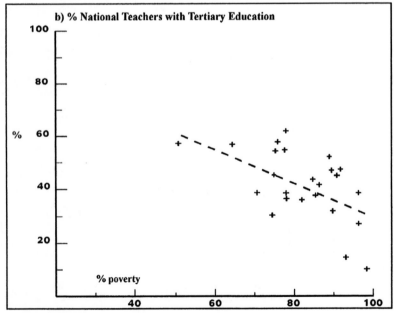

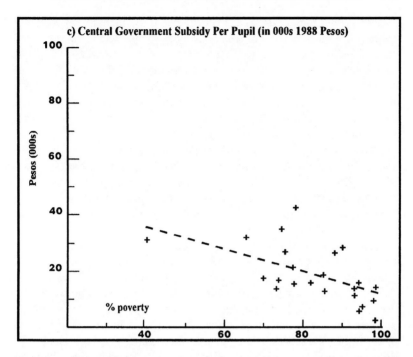

c) Central Government Subsidy Per Pupil (in 000s 1988 Pesos)

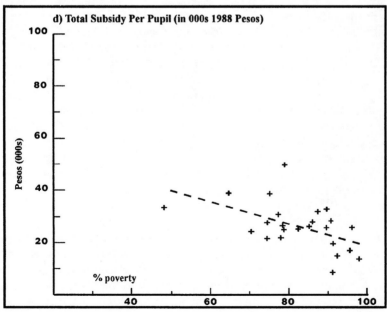

d) Total Subsidy Per Pupil (in 000s 1988 Pesos)

touch with teachers interested in transfers and ask them to pay a certain amount of money for the decree approving them. One variation of the sale of transfers is when two teachers swap places of work. This is in principle permitted by law. The corruption element comes when one of the parties, usually the teacher who is working in a remote area or in a rural school, makes a payment to the other for the exchange. In most cases there are intermediaries for the transactions and they receive a percentage of the amount exchanged.[34]

The cases of corruption identified in this chapter indicate that either a group of brokers decide to act independently from the existing political networks and to establish a particular network to profit financially from the transactions, or that some political group decides to collect cash for funding their activities, or for the personal betterment of all, or part, of their members.

The structure of power and the system of administration of public education based mainly on clientelism and corruption, as described above, has consequences for the distribution of state teachers and for the allocation of subsidies for education across the municipalities of the departments studied. It also has an impact on the quality of education delivered in public schools. Figures 3 and 4 (preceding pages) show the distribution of teachers paid by central funds, their academic qualifications, and the subsidy per pupil on education by municipality in the two departments studied.[35] The horizontal axes refer to percentages of municipal poverty. Each point represents a municipality and the straight lines are the regression lines, which indicate the trends for the whole sets of data in each department. The figures clearly indicate that there is a highly unequal and inequitable distribution of teachers paid by the central government across the municipalities (see Figures 3a and 4a). In some municipalities the central government pays almost all public teachers while in others only a few of them. The municipalities which benefit least from this unequal distribution are those which have higher indicators of poverty. Similarly, the distribution of national teachers with higher education qualifications is highly inequitable: the wealthier municipalities have a greater proportion of them than those in poorer municipalities (Figures 3b and 4b).

As a result, central government subsidies for education, in per pupil terms, are also unequally and inequitably allocated across municipalities. Wealthier municipalities receive greater central government subsidies, while poorer ones tend to receive lower subsidies (Figures 3c and 4c). The contribution from municipalities and the departments, though proportionally high in certain municipalities, is not enough to offset this inequality; and therefore, total subsidies per pupil are also highly inequitable (Figures 3d and 4d). The poorer the municipalities, the lower the level of total subsidy per pupil on education.[36]

The unequal and inequitable allocation of national teachers and central subsidies for schools in the two departments studied is a result of the departmental authorities' arrangements and decisions. These authorities have complete autonomy in the process. As Figures 3 and 4 testify, teachers and subsidies for education have not been allocated on grounds of equality, nor have they been allocated following redistributive criteria. Their allocation is a result of the clientelistic administration of public education. Teachers paid from central funds tend to be appointed or to be transferred to central municipalities, which happen to have better educational and social indicators. The rationale for recruitment and movement of teachers, which has nothing to do with educational needs but with clientelistic pressures, has left the poorer areas with few teachers paid by the central government. The few that there are possess lower qualifications. In this way, the unequal and inequitable features of public education tend, therefore, to worsen.

Conclusions

The systems of recruitment, transfers, promotions and other managerial aspects of public teachers and non-teaching staff in the educational sectors of many Colombian regions predominantly depend on political clientelism. Regional politicians control the key positions in the structure of power in the regional education systems. They monopolise access to all the administrative aspects in the lives of public teachers and control the distributions of teachers across schools and municipalities. In this way, they become an obligatory intermediary between the individual teachers and the educational administration.

Public teachers, and candidates for jobs in the education sector, are convinced by a series of tentative approaches of trial and error that nothing can be obtained from the existing power structure of educational administration without direct personal intervention by influential politicians. Senior teachers, supervisors and the staff of the regional or local educational agencies such as the SEDs and the FERs, together with activists in the regional political groups, are the middlemen, the brokers who arrange transactions between teachers and politicians. The latter use their connections at the centres of departmental or municipal decision-making on behalf of their clients. The goods exchanged in the clientelistic transactions are, on the side of the patrons, jobs, transfers, accelerated promotions and payments of social security rights, and on the client's side, increasing the numbers of political party followers and mobilising local support for the groups of their political bosses.

Regional politicians consider the public education system one of the best sources of political clientelism not only through the manipulation of the hiring of public teachers, but also because it gives them access to the control of the everyday administration of teachers' affairs. As a result, there is strong competition among regional political groups to control the departmental educational agencies, in particular the SEDs, which are responsible for administering most of the public teaching force, and the FERs, which manage the financial resources for departmental education. The highly fragmented structure of regional politics, and the high degree of competition among the political groups to obtain key positions in the departmental administration, explain the high turn-over of the directors and senior staff of these institutions.

From the beginning of the 1990s, the administration of national teachers was transferred to the municipalities. The implementation of this has been slow and uneven across the country, but by 1993 about 60 per cent of municipalities were administering most of their teaching force. The SEDs have therefore lost some of their previous power, but the degree of clientelistic transactions has not declined in the areas still under their control. The degree of clientelism at the municipal level has increased with the expansion of their functions. The decentralisation of the administration of national teachers to the local level has often resulted in the municipalisation of clientelism in public education.

In the struggle among regional political groups to control key positions in the departmental or municipal educational agencies, concern for the contents and effect of educational policies is minimal; the major criterion is the ability to control the use and distribution of the resources of the education system to consolidate political power. The recurrent complaints about the low level of technical development in the administration of the educational agencies, their lack of the minimum instruments to deal with educational administration, their inefficiency, the slow procedures in the administration of teachers' affairs, in a word, the 'mismanagement of public schooling', can be explained by the fact that their main orientation is not to meet the demands of the educational system but the demands of the clientelistic networks for power at the regional level. The mismanagement of public schooling, which in turn results in low coverage of education and in poor quality, is not, in other words, simply a consequence of oversight or administrative inefficiency. It is not simply a technical problem as is commonly thought, but a political one. The structures of educational administration serve less to improve schooling than to maintain and enhance the networks of the regional politicians controlling the educational agencies. The chronic dysfunction of the system is in reality a highly efficacious instrument for generating and maintaining political support for specific regional political groups.[37]

We have seen that most of the stated norms for the administration of public teachers do not work. Since both the general rights stated in the norms are denied and the legal avenues to obtain their goals are blocked, individuals seek to attain their particular goals through the personal intervention of political patrons, for which the price is political support. In this way, the teachers' rights are transformed into political favours. By the same token, the general channels stated by the norms to deal with teachers' affairs have been replaced by individualistic transactions to obtain particularistic benefits. The transformation of the universalistic criteria stated by the norms into individualistic transactions and particularistic benefits incurred in the administration of public teachers has been helped by the ministry's extraordinary incapacity to impose the national norms across the country.[38]

In this situation, it is not strange that corruption should have emerged. The selling of teaching positions or teacher's transfers has much in common with clientelistic transactions. The aims and nature of the transactions are the same: particular benefits and individualistic transaction. The difference resides in the nature of the goods exchanged. In both cases, there is a privatisation of the state's resources for particular aims. In a clientelistic relationship the aims of the brokers and patrons are political, in the case of corruption they are personal and economic. In any case, the clientelistic structure of the transactions in the educational administration facilitated, or perhaps encouraged, the emergence of corruption. In addition, again, the lack of control from the centre, given its characteristic incapacity for inspection in the regions, gives fertile ground for corruption.

Political clientelism is essentially a particular system for distributing public goods. In education, most of the goods are embodied in teacher employment. We have seen the consequences of clientelistic transactions in two departments. The predominant position of clientelistic politics in the administration of education has produced a highly unequal and inequitable distribution of public teachers, and consequently of subsidies in education across municipalities. Poorer and more educationally deprived municipalities tend to have relatively fewer public teachers paid by the central government, and fewer public teachers with high qualifications. Consequently, the poorer the municipality, the lower the central subsidies per pupil. These findings reinforce an argument expressed above: the obstacles for the improvement of education are not only financial and administrative, but political. With the current clientelistic structure of the distribution of public educational resources, major improvements in the quantity and quality of public education can hardly be expected.

In the final analyisis, the success in achieving the constitutional mandate of nine years' compulsory education for all children, and the ambitious goals of the *Salto Educativo* depend critically on the way the central government changes two major areas of the public educational system: the remarkable weakness of the ministry's instruments that link the centre with the regions, and the clientelistic structure of administration of public education which prevails in many departments. Without significant changes in these areas, the ambitious programmes of the Samper administration might be significantly unfulfilled, and the envisioned expansion and improvement of educational services might, again, be delayed.

Notes

1. All net enrolment rates are from DNP, 'Encuesta de Caracterización Socioecónomica – CASEN', provisional data, unpubl. Bogotá, 1995.
2. See Molina (1993) chapter 4; and The World Bank (1994b), chapter 3.
3. See DNP, 'El Salto Educativo' (Bogotá:mimeo, 1994), p. 5.
4. See World Bank (1994b), p. 82.
5. *Ibid*, table 3.3, p. 83.
6. See the criticisms made by the *Comisión del Plan* in the national press during February 1995.
7. For a review of education in Colombian history, see Safford (1976), p. 5; Helg (1987), p. 20; and Jaramillo Uribe (1984), p. 261. For a historical overview of the weakness of the Colombian state, see Chapter 1 by Marco Palacios in this volume.
8. Fresneda and Duarte (1984), p. 116.
9. See Loy (1979) and (1982).
10. As one Secretary of Government acknowledged in 1880, 'al director jeneral de instrucción pública se le ha abrumado de muchos i trascendentales deberes de pura iniciativa, pero no se le han dejado a su alcance sino mui reducidos medios de acción propia i de impulso directo: ni tiene a su disposición inmediata los fondos i elementos que son precisos para la

propagación de la enseñanza en donde quiera i en el momento en que la necesidad se haga sentir'. Quoted in *Memoria del Secretario* (1881), p. 17.

11. Helg (1987), p. 101.
12. Helg argues that the reforms were 'más declaraciones políticas de principios que expresiones de un cambio estructural'. Perhaps López himself at the end of his government arrived at a similar conclusion when he said: 'No dejaremos millares de escuelas, no terminaremos todas las normales, ni nos tocará inaugurar la Ciudad Universitaria, ni daremos de comer a la totalidad de la población escolar . . . ; pero hemos alcanzado ya el objetivo de crear un afán general en favor de la educación del pueblo.' Quoted in Helg (1980), p. 35. See also Lebot (1972), pp. 127–31.
13. Quoted in Lebot, (1972), p. 130. The weakness of the ministry in the regions could also be seen in the fact that during the 1940s it had just 18 inspectors to cover 8,300 schools dispersed throughout the country. See Helg (1987), p. 225.
14. Londoño remarks on this point: 'Before the 1950s, Colombia's allocation of spending for education was half what other countries at similar stages of development spent. The accelerated use of public funds for education that took place worldwide during the 1950s also occurred in Colombia. The turning point was 1957, after which public expenditures on education accelerated very rapidly. In fact, education expenditure almost doubled in a decade, reaching the international levels of the mid-1950s.' See Londoño (1990), pp. 57–8.
15. Here we are accounting both central and departmental funds to education.
16. Hanson (1983), p. 94.
17. See also Hanson (1989), pp. 46–7.
18. Ministerio de Educación (1971), p. 29.
19. Arnove reports some examples of the violations to the contracts between the departments and the ministry. He also quoted one of the FER directors talking about the little room for manoeuvre of the central government to punish trasgressors: 'Cuando el departamento no se ajustaba al contrato, el Ministro con frecuencia se enojaba y hablaba de suspender el pago mensual al departamento, pero nunca lo hizo. Usted debe recordar que él también es un político, y él debe trabajar con los gobernadores que también son políticos. El Ministro puede presionar a los governadores pero también está sujeto a las presiones políticas por parte de ellos.' See Arnove (1978), pp. 33–4.
20. See Hanson (1989), p. 45.
21. See Sarmiento et al. (1987); and World Bank (1994b), chapters 3 and 6.
22. Decree no. 2884 of 1994.
23. My research was located in one department of the Atlantic coast and another in the Andean region. Cubillos found clientelism in Cali's Secretary of Education; see Cubillos (1982). *El Tiempo*, 16 Aug. 1992 (p. 1E), presented evidence of 2,408 appointments of teachers made through clientelistic mediation in Bogotá during 1992. *Cambio 16*, 22 Nov. 1993 (p. 17), reported similar practices in Casanare and Arauca. See also Duarte (1995).
24. See Decree 2277 of 1979 (*Estatuto Docente*), Decrees 175 and 176 of 1982,

and the Ministry of Education's *Resolución* 20974 of 1989. For appointments in remote areas where no qualified teachers have applied, the authorities may appoint candidates without teacher-training qualifications. But candidates must have finished secondary education. In this case, the appointed teacher would have up to three years to obtain a pedagogical degree.

25. See Decrees 175 and Decree 176 of 1982. Teachers appointed without public competition to remote areas cannot be transferred to other areas. Teachers transferred or appointed to cities of more than 100,000 inhabitants must have worked previously, for at least two years, in smaller cities.

26. See Decrees 2277 and 2621 of 1979, Decree 297 of 1980, Decrees 250 and 897 of 1981, and Decree 177 of 1982.

27. Here we are following the concept of a 'universalistic model' of societal interaction explained by Eisenstadt and Roniger:

    The 'official' model of universalistic open-market or bureaucratic societies assumes that access to major markets, centres of power and the setting up of public goods (as well as, in principle, the public distribution of private goods) is vested in all members of the wider community, without regard to their membership in any other ascriptive hierarchical sub-units . . . Eisenstadt and Roniger (1984), pp. 169–70.

28. See Valenzuela (1977), especially part II, chapter 7. Valenzuela also points out that the individualistic transactions are conducted on the implementing side of the policy process, while collective ones are located at the legislative stage (see pp. 159–60).

29. See Eisenstadt and Roginer (1984) chapter 4; Valenzuela (1977), chapter 7; Clapham (1982); and Chubb (1982).

30. See *La Opinión,* Cúcuta, 17 May 1985, p. 3.

31. Examples of all these practices can be found in regional newspapers.

32. In most cases it is done despite the stated norms and limitations for teacher transfers: the obligation for teachers working in cities with less than 100,000 inhabitants to stay there at least two years and the prohibition on teachers appointed without *concurso* being transferred to areas other than that originally assigned.

33. See Duarte (1994).

34. Our interviewees also mentioned that the corruption in the concession of public contracts to buy goods or services for the education sector was common in the two departments studied. They claimed that an important portion of the contracts in education are allocated not to those who offer the best technical conditions and prices, but to those who have the best political support, or those who offer bribes. The contracts most exposed to bribes, as they claimed, were those for the acquisition of school furniture, textbooks, libraries, teaching materials, and school construction. For an analysis of this and other types of corruption in Colombian public administration see chapters 2–5 of Cepeda Ulloa (1994a). Another sphere of corruption is the selling of government scholarships distributed through

the so-called *'auxilios parlamentarios'*. An illustration of this was presented in one of the main national Colombian newspapers in February 1994. See 'Procuraduría Destituyó a Ex-Asistente del Senado', *El Tiempo*, 5 February 1994.

35. The figures used in this section are from Duarte (1995), section 5.

36. The coefficients and t-statistics of the regressions depicted in figures 3 and 4 indicate that there are negative and significant relationships between the percentage of national teachers, teachers' academic qualifications, and subsidies, on the one hand, and municipal poverty on the other.

37. Plank presents similar findings in his analysis of Brazilian public education. See Plank (1990), pp. 83–9; and Plank (1990b), pp. 538–59.

38. The national teachers' union, the Federación Colombiana de Educadores – FECODE, has been important at national level in achieving legislation that guarantees better salaries and stability for teachers paid by the central government. At the departmental level, the teachers' unions have usually been effective in organising support for the economistic goals pursued by FECODE at the legislative stage, but less successful in making regional agencies adhere to the national norms for the administration of public schooling. They are often internally divided, and in most cases, their role is limited to informing the regional press of irregularities found. However, it must be said that we know little about Colombian teachers' unions, and we still lack an adequate study of their role within Colombian education.

CHAPTER 7

COLOMBIAN HOUSING POLICY DURING THE 1990s

Alan Gilbert

For many years, Latin American governments sought to reduce their national housing deficits through the construction of public housing. A state agency was entrusted to build new homes for the poor; sometimes it was also responsible for removing slum and self-help housing. Gradually, governments began to realise that this approach was doomed to failure.[1] Governments could not build sufficient homes to satisfy the large numbers of families requiring better accommodation. The unwelcome consequence was that the numbers of families living in 'informal' housing were increasing through time.[2]

Recently, a new approach has been espoused in Washington which has become *de rigueur* in many parts of Latin America.[3] Broadly, this approach recommends that the state interfere less directly in the production of housing and restrict itself to modifying the wider macro-environment. It is a policy which enjoins governments to reform housing, land and financial sectors in ways that will 'enable the market to work'.[4] In Latin America, Pinochet's Chile was the pioneer of this kind of policy and, during the 1990s, Colombia has taken up important elements of this approach. The aim of this chapter is to examine recent Colombian experience and to reflect on the advantages and dangers involved in the new reforms.

This chapter contains five main sections. The first describes Colombian housing policy during the current and the previous governments. The second section attempts to show how the new policies conform with Washingtonian wisdom on how to tackle shelter problems and how to improve developmental practice. The third part examines some of the problems that Colombian practice encountered under the administration of César Gaviria (1990–94), and the fourth considers current policy under Ernesto Samper (1994–). Finally, the chapter raises some general issues about housing policy in a country like Colombia: specifically, the rationale for giving subsidies for housing, the desirability or otherwise of sites and services programmes, and the need for developing a rental housing policy.

Colombian Housing Policy since 1990

Until 1990, Colombia had adopted a typically Latin American approach to housing policy. The private sector built homes for the better off, a public agency provided homes for a small number of poorer families, and the poor provided their own homes through self-help construction on non-serviced and sometimes invaded land.[5] With the exception of 1970–74, when housing construction constituted one of the four basic planks of the national housing plan, and during 1982–86, when a major initiative was taken to increase housing construction for the poor, housing had always received low priority in national development policy.[6] During the 1980s, state agencies never managed to build more than 37,000 'social interest' units in any one year and, between 1987 and 1990, spending on social-interest housing amounted to only 0.54 per cent of the gross national product.[7] The almost inevitable consequence of such minimal spending was that self-help housing expanded throughout the country; invasions and pirate urbanisations provided the land on which most of the population built their own homes.

As in most other Latin American countries, the principal state housing agency, the Colombian Territorial Institute (ICT), was less than effective.[8] Certainly, it was widely criticised for its limited production, the low quality of its housing solutions, its high administrative costs, the political criteria determining the distribution of its housing units, the financial losses it made, and the fact that it often ignored local planning regulations.[9] Even the directors of ICT were sometimes vocal in their criticism of the job the Institute was doing, arguing that the agency could never perform effectively given the environment in which it was forced to operate.[10] When the Institute accumulated huge debts between 1982 and 1986, as a result of the way that the housing without down-payment plan was implemented, the time for radical change had arrived.[11]

In 1990, the overall approach to housing provision was modified substantially. The government of César Gaviria (1990–94) abolished ICT, replacing it with the slimmed down INURBE (National Institute for Social Interest Housing and Urban Reform), introduced a policy of giving direct subsidies to the poor, channelled these subsidies towards privately supplied housing options, and encouraged the private sector to supply more so-called 'social-interest housing'.[12] Housing policy under Ernesto Samper continued along similar lines although the new administration introduced several important modifications to its predecessor's approach. In particular, it changed the method of targeting the poor and gave much greater weight to settlement upgrading and community participation.[13]

Housing policy under *La Revolución Pacífica* attempted to tackle simultaneously two of the country's long-standing development problems: too much poor-quality housing and too little well-paid work.[14] It attempted to increase the housing supply by encouraging private investment in the housing sector, both by offering subsidies to buyers and by obliging the housing finance system to invest more in low-cost housing. Raising output would create more jobs in the labour-intensive construction sector and in related industries. On the demand side, state subsidies to lower income groups would allow more families to buy new homes and to improve their existing shelter. The programme anticipated the construction of 539,000 houses between 1991 and 1994, of which 72 per cent would consist of 'social interest housing'. Annual production of the latter would rise from an average of 35,000 units in the 1980s to 95,000 in the early 1990s.

Social interest housing would be accessible to those earning less than four minimum salaries, those without their own home, and those whose accommodation was poorly constructed or overcrowded, or lacked a title deed or services.[15] Families earning less than two minimum salaries would be eligible for a subsidy of up to fifteen minimum salaries and particular encouragement was given to families who were prepared to form groups to provide their own solutions through collective self-help programmes. Their solutions were expected to cost no more than 50 minimum salaries. In practice, this meant that little was being provided beyond a serviced site. Subsidies of up to twelve minimum salaries were also available to groups wishing to secure legal title to their land. Those earning between two and four minimum salaries would be eligible for a subsidy to buy a house with a value of between 50 and 135 minimum salaries (that is, between US$6,000 and US$16,200 at 1995 prices). To obtain a subsidy, families would have to be in possession of cash savings of at least five per cent of the value of the unit. A subsidy equivalent to twelve minimum salaries would be made available, a sum which could be supplemented by index linked mortgage loans from private lenders.[16] The subsidy would be held by a private trust company until the contract was signed when it would be passed on to the seller of the new unit. The beneficiary of the subsidy decided how to use the subsidy, but never received it directly.

When the Samper administration took over in August 1994, it continued to offer subsidies for poor home owners as a way of supplementing the demand for social interest housing.[17] However, it also modified housing policy in several important ways; according to one major national newspaper, changing course by 180 degrees.[18] First, it promised to increase low-income housing production; the new national plan anticipates that 606,000 housing solutions will be provided, of which 500,000 will receive subsidies and the rest will be eligible for special credit facilities. The number of subsidised families will rise significantly from the 211,000 recipients between 1991–94 to 500,000 between 1995–98.[19] Second, it changed the method of allocating subsidies. Instead of individual families applying directly for subsidies, poor families would be located through the *Red de Solidaridad Social.* The aim was to identify the most deserving by establishing local committees of interested parties. These would pick communities which were particularly poor and/or living in vulnerable conditions. Subsidies would be directed mainly at families earning less than two minimum salaries, although 84,000 would still be offered to families earning between two and four minimum salaries.[20] Individual families were still eligible to apply for subsidies, but many more would benefit through collective subsidy programmes (see below). Third, the kind of new housing solution available to the very poor was changed. Sites and services projects were out and most new solutions would take the form of 'basic units' and progressive housing. This was explained as an attempt to provide habitable homes for the very poor, rather than offering them mere plots. Fourth, much more emphasis would be given to squatter upgrading programmes and to improving the general environment of poor families. This was a response both to the continual growth of informal housing areas in the major cities and to the earlier failure of municipal government to put much effort into improving low-income areas. Greater efforts would also be made to implement the Urban Reform Law of 1989; a law which the current president had backed strongly. Finally, the whole housing and planning programme was to form part of the new national priority of creating a more participative form of democracy. The first page of the National Plan announces the goal of creating 'the new citizen': 'more productive in economic terms; more responsible in the social context; more participative and tolerant in the political . . . and, therefore, prouder of being Colombian.'[21]

Colombian Housing Programmes and the International Conventional Wisdom

The consensus on development policy in Washington shifted significantly during the 1980s and again in the 1990s. During the 1980s, the World Bank, USAID and the Inter-American Development Bank took on a pro-market, less-interventionalist stance; a line in keeping with the ideology of most governments in the OECD countries. However, increasing awareness that poverty in Africa and Latin America had grown significantly during the 'lost decade' of the 1980s soon persuaded Washington to modify that line. By the 1990s, much higher priority was being given to poverty alleviation and social development; social targeting was now approved practice among the development banks.[22] These shifts in policy have produced the following approach to housing.

Sector-wide reform Generally, there is now a strong commitment to institutional reform, sector-wide policies, better urban management and less government intervention, thereby 'enabling markets to work'.[23] Housing improvements cannot be achieved without facilitating change across the whole housing sector. Without changes in related markets, from land and building materials through to financial services, little would be achieved through individual projects. As the World Bank put it: 'projects that have been unable to deal with the overall regulatory, institutional, and economic environment have had a small or negligible impact on overall housing conditions'.[24] For example, if the middle class have no homes, building more units for the poor will simply lead to 'downward raiding'. In short, partial reform may even accentuate existing problems. Colombia moved strongly in the direction of sector reform by removing the requirements on the private sector to lend for social interest housing, by removing price and quantity controls which had discouraged the private sector from participating voluntarily in social interest housing, by attempting to improve the efficiency with which state funds were spent, and by offering subsidies to supplement the resources of low-income families.[25]

Reliance on the market The World Bank is determined to 'redirect developing-country governments from engaging in building, marketing, financing, and maintenance of housing units toward facilitating expansion of the private sector's role in such activities'.[26] The administration argued that Colombian policy before 1990 had been undermined by the exclusion of private sector construction and finance from the low-income field. The result, according to Hommes et al., was limited formal sector production and 'the proliferation of settlements on illegal lands'.[27] The new policy would lead to an expansion of housing production and reduce the housing deficit for the first time in years. Subsidies would continue to be provided, but in a much more explicit and transparent way than previously. As Giraldo explains: 'The new housing policy implied, among several fundamental changes, the disappearance of long-term state finance, generally provided through subsidised interest rates. Today, the only possibility of finance is through the Savings and Housing Corporations and . . . the commercial banks.'[28]

The private sector was to be much more fully involved in the provision of social interest housing. It would provide more housing, it would help finance home purchase by lending more to the poor, and it would help administer the subsidy programme through trust companies (*fiduciarias*). Local communities would be encouraged to participate more in the planning process and generous subsidies were offered to groups engaging in collective self-help programmes.

Subsidies for the poor would be shifted from a supply-based, state-run system to one that operated through demand. Subsidies would be offered only to the very poor. While families could use their subsidies to purchase new housing units, subsidies were also available for urbanisable lots, home improvements, titling and servicing. The private sector would be wholly responsible for building and financing housing units and for providing most urbanised sites.

Decisions about the kind of housing solutions to be offered would be left mainly to the market. Builders would be forced to offer appropriate solutions or risk attracting few subsidised purchasers – an approach far superior to the old system employed by ICT. The policy was clearly compatible with the ethos of structural adjustment, to privatise state and parastatal agencies on the grounds of greater efficiency. Housing finance would also be subject to fewer controls. Previously, the state had forced financial institutions to invest in social housing, an approach which had had harmful macro-economic consequences for the whole economy. Close scrutiny over the prices and number of credits also discouraged the private sector from participating in social interest housing.[29]

All these policy changes were continued under the Samper administration. The only substantial shift was that modifications to the subsidy allocation system meant that local communities, NGOs and municipal governments were to be more involved in identifying the beneficiaries of subsidies. Fewer subsidies were available for individual families through direct application.

Rolling back the state A foundation stone of structural adjustment

packages has always been a requirement to balance government revenues and expenditure. This demand has required the raising of taxes
and reductions in the budget. Expenditure has been cut through the privatisation of loss-making state agencies and through reduced
government expenditure. The lessons for housing are clear: governments should withdraw from direct shelter provision. Such an approach,
it is argued, will improve sector efficiency because 'unlike the private
sector, where market forces bring about an efficient provision of new
housing, publicly supported housing has no explicit mechanism for ensuring efficiency. In the private market the profit motive provides a
strong incentive for efficiency; the public sector lacks this discipline.'[30]
Government action should be reduced to a more limited, but vital, 'enabling' role. Government should seek to engineer changes in the
following areas: 'property rights development, mortgage finance, targeted subsidies, infrastructure for urban land development, regulatory
reform, organisation of the building industry, and institutional development'.[31]

Housing policy in Colombia under President Gaviria clearly followed this general strategy. The state stopped building houses. The
loss-making state housing agency, ICT, was wound up and the staff of
its successor institution, INURBE, slashed from 3,100 to 600.
INURBE's role was to be much more limited than that of ICT. The new
state agency would be a housing facilitator rather than a major player in
the building and financing of housing. Its main functions would be to
administer the subsidy programme and to advise local authorities on
various aspects of housing policy. The Gaviria government's expenditure on social interest housing, while much higher than that of the Barco
régime (1986–90), was much lower than spending under Belisario
Betancur (1982–86).[32] In 1984, spending on social interest housing was
332 billion plus compared to 147 billion plus in 1992. Of course, the
pattern of spending was very different; the Betancur government subsidised public homes, while the Gaviria government gave subsidies to
individual families to buy private sector homes or sites. *El Salto Social*
continued Gaviria's broad strategy. Subsidies were available to the
poor, INURBE would continue to act only as a 'facilitator', and state
intervention would concentrate on improving the physical environment
rather than on building new homes.

Decentralisation of the state The new political constitution of 1991
warmly embraced the goal of decentralisation. The Gaviria government
responded by increasing financial transfers from the centre to the mu-

nicipalities and departments by 125 per cent over a ten-year period.[33] The increased resources would allow municipalities to play a larger role in the housing programme, particularly in planning urban development.[34] Eventually, they would be responsible both for allocating subsidies and for financing the social housing programme. Such a shift was clearly compatible with the current international trend towards encouraging the decentralisation of government. The writers of the new constitution were also anxious to encourage popular participation in decision-making. The Gaviria government attempted to increase community involvement in self-help housing by offering higher subsidies (fifteen minimum salaries rather than twelve) to families who formed groups to organise self-help programmes.

These aims have been developed further by the Samper government, an intention clearly signalled by the title of the President's inaugural speech: 'The Time of the People'. The transfer of funds from the central state to the local state continues apace and responsibility for urban planning remains a municipal obligation. Increasing popular participation has become part of the national aim of helping to create a more participative form of democracy.[35] One of the principal objectives of the government, in a country where most Colombians now live in cities, is to create a new kind of urban society: 'a city of citizens'.[36] A primary function of the *Red de Solidaridad Social* is to encourage local communities to identify their priority needs.[37]

Squatter upgrading and sites and services During the 1970s, Washington pushed sites and services and squatter upgrading projects very hard. Recently, however, the former has fallen from favour. The current belief is that sites and services programmes do not work. As the World Bank argues: 'Site and service provision in principle is a replicable approach to the poor's shelter problem. But the difficulties public land-development institutions face in commercial operations have limited the effectiveness of such projects in most countries. Land has been difficult to acquire, and the operations have been subject to political pressures. Meanwhile, like all public enterprises, such entities frequently face weak incentives to serve their real clients.' As a result, 'the sites-and-services programmes of the 1970s and 1980s reduced the costs of shelter and infrastructure, but they did not usually reach the poorest households. Nor was cost recovery achieved.'[38]

Although Washington continues to accept that informal housing makes a significant contribution to improved shelter, it is putting more resources into settlement upgrading and service provision.[39] Squatter upgrading is fashionable in large part because it is seen to be cheap. As the World Bank puts it: 'Slum improvement projects . . . have proved effective, low-cost ways to improve the living conditions of the urban poor.' They 'were more successful in providing benefits to the poor while ensuring security of tenure. Cost recovery also worked relatively better than in the sites-and-services programmes. Instead of subsidising sites and services, unserviced settlements inhabited by the poor should continue to be upgraded.'[40]

In this sense, the Colombian programme's emphasis on sites-and-services programmes during the *Peaceful Revolution* was out of step with current thinking among the international funding agencies. It constituted an important element in the government's attempt to improve the lives of lower income groups. However, Colombian policy was compatible with thinking in Washington in so far as development of the projects was in the hands of the private sector.

Under Ernesto Samper, the earlier reliance on sites and services has been changed. Upgrading is in, sites and services are out. A number of reasons have been given for this closer approximation to international practice. Fundamental, however, is the belief that sites and service programmes failed to provide poor families with adequate housing quickly enough, that land speculators used the programme to make quick profits with minimum investment, and that, at times, sites and services developments were used merely as a cover for the expansion of illegal housing.

Targeted subsidies The realisation that, during the 1980s, poverty had increased in far too many low-income countries forced Washington to rethink its policy towards subsidies. The poverty alleviation strategy formulated by the World Bank in 1990 clearly accepted the role of subsidies but carefully prescribed the form that they should take. First, subsidies should be carefully targeted on those falling into the poverty 'safety net'. Second, subsidies would take a specific form. 'Preferably, subsidies should be one-time capital grants or housing allowances that have a finite duration or a built-in review procedure. Both types of subsidy allow families to seek housing in the market. Care should be taken to ensure that subsidies do not dampen supply response and lead to increases in house prices.'[41] Such an approach was clearly adopted in Chile during the 1980s and similar practice has been extended to other countries in the 1990s.

In Colombia, subsidies had been used widely by the national housing agency, ICT. Unfortunately, few of these subsidies ever reached the very poor. This was partly because the allocation system was so politicised; favoured families received subsidies even though they had relatively high incomes. However, the poor also lost out as a result of a structural feature of the system: ICT asked families for a guarantee that they could pay back a subsidised loan, something that was impossible for most low-income families. The result was that ICT normally provided housing for higher income groups and rarely developed programmes in the countryside where poverty was most obviously concentrated. When ICT tried to reach a lower income group, notably under the *Vivienda sin cuota inicial* plan of Belisario Betancur, the institute's financial state soon became chronic.[42]

Under *La Revolución Pacífica* housing subsidies were clearly targeted at the poor. One set of subsidies was available for families earning less than two minimum salaries and another for those earning between two and four minimum salaries. Families would only be eligible for a subsidy if they earned less than four minimum salaries and if their family did not own its own home. To encourage the poor to apply, subsidies could be used either to purchase a serviceable lot or a core housing unit (Decreto 599 of 1991).

Under *El Salto Social*, emphasis has been placed even more clearly on the poorest families. Of the one thousand billion pesos to be allocated in subsidies, 82 per cent are intended for those earning less than two minimum salaries.[43] More than two-thirds of the subsidies will be spent on settlement upgrading. In terms of numbers of beneficiaries, the balance shifts even more: 755,000 very poor families will benefit from upgrading compared to 158,000 from new housing units.[44] The new procedure for selecting beneficiaries will also benefit the poorest. *Mesas de Solidaridad Social* will identify those communities where at least 70 per cent of the community lack adequate housing.[45] Instead of individual families applying for loans, local committees will identify deserving communities. In addition, more resources will be allocated to poorer regions.

The Strengths and Weaknesses of Colombian Policy, 1990–94

This section attempts to present a critical balance of Colombian housing policies looking at the following issues: construction of new homes; the extent to which these programmes reached the poor; land and housing prices; rental housing and sharing; state decentralisation; the upgrading of existing settlements; sites and services programmes; the mechanism for delivering subsidies; and political interference.

Under the Gaviria administration some 100,000 social interest units were constructed each year compared to only 37,000 per annum under ICT during the 1970s.[46] The peak of state construction under ICT had been 63,000 units in 1984.[47] Of course, this comparison is unfair in the sense that ICT was building finished homes, whereas the annual total for the Gaviria administration included sites and services and upgrading schemes. In addition, the private sector increased its contribution in social-interest housing. According to Hommes et al., the private sector's share of investment in social-interest housing rose from zero between 1987 and 1990 to 62 per cent between 1991 and 1994. The overall result was that investment in social-interest housing rose from 0.54 per cent of Gross Domestic Product under Virgilio Barco to 0.84 per cent under César Gaviria.

There is no question that very large numbers of Colombian families applied for subsidies and loans. By the end of the administration some 300,000 subsidies had been allocated to Colombian families[48] and a total of 668,506 'housing solutions' had been provided. Of this total some 46 per cent were subsidised.[49] Unfortunately, the number of potential beneficiaries was the Achilles Heel of the subsidy programme. Too many families applied for subsidies and, when the Samper administration took over in August 1994, there was a queue of 150,000 families awaiting decisions by INURBE.[50] In Bogotá, there were four times as many applicants in 1993 as subsidies available.

In its favour, there can be little doubt that the majority of the subsidies went to families in need. Most public officials assert that it is inconceivable that higher income families made use of the subsidies.[51] There is also survey evidence to support the view that most of the subsidies approved by the end of 1993 went to poorer families: 30 per cent of subsidies to the poorest 10 per cent and 55 per cent to the poorest 20 per cent and 95 per cent to the poorest half. In the five largest cities, 22 per cent of the subsidies were allocated to those earning less than one minimum salary, 54 per cent to those earning between one and two minimum salaries, and only 2 per cent to those earning more than four minimum salaries.[52] However, more recent figures are less clear. Of the 668,000 solutions provided between 1991 and 1994, 58 per cent went to families earning up to four minimum salaries (US$480 per month in June 1995).[53] While this figure looks impressive it should be noted that 70 per cent of Colombian families earn 0–4 minimum salaries.[54] Of the subsidies offered by INURBE, it is claimed that some 88 per cent were destined for families in the bottom one-fifth of the income distribution, those earning around 3.5 minimum salaries or less.[55] According to Hommes et al., 57 per cent of INURBE subsidies went to those with less than two minimum salaries and 70 per cent to those below 2.7 minimum salaries. However, the World Bank reports that the Centro Nacional de Construcción survey shows that some 10–20 per cent of these subsidies may have gone to families with more than four minimum salaries.[56]

There are, however, a number of problems with these figures. The first problem relates to the accuracy of the income estimates. In making their applications to INURBE, families are asked to swear that they have declared their full income. However, the institution does not investigate the declared incomes. As such, it is likely that there is some underrecording of incomes. I am not suggesting that this underrecording is so extreme that it totally distorts the picture, but clearly some families are not so poor as they claim. A similar issue relates to the requirement that beneficiaries have no home of their own. Again there is no effective way of checking the applicants' veracity. The national property register is anything but complete and the *cédula,* the basic identity document of every Colombian, contains no home address. Hommes et al. admit the possibility of cheating when they argue that: 'it is necessary to refine the systems of verifying the levels of income and savings of the beneficiaries . . . these could be based on expost checks and ought to include sanctions that would discourage fraud.'[57]

The previous government also admits that there was a major difference between the incomes of families whose subsidy application was approved and the incomes of those who managed to use the subsidy. Of the subsidies taken up, only 6 per cent went to the poorest decile of families and 9 per cent to the next poorest. Most of the subsidies used went to those in the third to eighth deciles and 8 per cent to the richest 20 per cent.[58] Admittedly, the situation was much better in the urban areas where 29 per cent of the subsidies used went to the bottom quintile and a further 30 per cent to the next poorest quintile.

Most poor families failed to take up their subsidy for one of three reasons: they could not afford one of the available housing solutions, they could not mobilise enough money to put down a deposit, or they could not find a satisfactory housing solution. Certainly, few of the poorest families had sufficient savings or high enough incomes to make use of the subsidies to buy finished housing. For a family earning two minimum salaries, payments on a unit costing 50 minimum salaries would take about 46 per cent of its monthly income.[59] For a family earning one minimum salary, payments on a similar kind of house would

take up 92 per cent of its monthly income. Second, families earning between two and four minimum salaries and with enough savings to
qualify for a subsidy may have insufficient funds for the down-payment
on a home. Loans from the Savings and Housing Corporations (CAVs)
require a deposit of 30 per cent of the house price, a sum that is way
beyond the budgets of most low-income families. One-fifth of those
who had failed to take up their subsidy mentioned the barriers posed by
the lack of a down-payment.[60] Third, many families with a subsidy had
considerable difficulty in finding an appropriate housing solution. This
was particularly true at the lower end of the price range because few local authorities had encouraged the development of sites and service
schemes. This was a particular problem in Bogotá, although not in
Cali.[61] As a result of these difficulties, the final distribution of subsidies
was biased against the poor. Giraldo concluded in March 1993 that: 'the
present distribution of beneficiaries is the inverse of those in need: the
largest and poorest section of the population participates least; the less
numerous and the less poor participate more.'[62] This view is hardly contradicted by Hommes et al. when they admit that the focusing
mechanism could be improved.[63]

Let me turn now to land and housing prices. Increasing the amount
of investment in housing is always likely to increase the price of housing and particularly the cost of land. So far, no attempt has been made
to quantify the impact of the Gaviria administration's subsidy plan on
prices. Of course, evaluating the effect of the social interest housing
component on house prices is complicated by the fact that there was a
huge boom in housing construction between 1992 and 1994. The boom
was partly due to the housing plan but was more closely linked with
other elements of the national plan: the labour reform, the expanded resources of the housing and savings corporations, the growth of exports,
and the amnesty on monies held abroad.[64] The number of building licences for housing rose from an average of 403,000 square metres per
month in 1990 to 1,151,000 in December 1992. The production of grey
cement rose from 6,365,000 tons in 1990 to 9,209,000 tons in 1994.[65]

The boom in construction led to house prices in Bogotá rising by
between 35 per cent and 60 per cent, dependent on the quality of the estate.[66] During the slow-down of 1995, prices were increasing more
slowly and were expected to rise by 'only' 22 per cent. If such price
rises were replicated for social-interest housing, a subsidy of US$2,600
would not help a family purchase a dwelling in Bogotá.[67] Similarly, if
land prices rose at anything close to the rise in house prices, then the
cost of a serviced plot would have become prohibitively expensive.

Certainly, the rising cost of land has caused problems in cities with physical constraints on the supply of land, where the authorities have difficulty keeping up with the demand for services, where peripheral land is held by limited numbers of owners, and in urban areas where the local authorities have inflexible or inefficient licensing procedures. In cities with these kinds of constraint, the sites and services component of the Gaviria plan was badly hampered by a shortage of land. With land prices clearly rising very rapidly, few owners wanted to sell their land cheaply for sites and services programmes; they preferred to sell to builders developing housing estates.

The construction boom also raised the cost of building materials, a major difficulty for self-help communities on limited incomes. Between 1990 and 1994, the cost of grey cement rose by 195 per cent and bricks by 256 per cent. During the same period, housing costs in Bogotá rose by 165 per cent compared to a rise in consumer prices of 145 per cent.[68] With prices of housing, land and materials rising rapidly, the affordability problems referred to above clearly became worse. Small subsidies, especially when they are delayed (see below), are of little help to the poor under such circumstance. In Bogotá, the shortage of land was clearly a major problem for the sites and services programme.[69]

An implicit goal of housing policy in Colombia has long been to encourage every family to own their own home.[70] This approach was justified in the sense that most surveys report that Colombian families want to be home owners.[71] A partial consequence of this policy has been a substantial rise in the rate of home ownership in urban areas from 45 per cent in 1973 to 61 per cent in 1993. Housing policy under the Gaviria administration failed to do anything to reverse this trend. It certainly did nothing to help tenants and hastened the move towards home-ownership by offering a one-off subsidy to tenants wishing to buy a new home. That this was welcomed by the tenants is revealed by the fact that, nationwide, some 65 per cent of all subsidies allocated went to tenant families.[72]

I have argued elsewhere that to assume that all tenants want and are able to become owners is a naive approach given that no country has yet managed to achieve universal home ownership.[73] In Colombia, a rental housing policy is badly needed given that 34 per cent of urban families rented homes in 1993, and in Bogotá more than two-fifths of all families were tenants. If housing subsidies are offered to families in need, then tenants should be included whether or not they wish to become homeowners. For female-headed households, the aged and certain other categories of family, neither formal nor self-help ownership are options that can be readily taken up.

With respect to rental housing, the Samper government changed little. It failed to formulate a policy towards rental housing and has maintained the existing, but probably ineffective, rent controls.[74] No policy towards rental housing has been developed because there has been little political pressure to change existing practice. In addition, there is the problem that rental housing policy is conceived mainly as an issue of rent control. This is a sensitive issue in Colombia in so far as rents make up slightly more than 20 per cent of the basket of goods used to measure inflation. The fear is that any relaxation in rent controls would lead to rents rising even faster than they have done during the last three years. If that were the result, the explicit aim of reducing inflation would be under serious threat.

Anything that helps reduce excessive levels of government centralisation is welcome, particularly when it makes government more democratic by giving local people a say in the formulation and execution of policy. In this sense, the delegation of more responsibility over housing to local authorities in Colombia constituted a positive step. According to Hommes et al., the policy was also effective in so far as the Gaviria programme reached 270 of the country's 1,056 municipalities and no less than 175 municipalities put forward housing proposals to INURBE.[75] A major query about decentralisation, however, relates to the limited degree of democracy operating at the local level in Colombia. As both administrations have been well aware, few poor people contribute to debates about public policy. This is particularly true in regions suffering from political and economic violence. If decentralisation has increased the level of popular participation, then criticism of the approach must be muted. However, if top-down decision-making is still characteristic of most municipal and departmental administrations, a clear question mark remains over the success of the housing programme.

Successful decentralisation relies on competent management. Unfortunately, few Colombian municipalities are efficient and the more effective tend to be located in the major cities. Salazar claims that the decentralisation of functions to the municipalities occurred too rapidly and too many were unready to take up their new responsibilities. As a result, 'the municipalities and the departments did not make the necessary effort to work with the system'.[76] Since the incidence of poverty is highest in the countryside, where municipal government is at its weakest, decentralisation introduces a major flaw into housing policy. Those most in need of help are least likely to receive it. This recurrent problem soon reared its head under the Gaviria housing programme. As the National Planning Department soon recognised: 'the Rural Housing Programme has achieved nothing'.[77] On the positive side, however, the servicing of rural housing was much improved by the offer of contracts to private contractors.

The Gaviria government increased the number of informal sector housing solutions. Unfortunately, this emphasis did not always improve living conditions in the poorest settlements. This was partly an administrative problem, in so far as it was admitted during the first year of the plan that: 'the urban improvement programmes are badly delayed and only 37 per cent of the target has been implemented. With respect to the issue of legal titles, there is little reliable information, but the available data suggest that little progress has been made.'[78] Part of the problem in existing low-income areas was that the local authorities were less than diligent in helping to implement the programme. In Bogotá, for example, the local authority had little interest in upgrading poorer settlements. The authorities were reluctant to intervene because they did not wish to provide services in low-income areas as there was no mechanism through which they could recoup their expenditure. In places, too, problems were caused by the bureaucratic nature of planning procedures. Certainly, the Samper administration believed that the Gaviria programme had failed to tackle the servicing problems facing low-income settlements: 'The strategy has not been backed up by action intended to correct the environmental problems facing most subnormal settlements.'[79]

Between 1991 and 1994, 44 per cent of INURBE's subsidies were directed towards sites and services schemes.[80] This should have been a major strength of the programme. However, the Samper administration has been very critical of this aspect of its predecessor's housing programme. The principal concern is that far too few of the households receiving subsidies for a serviced lot managed to construct a decent home.[81] Of course, the weakness of this argument is that self-help construction always takes time. The fact that a family has failed to build a decent structure within a couple of years is hardly proof that they will not manage to do so fairly soon. To a government official, a slowly developing sites and services scheme may well look like a failure; to a poor family progress may be slow but steady. A second criticism is that too many urbanisers were providing 'urbanised sites' without a connection to the main service network.[82] In some cities, developers took up sites and services enthusiastically because they regarded it as an easy way of making a good return with very little investment. It is claimed that minimal investment led to excessive profits and high prices for 'serviced' land. The sites and services programme encouraged land speculation. A third weakness, particularly in Bogotá, was that the price of peripheral land was so high that few urbanisers were interested in using the property for sites and services programmes. The absence of such schemes explains why the number of subsidies used to buy urbanised lots in Bogotá was so low.[83] Finally, a general weakness in the programme lay in the failure of the local authorities to participate in the provision of serviced land. In part, this was because so few municipal authorities understood the opportunities offered by the Urban Reform Law and INURBE provided too little in the way of technical advice.[84] The problem was accentuated, however, because it was not in the interests of the municipality to provide land and services. If it authorised land for low-income housing development, the municipality would be required to provide services without receiving any return on its investment.

Many families were offered subsidies which they were unable to use. Indeed, up to March 1993, only 73 per cent of beneficiaries were able to use their subsidies. One reason for this limited take-up was that the process of granting subsidies took ten months for INURBE and fourteen months for other kinds of programme.[85] Given rapid inflation in house prices, a delay of this extent is sufficient to make the difference between success in purchasing a house and failure. The problem was made worse by the difficulty poor families had in obtaining loans. According to the current head of INURBE, the lack of credit for the poor is perhaps the basic failing of all Colombian housing schemes.

Perhaps the most embarrassing problem for the government was that the slow pace of disbursement and approval created a long queue for subsidies. By the end of 1994, some 150,000 applicants were waiting for their subsidy.[86] The response of the Samper government was to stop new applications and to change the subsidy system. This dealt with the major flaw in the subsidy programme, the fact that too many families were potential beneficiaries; since 70 per cent of Colombian families earn less than four minimum salaries, over five million families were potential beneficiaries.

One of the major aims of the new constitution of 1991 was to change the clientelistic nature of Colombian politics. The goal was to eliminate the trading of political favours for votes. Clearly, such a task could not be performed overnight and it is obvious that the impact of political manoeuvring explains the poor match between the regional distribution of subsidies and apparent need. Departments like Antioquia, Bolívar, Magdalena and Vichada received less than three subsidies per thousand inhabitants whereas Cauca received sixteen, Sucre 23 and La Guajira 34.[87] Although Cauca and Sucre are poor departments, this is no longer the case for La Guajira. Bolívar and Magdalena are both poorer than La Guajira but received few subsidies.

Housing during the Samper Government

As already suggested in the previous section, housing policy under the Samper administration has maintained the essentials of that of the Gaviria government but has modified several significant features of the programme. Clearly, the programme is too recent to be evaluated properly. What follows are merely suggestions as to the likely outcome of some of the major shifts in policy. In particular, I will be looking at subsidies, the number of housing solutions, settlement upgrading and improving the environment, the shift from sites and services, and the neglect of rental housing.

The long queue of families expecting to receive a housing subsidy could have had serious political repercussions. That problem was resolved in January 1995 by stopping any more families applying directly for subsidies. Action is now being taken to reduce the list as quickly as possible although it still contained 127,000 families in June 1995.[88] The Samper government also changed the method of allocating subsidies. The change was apparently made because of doubts over whether subsidies for new homes and for serviced sites had actually been reaching the poor. It was also modified in order to encourage a greater emphasis on settlement upgrading. However, there must also be some suspicion that the change was made because the government could simply not afford to give subsidies to all who were applying.

The method of identifying new beneficiaries still seems to be going through teething problems. Setting up local committees of the *Red de Solidaridad Social* has taken time. This has created problems for INURBE in terms of giving it insufficient time to plan its budget for the following year. It is also less than certain whether the new application procedure avoids the traditional problem of political machination. It is certainly not entirely clear whether the new collective procedures for applying for subsidies are either transparent or entirely fair (see below). Some claim that the strength of housing NGOs in Colombia will guarantee that the new *Mesas de Solidaridad Social* will work. Dedicated professionals with their feet firmly based in the community will prevent the entry of too much blatant politicking. At the same time, there must be some danger that professional politicians will seek to get their hands on the available subsidies and credits.

Whether the government can benefit all of the 755,000 families they promise to help is somewhat doubtful. The number of promised solutions is certainly highly ambitious and cuts of over US$600 million have already been announced in government expenditure in an effort to keep inflation within reasonable limits.[89]

In so far as much more emphasis is being put on settlement upgrading, a policy which currently receives universal support from development bankers, planners and academics alike, the new policy can hardly be criticised. Certainly the recognition given to better urban planning and service provision is wholly welcome. Without an appropriate response from the local planning and servicing authorities no housing programme can resolve the shelter problem. The difficulty, of course, is that because urban planning is devolved to the municipalities, its quality depends upon the latter's competence. Unfortunately, the local authorities in Colombia are less than efficient and many question their ability to plan and to provide services and infrastructure.[90] Nor is their technical competence likely to be raised greatly by the help provided by the limited staff of INURBE and the newly established commissions for public services. Despite the laudable ambitions of the current administration to improve the quality of the urban environment, the deficiencies of Colombian local government may yet undermine that goal.

The decision to reduce the emphasis on sites and services projects may rebound on the government. Even if the government is correct that the sites and services component of the Gaviria government did not work well, was it sensible to remove this element from the programme altogether? Sites and services programmes are not simple to administer, but they do have the potential to reach large numbers of families. Such projects may not always work quickly or well, but that does not mean that they do not work at all. There is no real alternative to self-help housing because few poor Colombians can afford the cost of a finished house. Even with the help of a subsidy, households earning two minimum incomes would need to pay nearly half of their monthly income to service the mortgage, those on the minimum income nearly all. Under such circumstances, there is therefore no choice but to support self-help housing. The great challenge to government in Colombia is to make enough semi-serviced land available to the poor at prices they can afford. If government fails to meet this challenge it will face a continuing wave of illegal and irregular forms of land occupation.

Under the Samper programme, fewer tenants will become owners because fewer subsidies are available to purchase housing. Tenants are clearly ineligible for collective improvement grants because they do not own the home in which they live. As such, settlement improvement will go on around them. Of course, they will benefit from upgrading in so far as water or road paving is introduced into their settlement. On the other hand, they may pay indirectly for the improvements through higher rents. Since tenant replies to questionnaires in the late seventies suggested that tenants were far less interested in *barrio* improvements than owners,[91] this is a potential weakness in the programme.

Conclusions

Three general issues are raised by Colombian housing policy during the 1990s: why subsidies are given for housing, the future of sites and services programmes, and the need for rental housing. Some general thoughts on these issues form the substance of the rest of this chapter.

Why give subsidies for housing? IMF adjustment policies discourage governments from offering general subsidies for public services. Besides the problem of cost, subsidies are deemed to be inequitable because the poorest households do not receive them. Subsidised prices discourage the public utilities from expanding capacity and it is the poor whose homes normally lie beyond the service network; in urban areas, those living in peripheral and illegal housing areas.[92] What makes the offer of subsidies still more inequitable is that regressive taxation systems sometimes mean that the unconnected are paying taxes which finance the subsidies going to more affluent, connected households.

Of course, the IMF and the World Bank accept that general subsidies should be offered for merit goods. Vaccinations against disease, minimum charges for small quantities of water consumption and free primary education represent sensible investments because the economic benefits deriving from better health and higher literacy are much greater than the cost of the subsidy. For non-merit goods, however, subsidies should only be offered to groups in particular need. Social targeting has been the major difference between early and later structural adjustment packages, and has been seen as a major success story in several Latin American countries where, despite plummeting household incomes, targeted subsidies have helped to keep infant mortality on its downward path. Targeted subsidies are essential for services such as water delivery, especially where users are being charged the full commercial cost of the service. Full cost recovery can lead to worry-ingly high levels of disconnection; a phenomenon experienced after the privatisation of water and electricity in Britain and Chile. For the poor, the case for subsidising both the capital cost of installing a service and for small amounts of subsequent consumption seems incontrovertible.[93] Subsidies for installation are necessary to help upgrade infrastructure in low-income areas. Without subsidies, some families will be unable to pay for the cost of installation which will undermine some of the ben-efits to be accrued from service improvements. Minimum levels of consumption should also be subsidised to prevent 'self-rationing', such as families opting out of the use of essential services, for example, drinking water. If prices are set above minimum income levels, the lack of a subsidy may well lead to low-income settlements using illicit means of acquiring the service, for example, bypassing meters and tap-ping into public electricity lines. Such subsidies should be paid by higher charges to other consumers, particularly those who use large quantities. The supermarket principle of giving discounts to large pur-chases should certainly not apply in the infrastructure field.

If a case can be made for offering subsidies for certain kinds of merit goods, what is the case for giving subsidies directly for housing? Subsidies can certainly help in generating employment, particularly within the construction industry and in related building-materials sec-tors. Whether it is more generative of employment than other kinds of investment, however, is open to question. Subsidising the building of finished houses is controversial because it offers a relatively high-cost solution in an environment where there are relatively few resources and many potential beneficiaries. Although building formal sector homes creates jobs in the construction sector, the homes created do not often reach the poor. Latin American experience shows that building homes is problematic because poor families cannot afford the necessary outlays. Building finished houses is a very expensive form of shelter solution and, without subsidies, the poor have benefited little from such pro-grammes. But, if the state offers a subsidy, limited government funds mean that relatively few units can be constructed. Unlike slum-upgrad-ing, building finished housing offends the notion of 'giving less to more', a notion that is critical at the current conjuncture of declining state expenditure and falling real incomes among the poor.

There is some justification for giving subsidies to low-income housing in so far as this may help to reduce the proliferation of illegal housing solutions. The availability of subsidies to low-income families allows builders and developers to raise prices, thereby covering the cost of providing infrastructure and services. If the explicit subsidy is less than the cost of servicing land on difficult terrain, it represents a real investment rather than a subsidy for consumption. Arguably, however, it constitutes a subsidy for infrastructure and services rather than for housing.

The risk involved in offering subsidies for housing is that part of the subsidy will be absorbed by the supplier as additional profit. Giving subsidies to low-income families for self-help construction may simply result in higher land prices. Unless subsidies result in some qualitative improvement in the housing solution offered, for example, by tempting the supplier to offer legal, subsidised solutions in place of illegal, un-subsidised solutions, there is little justification for subsidies. A second danger with subsidising housing is that the beneficiary will either divert the subsidy to some other purpose or pass part of the subsidy on; say, by renting out the property acquired with the subsidy. One way of avoiding this kind of problem is by giving the subsidy on a once-only basis to the family, a current Chilean practice.[94] An alternative is to direct the sub-sidy to the builder or developer on behalf of the beneficiary, as in current Colombian practice. A third danger with subsidies is that it is very hard to reach the very poorest families through housing subsidies. This has been evident in Chile where the requirement to have savings has excluded many poor families. In Australia, Britain and the United States, of course, subsidies in the form of income-tax relief on mort-gage interest payments has led to the better off receiving most of the benefits. There is now widespread acceptance that this is both an ineq-uitable and a very expensive method of improving housing.[95] Not only is such tax relief expensive, it is also counterproductive because such subsidies are partially capitalised in higher prices.[96] Tenants and the poor clearly lose out: capitalisation of the subsidy 'results in higher rents but renters, unlike owners, receive no benefits to compensate them for their housing costs'.[97]

Generally, I believe a better case can be made for subsidising the provision of infrastructure and services rather than for subsidising the purchase of housing units. Subsidies should not be given for the pur-chase of finished homes since it is only the better off who can afford such housing. If subsidies are to be offered for housing *per se* it is much better is to offer subsidies to families for minimum solutions. Subsidies should be directed to families selected according to need. Perhaps even better to direct subsidies away from housing towards service provision. This is particularly important at the current time. No one in Colombia needs reminding that the cost of electricity and water is rising. Because of drought, interest payments on the foreign debt and sheer incompetence on the part of some agencies, tariffs have risen markedly in recent years.[98] In future, tariffs need to rise even more because the government is committed to reducing subsidies and it is electricity, water and sewerage that have received most of the subsidies. In 1992, the World Bank calculated that urban households received subsidies for these services equivalent to 7.5 per cent of total government expenditure and 1.8 per cent of GDP.[99] Arguably, there is little wrong with this pattern of expenditure providing that the subsidy reaches the poor and it does not encourage excessive consumption.

With respect to equity, although Colombia has a long-established policy of cross-subsidising the poor, its tariff structure does not work well. The richest households have received subsidies on electricity, water and sewerage while many of the poor, particularly those without a legal connection, have received no subsidy. With so many utilities making large losses, it is inevitable that general tariffs will rise. Such rises will hit the poor unless a sensible tariff structure is established. If cross-subsidies and even general subsidies are not provided, the danger is that poor households will either engage in payment boycotts or will employ self-rationing. Neither is a desirable outcome and, arguably, it is more important to subsidise basic services than provide subsidies for housing.

The most effective way of making land available to the poor is through sites and services schemes. Unfortunately, few Latin American governments have introduced such schemes in an effective and large-scale manner. It appears that there is even some disillusion with sites and services projects among the major funding agencies.[100] Such schemes have been criticised on the grounds that they are not popular with the beneficiaries – governments prefer to build finished houses and the public criticise such schemes as official slums, and sites and services do not reach the poorest. Most doubt, however, seems to relate to the ability of the public sector to run such projects effectively.

While some of these criticisms are valid for particular schemes, it is clear that many poor families want serviced plots. In a recent survey conducted in Colombia's five major cities, for example, 45 per cent of families eligible for a government subsidy said that they were looking for a serviced lot and a further 10 per cent were looking for a plot that could be serviced in the future.[101] By contrast, only 11 per cent were looking for a core house and 13 per cent for a basic housing unit. If sites and services schemes elsewhere have failed to generate interest from the poor, it is because those schemes have failed to offer the poor what they really need. Too many schemes have offered standards far above those that people require, in locations where people do not want to live, and at prices which they cannot afford. The sensible response is not to eschew this essential and unavoidable approach to housing improvement but to learn from past errors.

For many families, renting provides a decent and sensible housing solution, particularly in the short term. To date, however, government intervention in rental housing has tended to be counterproductive. Rent controls have contributed to the decline in private rental investment particularly for middle- and upper-working-class groups. Building regulations have had a similar effect.[102] In addition, few governments have attempted to increase the rental housing stock. Certainly, no Latin American government has built housing for rent in the past twenty years and few have given any incentive to private companies interested in building rental housing. Most governments have failed even to mention rental housing in their policy statements.

Apart from a general desire to remove rent controls, there appears to be little in the way of a rental housing policy emerging either from Washington or from within Latin America. This seems to be a major gap in housing reform given the huge numbers of tenants living in the region's cities; some four million households, for example, live in rental accommodation in Mexico City alone.[103] In addition, there is evidence to suggest that whatever households say about the desirability of owner-occupation, many refuse this option even when they have the resources to buy a self-help home.[104] Rental housing should be encouraged because it is a cost-effective shelter strategy. As Hansen and Williams argue:

> increasing the supply of rental units by encouraging homeowners to rent out rooms and add rental units may be the most efficient way to increase shelter in third world cities. Two factors underlie this argument. First, adding rental units to existing housing means that no additional land costs, which can account for 50 per cent of total dwelling costs, are incurred. Labour and materials are the only major inputs. Second, as a result of higher density development, homeowners and renters combined on the same lot can better afford basic services such as water. Thus the prospects for cost recovery of infrastructure investment are greater than in less dense, low-income communities.[105]

There are various ways in which rental housing could be encouraged. Appropriate mechanisms would include targeting credit towards landlords, reducing rent controls, offering tax relief to landlords on rental income, establishing an efficient arbitration service between landlords and tenants, and, perhaps most importantly, improving the quality of transport and infrastructure in low-income settlements.[106] Since most landlords and landladies differ little in terms of their income from most of their tenants, equity is not a significant issue. Since rental housing tends to offer tenants better location, services and infrastructure than does self-help housing,[107] support for rental housing promises to improve the quality of shelter in most cities. Finally, direct investment in rental housing will help to increase housing densities, thereby reducing suburban sprawl and illegal forms of land occupation.

There can be little doubt that Colombian housing policy before 1990 left a great deal to be desired. Too few subsidies reached the poor. Too much public housing construction was inefficient and allocation procedures were highly politicised. State programmes failed to reduce either the quantitative or the qualitative housing deficit. The numbers of families living in informal housing continued to increase both absolutely and relatively. And, when a major effort was made to reduce the initial cost of buying a formal sector home, the plan destroyed the principal state housing agency.

The modifications in housing policy made in the 1990s included some real improvements. The new system of subsidies did reach the poor. The allocation mechanism was much more transparent and equitable. Private sector investment helped to increase the resources flowing into social-interest housing. The new approach also recognised the need for more investment in infrastructure and services; a proper housing solution clearly requires much more than improvements to the home alone.

Nevertheless, questionable elements remain in the new policy. First, it is not certain that the provision of subsidies for housing units is better than giving subsidies for infrastructure and services. Second, given the large numbers of tenants, it is very short-sighted not to formulate a policy towards rental housing. Third, the market may offer better value housing than that provided by ICT but that still leaves the huge problem of what to do about rising land and material prices; so far, the Urban Reform Law has not been used sufficiently to counteract the unfavourable face of the market. Finally, neither the Gaviria nor the Samper government has managed to recognise the huge administrative problems involved in supplying large numbers of housing solutions. The goals have probably been overambitious with the danger that resources are stretched and too little is done properly.

Notes

*I should like to thank the following government officials and advisers, both current and retired, for talking to me so honestly about past and present policy and for providing me with so much useful information: Jairo Arias, Luis Mauricio Cuervo, Diego Fernández, Fernando Gaitán, Fabio Giraldo, Samuel Jaramillo, Samuel Eduardo Salazar and Enrique Uribe.

1. See Gilbert and Gugler (1992); Matthey (1990); Shidlo (1990); Skinner et al. (1987); Ward (1982); Valença (1992); and World Bank (1980).
2. I use this vague and unsatisfactory term to cover all forms of 'self-help' housing. This includes housing built, or at least designed and contracted, by the poor whether on legally acquired land or land obtained through invasion, semi-legally through purchase or through government connivance and rule bending.
3   See World Bank (1993), and Harris (1992).
4. World Bank (1993).
5. See Collier (1976); de Soto (1989); Gilbert (1994); Hardoy and Satterthwaite (1989).
6. DNP (1972 and 1983); Gilbert and Ward (1985); Jaramillo (1982); Molina (1990); Murillo and Ungar (1982); and Robledo (1985).
7. Hommes et al. (1994), p. 162.
8. Gutiérrez (1989).
9. Castro (1989); Robledo (1985); and Ortiz (1995).
10. Reading the annual report of ICT offers a highly instructive critique of why the institute could not possibly have accomplished its goals. The criticism of how high land prices forced the Institute to buy unserviced and peripheral land, and thereby spend most of its budget on infrastructure rather than housing, is particularly interesting. Several directors enjoined the Minister of Development to take action on land prices. See Pacheco (1989).
11. Under Belisario Betancur, a major effort was made to make lower income housing units available to the poor. The key plank in this effort was to remove the barrier of the housing deposit. The Housing and Savings Corporations were expected to lend a proportion of their savings for social-interest housing.
12. DNP (1991 and 1993).
13. DNP (1994a).
14. The Peaceful Revolution was the name given to César Gaviria's national plan. It was a neo-liberal approach to development which emphasised trade liberalisation, market reform and labour deregulation.
15. The minimum salary since 1 January 1995 is $3,964.45 per day. The official exchange rate on 24 June 1995 was 822 to the dollar. Hence the monthly minimum salary was US$120 per month assuming a working month of 25 days; the average working week for industrial workers is 48 hours.
16. UPAC is the indexed mortgage loan and savings system created in 1972. On 24 June 1995, one UPAC was worth $7,137.19 or US$8.68.
17. DNP (1994a), p. 3.
18. *El Tiempo*, 8 Oct. 1994.

19   See DNP (1994a), p. 1; and DNP (1995), p. 134.
20. DNP (1995), p. 135.
21. See Velásquez (1995); Forero (1995); and DNP (1995), pp. 1–2.
22. Iglesias (1992), and World Bank (1990 and 1992).
23. World Bank (1992).
24. World Bank (1993), p. 53.
25. Hommes et al. (1994), p. 161–2.
26. World Bank (1993), p. 62.
27. Hommes et al. (1994), p. 161.
28. Giraldo (1993), p. 45.
29. Hommes et al. (1994), p. 162.
30. *Ibid.*, p. 90.
31. World Bank (1993), p. 62.
32. Vélez (1994), p. 101.
33. Hommes et al. (1994), p. xv. See also Chapter 4 in this volume.
34. DNP (1992b).
35. Velásquez (1995), Forero (1995), and Chapter 3 in this volume.
36. Ministerio de Desarrollo Económico (1995), p. 5.
37. DNP (1995), p. 134.
38. World Bank (1992), pp. 7.10 and 3.13.
39. USAID (1992), and World Bank (1993). There are, of course, exceptions as, in Mexico, where support has been given to a low-income housing finance programme and in Chile, with continued support for core-houses and low-income units.
40. World Bank (1992), pp. 7.10 and 3.13.
41. World Bank (1993), p. 126.
42. Pacheco (1989).
43. DNP (1994a), p. 8.
44. However, this estimate is based on the somewhat questionable assumption that 258,500 subsidies will benefit 775,000 families because each subsidy given to one family will help two other families by improving the settlement, e.g. through that part of the subsidy directed to community programmes such as road paving.
45. DNP (1994a), p. 4.
46. Hommes et al. (1994), p. 162.
47. DNP (1990), p. 12.
48. DNP (1994b), p. 24.
49. Hommes et al. (1994), p. 163.
50. Salazar (1994), p. 32.
51. It is admitted that, at first, some middle-class families did apply for subsidies. However, when they realised that they could not use the funds for improving their own home or to buy a car, they ceased to apply.
52. Giraldo (1993), t. 7.22.
53. DNP (1994b), p. 22. Assuming that the 91,386 rural families were all earning less than five minimum salaries. For urban areas alone, 51.8% of solutions had gone to low-income families.

54. Salazar (1994), p. 29.
55. Clearly, there has been some shift in the basis of the calculation. If 70% of Colombian families earn less than five minimum salaries, these figures cannot be correct.
56. See DNP (1994b), p. 24; Hommes et al. (1994); and World Bank (1994), p. 112.
57. Hommes et al. (1994), p. 171.
58. Giraldo (1993), t. 7.38.
59. Assuming an interest rate of 34 per cent and a 20-year repayment period, with a 5 per cent downpayment and 15 minimum salaries subsidy (calculations by T. Persaud of the World Bank). Later figures cited in World Bank (1994: 114) reduced the interest rate to 28 per cent and produced affordability rates of 39 per cent and 77 per cent of income respectively. In practice this rate was much lower than that which was operating in June 1995; 12–17 per cent plus monetary correction of 26 per cent, i.e. between 38 and 43 per cent (*El Tiempo* 24 June 1995: 4B).
60. Giraldo (1993), ts. 7.32–3.
61. In Cali, the municipality developed its own sites and service schemes as well as encouraging legal developments by former pirate developers: the *Calimío* and *Desepaz* programmes.
62. Giraldo (1994), p. 48.
63. Hommes et al. (1994), p. 171.
64. Giraldo and Cortés (1994). The amnesty led to a massive repatriation of capital from abroad, a process no doubt amplified by the laundering of drug monies.
65. *Revista del Banco de la República,* Jan. 1995, pp. 286 and 289.
66. *Dinero* (June 1995), p. 30.
67. June 1995 subsidy is 300 UPACS for the purchase of a basic unit. One UPAC was worth US$8.68 on 25 June.
68. Fortunately, the minimum salary rose by 190%, although earnings in the low-paid retail trade only increased by 47% (*Revista del Banco de la República*, Jan. 1995).
69. Giraldo and Cortés (1994), p. 40.
70. Statements by national presidents referring to the political benefits of home ownership can be traced back at least to Mariano Ospina Pérez (1944–48). See Laun (1976) and Gilbert and Ward (1985).
71. Such statements are not always to be taken at face value; see Gilbert (1993).
72. Giraldo (1993), t. 7.24.
73. Gilbert (1993).
74. The current rent control legislation dates from 1985. It decrees that rents can only rise by 90% of the rise in the national price index for the previous year. Between January 1993 and February 1995, rents rose by 29% compared to the consumer price index of 22% (*Banco de la República*, 1995, p. 16). Between December 1988 and March 1995, rents rose 3.25 times compared to 3.31 times in prices as a whole (*Boletín de Estadística,* 504, Mar. 1995). These figures, and especially the most recent data, suggest that the rent control policy, which restricts rent rises to 90% of the rise in consumer prices, is not working. As such, Colombia seems to be obtaining the worst of both worlds; it is seemingly discouraging

landlords through the wording of the law, while failing tenants by the weaknesses of its implementation.

75. Hommes et al. (1994), p. 169.
76. Salazar (1994), p. 29.
77. DNP (1992a), p. 16.
78. DNP (1992a), p. 15.
79. DNP (1994a), p. 3.
80. Salazar (1994), p. 29. Of the remainder, 8% were for basic units, 19% for minimum housing and 19% for *barrio* upgrading.
81. DNP (1994a), p. 3.
82. Seemingly, a full service network was often provided within the settlement, but no connection made to the city's water or drainage network because the water company was unable to provide the service.
83. Most of the subsidies were supplied through the *Cajas de Compensación* which dealt with higher income families. In Cundinamarca, the department that contains Bogotá, some 49,715 subsidies were allocated between 1991 and 1993, of which INURBE was responsible for only 28%.
84. Salazar (1994), p. 29.
85. DNP (1994a), p. 3 and Salazar (1994), p. 29.
86. INURBE (1995).
87. Hommes et al. (1994), p. 167.
88. INURBE (1995).
89. *El Espectador*, 27 June 1995.
90. See Bell's chapter in this volume (Chapter 4).
91. Gilbert and Ward (1985).
92. Linn (1983).
93. Herbert and Kempson (1995).
94. Echegaray (1992), Kusnetzoff (1990), Persaud (1992), and Richards (1994).
95. Bramley (1993), Megbolugbe and Linneman (1993), p. 673.
96. Bramley (1993), p. 26; Flood and Yates (1989), p. 208.
97. *Ibid.*, p. 208.
98. Gilbert (1990), Ochoa (1989), and Yepes (1993). During 1993 and 1994 the price of public services rose by 33% and 24% compared to the overall rise in prices of 23% for both years. Between December 1988 and March 1995, public service tariffs rose in current prices by 3.54 times, the general price index by only 3.31 times.
99. World Bank (1994), p. 82.
100. World Bank (1993).
101. Giraldo (1993).
102. Gilbert and Varley (1991).
103. Coloumb and Sánchez (1991).
104. Gilbert and Varley (1991).
105. Hansen and Williams (1988), pp. 316–7.
106. UNCHS (1989).
107. Lemer (1987).

PART III

THE STATE AND THE
ECONOMIC *APERTURA*

CHAPTER 8

THE COLOMBIAN *APERTURA*: AN ASSESSMENT

Jorge Ramírez Ocampo

To understand the nature of the economic reforms adopted under the Gaviria administration (1990–94), it is important to bear in mind that Colombia has had a relatively long tradition of sound economic policies. These allowed the country to avoid the debt crisis and the painful consequences of the so-called 'lost decade', experienced by other Latin American countries during the 1980s. The *apertura* – as the process of economic reform came to be known – was therefore a significant change in direction, from the import-substitution model to a policy of competition and reduction of tariff and non-tariff barriers to trade. It was not a revolution in which every existing institution was destroyed and an entirely new economy was created.

This tradition of sound economic policy has not been the rule in Latin America. This is probably the main reason for Colombia not having experienced any hyper-inflationary periods in our recent economic history and for the lower costs incurred during the transition to the new model. It is also the main reason for optimism regarding the future of the Colombian economy. In Colombia one should expect gradual change, instead of revolutions. It is very unlikely that we will be faced with an 'aguardiente crisis' similar to the 'tequila effect' experienced by Mexico after the crisis of December 1994. In this chapter, I will discuss in separate sections 'the good, the bad and the ugly' sides of the *apertura*. This will be followed by some comments on the prospects for future developments. [1]

'The Good': Structural Reform

By the end of the 1980s it was clear that the import-substitution model had lost its usefulness for the development of Colombia. The possibility of keeping a reasonable growth rate based only on the requirements of domestic consumption did not exist. Whenever the authorities tried to accelerate economic growth through an increase in domestic demand, the inflation rate increased and subsequently a restrictive macroeconomic policy had to be applied. Colombians were facing a 'stop-go' situation, similar to the one experienced by the United Kingdom during the 1960s and 1970s. In those circumstances, the possibilities of maintaining a sustained rate of growth of more than 3.5 per cent were far from being achieved.

In a document prepared under my co-ordination in 1989, we included some projections with 'optimistic' and 'pessimistic' scenarios for the decade 1989–98.[2] In each case we tried a policy of import substitution and one of *apertura*. In the optimistic scenario, in which the world economy would grow at an annual rate of 5 per cent, and prices for the main commodities exported by Colombia would be relatively high, the rate of growth would have been high with either of the alternative policies. However, the rate of growth would have been substantially higher with *apertura*: by the year 2000, economic growth would have been more than 8 per cent with *apertura*, while it would have been only 5.5 per cent with the previous strategy of import substitution.

In a pessimistic scenario, on the other hand, the average annual rate of growth following *apertura* policies was estimated at around 4.1 per cent. In contrast, with a policy of import substitution, the results were apparently discouraging: the economy would have been able to grow at only 1.3 per cent per year. This would have meant a reduction of income *per capita* during the decade, because the drop in domestic savings and limited access to international finance would have reduced the level of investment. Since the likelihood of the 'pessimistic' scenario was greater than the 'optimistic' one and since the results, in terms of growth, were better with *apertura* in either scenario, we strongly recommended this policy with all the institutional reforms required to apply it successfully. Our voice was only one in a chorus in which the World Bank, the Inter-American Development Bank, the Banco de la República of Colombia (Central Bank), several other research institutions and individual economists all agreed that a change of direction in Colombian economic policy was long overdue. *Apertura* was therefore necessary.

A *sine qua non* for the success of *apertura* was the implementation of several fundamental institutional reforms that would allow more flexibility for the business community. In 1990, at the beginning of the Gaviria government, the main efforts were oriented towards this end and most of the proposed reforms were passed by the appropriate authorities. Although Armando Montenegro examines the reforms in some detail in Chapter 9, I will briefly outline the major ones.[3]

Commercial reforms Import licences were eliminated for all goods except a minor percentage of imports (about 5 per cent), mainly security or chemical products related to the processing of narcotics. Average tariffs were reduced from 47 to 11.5 per cent. Export incentives were cut to a minimum. In addition, customs procedures were simplified. Unfortunately, with the absorption of the customs function by the Internal Revenue Service, the control of smuggling was relaxed and the amount of contraband increased substantially. A new Foreign Trade Ministry was created and the export promotion fund (Proexpo) was split into two new institutions: a foreign trade bank (Bancoldex) and an agency specialised in non-financial export promotion (Proexport-Colombia).

Labour reform A greater flexibility was introduced by changing the existing legislation. Private severance pay funds were created for the management of the reserves that each company must establish for payment at the time when labour is made redundant (the so-called *cesantía*). Before the reform, companies had to establish their own reserves and make a retroactive adjustment to the balance of the severance-pay reserve of each worker. This adjustment was done by multiplying the amount of salary adjustments by the number of years of employment at the company and was applicable even if the employee had received the outstanding amount for the acquisition of his house. This provision created a contingent liability which was very difficult to evaluate. This reserve is equivalent to one month's salary per year of employment. Now the companies pay the equivalent of one month's salary at the end of each year to the new financial institutions which pay commercial interest on the outstanding balance of each employee. Work contracts started after the end of 1980 can now be terminated without a special penalty which was provided for when employees completed ten years of employment at the same company. Greater rights were conferred on trade unions and, in accordance with the 1991 Constitution, social organisations now have preferential access to pre-privatisation share purchasing in public companies.

Foreign exchange reform Import and export of capital can now be carried out without the intervention of the Central Bank or the Planning Department; commercial banks and other private financial institutions were authorised to trade in foreign exchange. The rate of exchange is no longer fixed daily by the Central Bank, but is the result of market forces, within a 14 per cent band.

Financial reform Financial institutions were deregulated. Specialisation of financial institutions was eliminated; they may diversify their services within the same institution. Entry limitations were reduced in order to increase competition. Additionally, foreign ownership restrictions were eliminated. Foreign investors may own 100 per cent of financial institutions. Meanwhile, supervision by the Bank Superintendence was strengthened. Since the reforms, a greater capitalisation and higher reserve requirements have been established in order to strengthen the financial structure of these institutions.

Foreign investment reforms For many years, especially after Decision 24 of the Andean Pact was adopted in 1972, the attitude of Colombian authorities towards foreign investment had not been enthusiastic. Many restrictions were imposed on foreign capital. The Planning Department, for example, had to approve the investment beforehand. This process usually took several months. There was a limit for the remission of profits. 'Mixed' companies (with more than 50 per cent of foreign capital) did not benefit from any advantages of the Andean Pact unless they made a formal commitment for conversion to 'national' companies with a greater share of local capital. The share of local capital in banks had to be greater than 55 per cent. In 1990 most of these restrictions were eliminated, and now foreign investment is allowed without previous authorisation, except for a few activities which are clearly defined; there is no limit on remission of profits and foreign interests, as already stated, may own 100 per cent of local banks. There is only an *a posteriori* registration requirement in order to maintain remittance rights. Tax treatment of foreign investment in venture capital is still less favourable than that accorded to local investors, but the 1992 tax reform provided for a gradual reduction in the discriminatory provisions. On the other hand, portfolio investment has an unconditional tax exemption, which, in my view, goes too far because it stimulates imports of short-term, speculative capital.

Central Bank reform The Junta Monetaria was eliminated and an independent Banco de la República Board (the Board) of seven directors was created in the constitutional reform of 1991. Five directors of the Board are appointed by the President of the Republic for a fixed period of four years. After the first four year period, the President will change one director each year. The Minister of Finance acts as chairman of the Board and has only one vote. The Board appoints the general manager of the Banco de la República who is himself a director of the Board and has voting rights. According to the Constitution, the Board of the Central Bank and the government have the obligation to co-ordinate economic policies. The reform of the Central Bank has proved to be one of the most important changes among the new economic institutions of Colombia.

Tax reforms Double taxation for shareholders of companies was eliminated in 1986. Capital gains tax for stock-exchange earnings was eliminated. Tax exemption for the equivalent of Value Added Tax (VAT) on capital goods was introduced. VAT was increased from 10 per cent to 14 per cent. An income tax surcharge equivalent to 25 per cent of the ordinary rate was established. The current rate for corporations, including the surcharge, is now 37.5 per cent.

Social security reform Private firms may participate in the provision of health services and pension funds. The severance payment savings (*cesantías*) are now administered by private firms. These reforms allow for the mobilisation of savings to finance production projects. According to a recent study,[4] the total savings accumulated in these funds will be between 12 and 22.5 per cent of Gross Domestic Product (GDP) by the year 2010 and up to 54 per cent of GDP by the year 2025.

These radical institutional reforms have been generally well accepted. In a 1994 public opinion poll, over 60 per cent of a sample of businessmen considered the reforms positive. As a result of the implementation of *apertura*, there have been some important results which may be summarised as follows.

Private investment, which had dropped below 9 per cent of GDP, increased to 17 per cent in 1994. The reasons for this increase may be attributed to the general acceptance of the reforms, to the availability of foreign credit and to the decreasing cost of capital (because of the reduction of tariffs, the appreciation of the currency and the reduction of interest rates between 1992 and the first half of 1994). Productivity of labour has increased 6 per cent a year. This increase was the result of a higher use of capacity and of the modernisation of equipment which was forced by greater competition. GDP growth returned to the ratio which had been obtained during the sixties and seventies. Government expenditure contributed substantially to this acceleration of the growth rate, as we shall see later on.

'The Bad': Low Savings and High Debt

As mentioned above, the driving force of growth during 1990–94 was government expenditure. The average share of central government current expenditure during the 1970s and the 1980s had been just under 6 per cent of GDP and average public investment had been 7.5 per cent, for an overall share of central government expenditure of around 14 per cent. Since the outset of the Gaviria government, fiscal expenditure began to grow at a much faster rate than GDP. By 1994 the central government was absorbing almost 22 per cent of GDP, of which almost 14 per cent went to current expenditure, while fiscal investment remained at traditional levels.

To some extent this huge jump was the result of the decentralisation of resources imposed by the 1991 Constitution. It was also an answer to the need to allocate more resources in the area of security and to strengthen the judicial system. These were urgent needs, approved by the vast majority. The improvement of infrastructure and pressing social issues demanded attention as well. These are the reasons that help to explain why a majority of the private sector supported an increase of taxes as described above.

However, it was always understood that a substantial part of those taxes should be saved in order to maintain a reasonable balance between aggregate supply and demand; otherwise the need to control inflation and maintain an equilibrium exchange rate would be frustrated. The rate of growth of government expenditure was almost 12 per cent per year, compared with less than a 5 per cent increase of GDP between 1991 and 1994. Unfortunately, the efficiency of governmental agencies did not improve. The fiscal surplus was below 1 per cent of GDP, except in 1994 when the proceeds of privatisations were large. The government surplus did not contribute to the stabilisation of the economy.

As mentioned above, the independent Banco de la República Board has, as its main goal, the control of inflation. The instruments given to the Board by the Constitution and by law for this purpose are the control over monetary and exchange rate policies. When the *apertura* programme was launched, many of us thought that the opening of the financial market should take place only when the commercial *apertura* was consolidated. But this opinion was not shared either by the government or by the Board. By the middle of 1991, the financial market had been opened. As a result, monetary and exchange rate policies were no longer independent: they were both subject to the pressures of international financial movements. In these circumstances the only available instrument for inflation control was fiscal policy. But, as we have seen, government expenditure was increasing significantly.

In these circumstances, the Board allowed the revaluation of the currency, since it was unable to obtain the co-operation of the Executive to reduce public expenditure. But such a policy was dangerous. The high local demand for money resulted in an increase in interest rates. At the same time, the low international cost of money and the reduced level of nominal devaluation made foreign credit very attractive. As a result, the control of money supply became almost impossible as short-term capital inflows were stimulated. In 1992 the Board tried to control capital inflows by reducing interest rates. This was not enough. In fact, from 1991 to the last quarter of 1994 the rate of growth of money supply (M1) was above the range established as a goal by the Board.

The growth of private consumption did not help either. As a consequence of the release of reserves for severance pay, the opening of imports and access to foreign credit, the private sector had the opportunity to increase consumption substantially. The rate of private savings dropped to the lowest level ever, while a huge private deficit of over 6 per cent of GDP was registered in 1994.

The reaction of the authorities, at the request of producers associations, such as ANALDEX (Asociación Nacional de Exportadores), was to penalise short term international credit with very high reserve deposits. Such deposits were first applied to credits of less than eighteen months; then of less than three years, and finally, after the inauguration of the new government in 1994, to credits of less than a five year term. Any correction had come too late. From 1992 to 1994, private international debt went from US$3.5 billion to US$8.5 billion.

At the beginning of the *apertura* process the rate of devaluation had been high, exports had grown fast and imports stagnated. This resulted in a current account surplus and a substantial increase in international reserves which, by the end of 1991, were the equivalent of fifteen months of imports. With the appreciation of the peso and the liberalisation of capital markets, this situation was reversed after 1992. Imports increased very fast; the rate of growth of non-traditional exports was reduced and traditional exports suffered the effect of lower international prices. As a result, there was a sharp deterioration of the balance of trade, which went from a surplus of more than US$2.3 billion in 1991 to a deficit of US$2.4 billion in 1994.

The current account of the balance of payments showed an even greater reduction, since it went from a surplus of US$2.5 billion in

1991 to a US$3.0 billion deficit in 1994. This represented a collapse of more than 10 per cent of GDP. Since 1991 a surplus in the capital account of the balance of payments has compensated the deficit in the current account and international reserves have remained at around US$8 billion, which amounts to 8.8 times the monthly imports of 1994.

It must be understood that in the developments that I have described up to now expectations created by the oil discoveries in Cusiana and Cupiagua played an important role. As a result of the increase in government and private expenditure, total national savings dropped from more than 20 per cent in 1990 to 15 per cent of GDP in 1994, while investment was at its highest historical levels (23 per cent of GDP). There was, therefore, a domestic deficit equivalent to almost 6 per cent of GDP which was financed with the transfer of international savings. Fiscal policy did not fulfil its anti-cyclical role. This imbalance was responsible for unsatisfactory results in the control of inflation and for appreciation in the currency.

In Colombia, according to Calderón, an increase of 1 per cent in the share of government expenditure in GDP results in a 3 per cent appreciation of the currency if it is financed by taxes.[5] If it is financed by public debt, the appreciation goes up to 4 per cent. It is not surprising, therefore, that there has been a significant appreciation in the Colombian peso. The Purchasing Parity Index (100 in December 1986) used by Banco de la República to measure the real rate of exchange was 93 in January 1995 (7 per cent below the equilibrium level). But this index only takes into account the prices of tradable goods, which tend to become relatively cheaper during revaluation periods. The Exporters Association calculated an index that takes into account the impact of non-tradable goods on the cost of production. Taking the same basis, this index was 76 in January 1995, showing an appreciation in the peso of 24 per cent compared with the basis.

In order to understand these decisions of the Colombian authorities, we must remember that the position of the leading multilateral agencies, led by the IMF, was to support the theory of the control of inflation through the foreign exchange rate anchor, following the models applied in Argentina and Mexico with apparent success. The international financial world seemed to be satisfied with this model. They were willing to pump in ever greater resources to keep the system running. The new strategy collapsed when the Mexican government was forced to devalue and to abandon the control of the foreign exchange market because their foreign reserves had been exhausted. This led to a sharp revision of recommendations by the IMF. Stanley Fisher, for example, has recognised that it was a great mistake that resulted in huge costs particularly in the case of Mexico. In February 1995, *The Economist* stated: 'Many economists agree that removing capital controls can be dangerous if an emerging economy has not yet liberalised prices and trade.'[6] In that case, large inflows of foreign money serve only to promote the wrong sources of investment and output. Many argue that the removal of capital controls should therefore be applied towards the end of the process of economic reform. In a document issued by the World Bank in November 1994, Vittorio Corbo and Leonardo Hernández addressed this issue and arrived at similar conclusions – governments in developing countries should be concerned about capital inflows for several reasons:

> The appreciation of the real exchange rate can put in jeopardy the success of the recently implemented trade liberalisation reforms; the increase in domestic inflation can erode the credibility of the undergoing price stabilisation programs . . . Those countries that show a decreasing pattern of government consumption – as a percentage of GDP – are also those that show a lower real exchange rate appreciation, while those countries that show an increasing share of government consumption in GDP are the same that show the highest real exchange rate appreciation . . . Sterilized intervention is most effective when it is accompanied by fiscal restraint. However, it does not seem to be a sustainable policy . . . as sterilized intervention tends to exacerbate capital inflows rather than to ameliorate them. This occurs because it tends to increase the difference between domestic and foreign interest rates . . . An increase in public sector savings seems to be the only sustainable policy to protect the real exchange rate in the long run.[7]

Of course the Colombian model has some advantages compared to the Mexican one. Above all, the country's democratic system allowed the private sector to criticise government decisions (which we did), and public policy was subject to the checks and balances of public opinion. I do believe that this has been a key factor in avoiding the extreme path to which the Mexican economy was subjected. As a result of those pressures there were some efforts to control foreign credit and to avoid a faster increase in government expenditure. In the end Colombia was in a much sounder situation than Mexico. And the country was not at any risk of facing an international crisis. Perhaps we can say that Colombia was lucky to receive a warning from the Mexican collapse. I am certain that we have learned the hard lesson.

And 'the Ugly': 'Dutch Disease'

'Dutch disease' is a situation in which there is excess supply of foreign exchange as a result of an increase in the price of a commodity, or of a large flow of speculative capital to an economy that is not sufficiently diversified. This excess supply of foreign exchange generates an appreciation in the local currency that reduces the competitiveness of tradable goods.

This process started in Colombia with the inflow of speculative capital stimulated by the success of the structural reforms mentioned in the first section of this chapter, and by the trend to invest in emerging markets that appeared in international financial centres during the early 1990s. This was aggravated by the large differential between local and international interest rates, the hasty opening of the capital market and the expectation of an oil 'bonanza'. It is also relevant to mention money laundering from drug trafficking as a complicating factor in this picture.

The revaluation of the peso produced a fall in the relative prices of tradable goods compared with non-tradable goods of the order of 25 per cent. This is the result of demand pressures not reflected in the price of tradable goods because they are imported with cheaper foreign currency, while the price of non-tradable goods rises, since they are not subject to international competition. As a consequence of this change in relative prices, there was a change in resource allocation because the non-tradables sector became more profitable. The rate of growth of tradable goods has been 2 per cent per year since 1991 while that of non-tradable goods has accelerated to 7.2 per cent and has explained almost all of the growth of GDP.

We started, therefore, to experience the symptoms of 'Dutch disease' which can be summarised in the following characteristics: a substantial increase in international reserves, which went from US$4.5 to US$8.0 billion between 1990 and 1993; a sharp revaluation of the currency; and an accelerated increase of imports which increased 150 per cent between 1991 and 1994. In addition, the rate of growth of non-traditional exports, which had been 21 per cent from 1985 to 1991, dropped to 8.5 per cent during the next three years. From 1991 to 1994 the share of exports of total industrial production was reduced from 17 to 15.4 per cent and the diversification of exports, which had been reasonably strong, was stopped.

We had a substantial deficit in the trade balance (US$2.4 billion in 1994) and an even greater deficit in the current account of the balance of payments of almost 5 per cent of GDP in 1994. This situation was not solved by the increase in international coffee prices nor is it likely to disappear during the next four years with the greater exports of oil. Domestic demand has grown by 11 per cent per year. Much faster than GDP.

The public sector has been the most dynamic sector of the economy and has created severe problems for the control of inflation and the maintenance of an equilibrium real exchange rate. The profitability of tradable sectors has been dropping consistently since 1991. It is rather frustrating to see how short-term economic policies have hampered the economy from harvesting all the benefits of the well-oriented and courageous structural reforms carried out by the Gaviria administration. The need to revise short-term policies had been clear for some time and was widely discussed during the 1994 campaign. The new developments in Mexico have made it inevitable.

There is also the problem of drug trafficking. This is, of course, a very serious problem not directly related to the *apertura*, but which in some ways may have been aggravated by the liberalisation of the foreign exchange market and by the incorporation of the Customs Administration to the 'Administración Nacional de Impuestos' which has almost eliminated smuggling control. Some people consider that the Colombian economy has not suffered the economic crises of other Latin American countries because of the large inflow of drug money. This is a mistake. Mauricio Rubio estimated in a recent study that the cost of crime to the Colombian economy had been 6,000 billion Colombian pesos.[8] This is a conservative estimate because it takes into account only reported crimes and it does not evaluate some types of delinquency such as car theft and the cost of corruption to the state. On the other hand, the rate of crime in Colombia has increased substantially since the late 1970s, when drug trafficking began to be a serious problem. From 1980 to 1993, the number of homicides increased from 25 to about 80 per 100,000. The effect of this increase on the rate of growth in the economy, through the reduction of productivity and the discouragement of private investment, is estimated by Rubio at an average of 2 per cent of GDP per year, since 1980. The accumulated effect of this reduction in the rate of growth on *per capita* income was the equivalent of one-third of the level reached in that year. In 1993, therefore, the level of *per capita* income would have been US$2,000, instead of the US$1,500 registered that year, had it not been for the increase in crime induced by drug trafficking.

The damaging consequences of drug money on the economy are brought about through several mechanisms. The 'demonstration effect' on luxury and wasteful consumption has contributed to a reduction in the rate of savings and has promoted imports of luxury goods that are beyond the country's means, and even those of most families involved. The increased demand for non-tradable goods, such as real estate, has contributed to creating inflationary pressures. The greater availability of foreign currency obtained through money laundering has had a significant effect on the appreciation of the Colombian peso and has, therefore, contributed to increase the risk of 'Dutch disease'. The main procedure used for money laundering in Colombia has been contraband which has seen a huge increase and has been one of the most damaging recent developments, both from the point of view of corruption of government officers and of unfair competition against local producers.

The conclusion from this analysis is, therefore, that drug trafficking and drug money have not contributed to protect the Colombian economy from the crises suffered by Latin America during the last fifteen years. On the contrary, the Colombian economy has been able to overcome those crises successfully in spite of the very damaging consequences of drug trafficking on the economy and, in particular, on productivity, investment and the rate of growth of GDP.

Perspectives on Prospects for the Future

Colombia now faces an interesting prospect. The short-term policies have resulted in many distortions of the economy and in an appreciation of the peso; in dangerous symptoms of 'Dutch disease', and in reduced effectiveness of inflation control policies. But at the time of writing this chapter, it maintains a sound set of economic indicators while it has managed to introduce fundamental reforms which have been well accepted by public opinion and by the business community.

The prospects for economic growth until 1998 are good (5.6 per cent per year according to the Planning Department)[9] This optimistic outlook is based upon the oil development in Cusiana and Cupiagua; the high investment rate of the private sector during the last few years (especially in the industrial sector); and access to neighbouring markets obtained as a result of trade negotiations. The impact of the 'tequila effect' on the Colombian economy has been felt through the frustration of the commercial expectations which had been built up for trade with Mexico, and in the greater difficulty in obtaining international credit. This limitation is affecting not only the amount of credit available for the private sector, but also the increased interest spread as a result of the so called 'Latin American risk'. A large proportion of capital inflows will come from direct investment, which is programmed for the development of the oil fields. Foreign credit is expected to come mainly from multilateral and governmental sources. On the other hand, the lower pressures of speculative capital and the greater risk perceived by international banks have had the positive effect of reducing the process of currency appreciation.

The projections for the balance of trade assume a gradually reducing deficit as a consequence of the development of the new oil fields, a rather stable international oil market and a reduction in the growth rate of imports. The current account, on the other hand, shows a large deficit (four to five billion dollars per year) until 1998. Foreign debt is not expected to become a problem in the Colombian economy since it will represent a declining proportion of GDP and the percentage of total exports required for debt service will fall.

There are, however, several limitations that have to be taken into account. The reduction of inflation below 20 per cent is proving very difficult because of the inertia in the adjustment of prices and salaries that has been built into the economy. The Samper government initially proposed a 'social pact' with the participation of workers and the private sector in order to curtail inflationary expectations. The pact includes a commitment by the government to maintain within agreed limits the prices and rates over which it has control (public services). There was a commitment to obtain a fiscal surplus of up to 1.2 per cent of GDP in 1995. The results of the pact were positive during January 1995. But the reduction of inflation in the following months was modest because of the increase in tuition fees at the beginning of the school year and the effect of a very dry season on the supply of food. The control of inflation will require a great deal of austerity in the adjustment of salaries and a very severe control of public expenditure, together with a limitation on the rate of growth of private consumption. Our main concern in this field is that the amount of public expenditure programmed in the Development Plan does not seem to be consistent with the proposed reduction of inflation to single digits before the end of 1998.

The very high rate of consumption which has prevailed in Colombia during the last few years has reduced sound sources of investment financing. It is very important to re-establish our traditional levels of private savings because, as mentioned above, it dropped from 14 per cent in 1990 to 6 per cent in 1994. This is particularly urgent in view of the reduced availability of international financial resources for Latin American countries after the Mexican crisis. Another restriction on economic growth will arise from the limited availability of skilled labour. Labour costs for the industrial sector have increased 40 per cent more than the producer price index since 1992. This has been one of the most scarce factors of production during the last few years.

Public expenditure will continue to be very dynamic during the next four years. Total expenditure for the non-financial public sector will grow, according to the *Salto Social*, from 30 to 33.6 per cent of GDP. The two main sources of this substantial increase will be a greater rate of investment and larger transfers to local governments required by the 1991 Constitution.

The *Salto Social* development plan states that investment will be oriented towards the solution of social needs and to the construction of infrastructure which is urgently required, since the density of roads in Colombia is very low (309 km per million inhabitants, compared with 683 km per million inhabitants as an average for medium-income countries). According to the Planning Department, this limitation represents a tariff on imports equivalent to 12 per cent of their value and the equivalent of a tax on exports of 8 per cent. The *Salto Social* has included investments in roads, energy and communications equivalent to 9 per cent of GDP during 1994–98.

Transfers of resources to local authorities required by the 1991 Constitution are expected to reach 40 per cent of current central government income by 1998. But the provisions for the delegation of responsibilities to those authorities have been opposed by local governments. There is, therefore, a duplication of expenditure which strongly limits the capacity of the public sector for austerity.

One further restriction faced by the Colombian economy is violence. We have been living in a violent atmosphere for many years, and we have learned how to maintain a sound economic and social policy within that limitation. But, it is clear that violence creates a serious limitation for our economic and social development because it inhibits long-term investment. Unfortunately, violence is now harder to control because there is an alliance between drug dealers and a guerrilla element that has lost its political principles and become an enforcing organisation for drug trafficking.

The development plan proposed by the Samper government attempts to solve these problems based on three strategies: first, sound macroeconomic policy; second, a strategy to increase productivity in order to build up a competitive economy through investing in science, technology and infrastructure, and by giving special support to the export, agricultural and industrial sectors; and finally, by adopting an active employment policy based on the improvement of professional training programmes, the plan proposes to create 1.5 million new jobs.[10] The goals of the new macroeconomic policy are to avoid any further appreciation of the currency and to move gradually towards an equilibrium rate of exchange.[11] As noted above, one of the main problems of the short-term policies applied during the Gaviria administration was the sharp revaluation of the peso, which resulted in a deterioration in the competitiveness of tradable goods. The Samper government shares this concern and considers that a reasonable support of the rate of exchange is '*uno de los requisitos esenciales para que tenga éxito el proceso de internacionalización de la economía*'.[12]

One of the main reasons for revaluation has been the large increase in private foreign debt, as mentioned above. The government and the Banco de la República have, therefore, increased the minimum term for obtaining foreign credit from three to five years, without establishing large reserve deposits of up to 100 per cent. The only exceptions to this rule are credits for imports, which can be obtained for four months without deposit, and short-term working capital credit for exports.

Another reason for revaluation has been the increase in domestic demand which has been the main obstacle to the control of inflation and has been responsible for the maintenance of high interest rates. The plan proposed, therefore, to avoid any fiscal deficits and to promote the recovery of traditional levels of private savings, as we shall see below. The gradual recovery of equilibrium in the real rate of exchange is now more likely, as a consequence of the change in the international financial climate that has resulted from the Mexican crisis. In November 1994, several economic analysts included in their projections a continued increase of private debt with greater accumulation of foreign reserves until 1998. Now those same analysts foresee an entirely different development. According to the projections presented at a seminar organised by ANIF (Asociación Nacional de Instituciones Financieras) and Fedesarrollo at the end of February 1995, there will be a gradual reduction of international reserves, which will drop to just over five billion dollars by the end of 1998. In the original scenario the likelihood of further appreciation of the peso was almost inevitable. In the new situation, the gradual recovery of the equilibrium real foreign exchange rate will take several years, but it is not impossible.

There is a need to strengthen domestic savings which are essential for sound investment finance. This goal is also necessary to avoid the harmful influence of hasty expenditure of the foreign exchange earned from the temporary increase in the price of coffee and from the new oil fields. In order to avoid the 'Dutch disease' effect of large inflows of foreign currency from the temporary price increase of coffee the Gaviria government established a fund abroad, in US dollars, that will be gradually converted to pesos, as necessary, for financing the domestic operations of the coffee sector. The strategy adopted for the additional oil income is similar. The government has presented a law designed to create an 'Oil Stabilisation Fund' that will keep the reserves in foreign currency and will deliver them to the National Royalty Fund and to local governments to which the Law has allocated such resources. This initiative originated with the previous government.

The strategy for recovering traditional levels of private savings includes the implementation of the social security reform allowing for the creation of private pension funds; the restriction of short-term foreign debt explained above; the strengthening of the capital and financial markets; and the participation of private investors in some public service companies.

It should also be noted that if the efforts to reduce inflation were to be successful, the inherent stability of the economy would be an important factor for encouraging greater long-term savings. The Colombian experience has been that one of the main obstacles for the control of inflation has been the negotiation of salaries and prices based upon previous rates of price increase. This has resulted in a strong reference to previous rates of inflation for the adjustment of salaries and prices that has made it extremely costly to control inflation. The Samper government, therefore, invited workers and employers to make a special effort in order to be able to reduce the rate of inflation from over 22 per cent which was registered in 1994 to single figure levels in 1998.

There is also a need to consolidate the *apertura* in order to maintain international competition as the main force for the allocation of resources. Both the government and the private sector understand that there is no way back in this respect. On the contrary, it is necessary to carry on with a stronger participation in the World Trade Organisation. It is also necessary to continue the application of an active trade policy and the process of regional integration, as well as our efforts to participate in the North American Free Trade Agreement (NAFTA). On the other hand, it is urgent to re-establish the function of customs control on illegal imports of goods and the protection of domestic production against unfair competition.

It is very important to maintain a policy of attracting direct foreign investment. It must be understood that international capital brings not only foreign savings, but also up-to-date technology and access to international markets. The proposal presented in the plan also invites foreign capital to participate in the new concession system for the construction and administration of public works, including roads, energy generating facilities and telecommunications.

As can be seen, these goals proposed by the plans of the Samper administration are about to obtain stabilisation and economic growth at the same time. The only part of the puzzle which does not seem to fit is the planned public expenditure foreseen for the implementation of social investment and infrastructure. As a result, the participation of central government investment and transfers in GDP is proposed to increase from 7.2 per cent in 1994 to 10.5 per cent in 1998. It is very difficult to understand how this goal can be consistent with the five macroeconomic objectives described above.

Public debate in Colombia has been very active during the last few years. This is an important advantage of Colombia's democratic system. The National Planning Council created by the Constitution presented some of these inconsistencies to Congress during the discussion of the *Salto Social*. The government has accepted the objection and is in the process of preparing a tax reform which will be painful, but will avoid some of the pressures for further increases in expenditure, because the draft law approving the plan states that the investment programme will have to be reduced to the level of available resources.

Conclusions

Economic growth has been positive in Colombia during the last forty years. Even during the 1980s, the so called 'lost decade' in Latin America, the Colombian economy registered an increase in *per capita* income. There is no other country in the region with a similar record. This performance has been the result of a sound economic policy, which has been consistently maintained regardless of changes in government.

It is also noteworthy that the reforms required to open up the economy were carried out in a very short period of time. In contrast with other Latin American countries, the shock produced by these reforms did not result in a reduction in real salaries or a sharp deterioration of income distribution.

Structural reforms were carried out in a wide range of economic institutions. They included a liberalisation of foreign trade policy; the introduction of flexibility in labour legislation; a reduced level of government intervention in the financial and foreign exchange markets; reforms in international investment provisions; the creation of an independent Central Bank board of directors; a tax reform, and a reform in social security that will generate large institutional savings during the next decades.

The structural reforms were followed by very active commercial negotiations in order to consolidate access of Colombian exports to a wide range of markets either through free trade agreements or by obtaining trade preferences in the United States and the European Union. The most important result of this change in the development model has been an initial acceleration of economic growth and a substantial increase in private investment which has reached the highest levels of GDP participation on record. This investment has been oriented to modernisation of industrial equipment and has contributed to large increases in productivity.

These structural reforms have been well accepted by public opinion and have been generally maintained after the change of government. We believe that it is almost impossible for Colombia to return to the previous closed economy model.

During the last few years, government expenditure has increased at a very fast pace and has become an obstacle for the control of inflation and for the maintenance of an equilibrium real exchange rate. The result of this currency appreciation has been a deterioration in the current account of the balance of payments, and a loss of dynamism in the tradable-goods sectors that could put the Colombian economy at the edge of suffering a severe bout of 'Dutch disease'.

The beginning of the extraction of oil from the new fields in Cusiana and Cupiagua make this danger even greater. But it creates important opportunities for the acceleration of the growth rate, for the improvement of infrastructure and for an increase of social investment. The Samper government is in the process of obtaining approval from Congress to create an Oil Stabilisation Fund that will allow a more gradual use of these resources and will assure a more sound investment of the oil proceeds.

Among the economic goals of the new government the recovery of an equilibrium real exchange rate has the highest priority. They have adopted several provisions to restrict short-term foreign credit and to promote private savings in order to stop currency appreciation. The Mexican crisis, which has reduced the pressure of speculative financial movements towards Latin America, has helped in the correction of this problem.

The main problem in the near future is the very high increase in government expenditure that has been proposed by the new government for the next four years. Our recent experience shows that this is not consistent with the other economic policy goals that have been proposed. But it is fortunate that during the debate in the National Planning Commission and in Congress this problem has received wide attention. The government has, therefore, accepted that the rate of public expenditure and investment will be reduced unless the government can increase available resources, either through an improvement of tax administration or through a tax reform that has been proposed to the Congress.

Drug trafficking and money laundering remain a heavy burden on the Colombian economy, because they induce luxury consumption, promote unfair competition through smuggling and undervaluation of imports, inhibit the control of inflation and an adequate foreign exchange rate adjustment, and stimulate the corruption of public officers through bribes and menaces. Some people who analyse Colombia from far away, and who have not experienced the violence and arrogant exhibition of waste promoted by drug lords, may think that the explanation of the relative success of the Colombian economy is a consequence of the availability of drug money. On the contrary, the most damaging influences on the economy originate from drug trafficking and related crimes.

Notes

1. Two works by Fedesarrollo have been particularly useful; Fedesarrollo (1994) and (1995).
2. Caballero Argáez and Ramírez Gómez (1991).
3. Some of these reforms are also discussed by Montenegro in Chapter 9.
4. Lora and Helmsdorff (1994).
5. Calderón (1994).
6. 'Capital Punishment', *The Economist,* 4 Feb. 1995, p. 72.
7. Vittorio and Hernández (1994).
8. Rubio (1995), pp. 101–29.
9. Presidencia de República (1994), p. 43.
10. *Ibid.*, p. 18.
11. *Ibid.*, pp. 44–53.
12. *Ibid.*, p. 44.

CHAPTER 9

REGULATION AND DEREGULATION: THE PROCESS OF REFORM IN COLOMBIA, 1990–94

Armando Montenegro

The constitutional and legal reforms undertaken from 1990 to 1994 drastically altered the roles of government and the private sector in the Colombian economy. These reforms aimed at strengthening the presence of government in long-neglected areas: security, justice and services for the poor. Meanwhile they sought to encourage the private sector to enter into and compete in previously protected markets, and expand its role in areas such as public utilities, social services and infrastructure. Within this context, two elements of these reforms stand out: a massive effort to deregulate vast areas of the economy, and a simultaneous decision to create new institutions for regulating the expanded private sector activities within a competitive environment.

Deregulating the secluded Colombian economy had become imperative. Statistical evidence repeatedly showed that overregulation and government prohibitions were strangling economic activity; they were also acting as disincentives to innovation, investment and growth. For this reason, deregulation was extended to trade, capital, and labour markets, as well as to infrastructure, social and public services. More precisely, this effort was aimed at eliminating barriers of entry and establishing, when possible, simple and general competitive rules.

Alongside this significant effort to deregulate the economy, a demand for a new type of state intervention arose: competition had to be protected, monopolistic and oligopolistic abuses curtailed, and natural monopolies – public and private – carefully regulated. Therefore, certain institutions had to be wholly restructured in tune with the reforms. Likewise, other regulatory institutions had to be established to set tariffs and market standards, and to protect competition.

This chapter examines the deregulatory effort and the institutional transformation accomplished by the Gaviria administration during the 1990–94 period. The text is divided into three parts: the first part provides a general description of the Colombian regulatory situation up to 1990. The second examines the most important developments of the process of reform; and finally, the third part outlines questions and challenges concerning their future. Before entering into the subject proper, however, a limitation must be acknowledged. Regulation is a rather imprecise term; it generally refers to government's actions affecting business in topics such as monopoly control, industrial and trade policies, as well as a multiplicity of public interventions over a variety of issues – environment protection, driving speed limits, security in the working place, health, etcetera. This paper is confined to regulation associated with capital, trade, labour and public utilities; it also deals with protection of competition in various markets.

The Previous Regulatory System

What was the Colombian regulatory situation before the 1990–94 reforms? In this section I will first outline the general institutional conditions that shaped Colombian regulation by the end of the 1980s and, second, I will look at the most relevant features of the regulatory system and, in particular, how this affected the evolution of the country's economy. Three basic conditions must be examined with regard to the Colombian situation before the 1990 reforms: (i) the division of labour and responsibilities between the government and the private sector; (ii) the position of regulators *vis-à-vis* those in other positions of government and private business firms; and (iii) the personnel, the technical capacity, and in general, the technology available to the country for effectively carrying out the government's regulatory responsibilities.

By the end of the 1980s, disorder prevailed in the distribution of roles between the public and private sectors. Many of the most important traditional roles of the state were being performed by the private sector, amidst a confused and often violent environment. The most noticeable were security and justice, where the Colombian state has never been able to impose its natural monopoly. High levels of impunity, violence, the expanding activities of organised crime, and the persistent challenge of various armed groups proceeding from all kinds of ideological orientations have long dominated Colombia.

While private groups made incursions into activities traditionally restricted to the state elsewhere, the Colombian government used some of its energies and resources undertaking endeavours within the realm of the private sector. Indeed the government, directly or through its various enterprises, created, invested or promoted public firms in industry, luxury hotel construction, air and river transportation, banking, trade of agricultural goods, ports, gambling, gas stations, cattle vaccine production and in many other activities.[1] However, the extent of the Colombian government's intervention in these areas was less prevalent than in the worst Latin American examples.

Where private and public sector agents coexisted, the rules of the game were not that clear. In general, public or mixed firms (state agents with private participation) usually received a special treatment from the government, hindering fair competition in the eyes of possible competitors. For example, state banks controlled over 50 per cent of banking business, enjoying regulatory advantages, especially in mobilising a substantial volume of government funds. Likewise, those firms in which the Empresa Colombiana de Petróleos (Ecopetrol) – the state oil holding – held equity investments[2] were viewed by their occasional competitors as enjoying a preferential treatment regarding financial and commercial matters.

The production of some goods and the provision of important services were preserved as state monopolies: alcoholic beverages, lotteries, telecommunications, electricity, and most public utilities. Some of these monopolies (ports, power generators, electricity and water supply) had in fact been run as private companies in the past.[3]

This private-public division of labour had significant consequences regarding the regulatory regime. Where the government simultaneously played the roles of both competitor and regulator, distinct conflicts of interest arose. Very often, the private sector justifiably felt that, facing unfair competition from state companies, there were no institutions to which they could take their complaints. Where the government established perfect or near-perfect state monopolies, there was no protection for the consumers. Only in those areas where there was a network of local public monopolies administered by regional firms, was there a weak, but growing body of regulatory authority, as for example, in the National Tariff Board.

In regulating businesses, certain practices and traditions fostered intimate relationships between regulators and the regulated. In many instances, the distinction between private and public roles was not clear-cut. On the contrary, government intervention over the private sector was characterised by a complicated network of contacts and exchanges between public officials and the major producer associations. This was directed at producing 'negotiated', 'concerted', or 'consulted' policies. State intervention in the economy often provided an 'umbrella' for partnerships between the government and influential groups, usually representing the largest productive sectors.

Some crucial aspects of existing regulatory arrangements are

worthy of further consideration. The system was centred around the executive branch, without scrutiny of Congress, the press, or any other
agency of control.[4] Moreover, fiscal and quasi-fiscal rents were assigned without being incorporated into public budgets. To this end, a
multi-purpose, and certainly quite heterodox, Central Bank was instrumental in Colombian policy-making. In addition most subsidies and
fiscal transfers to private groups were treated as simple mechanisms for
income and wealth distribution; and they were not aimed at fostering investment, innovation and growth. Finally regulatory decisions were
made, one by one, in different policy scenarios, in a fragmented fashion, without a coherent framework. Thus, in many instances, public
policies were established simply to compensate for the negative impact
of prior decisions made in other scenarios. For example, certain export
subsidies were deemed necessary to compensate for quantitative restrictions and high tariffs, as well as for labour regulations and
regulation-induced infrastructure inefficiency.

In some academic circles it has been argued that Colombian regulations could be explained by the 'capture' model which maintains that
regulation is 'acquired by the industry and is designed and operated primarily for its benefit'. Others explain Colombian regulations by using
the 'rent seeking' approach, which regards policies as the result of lobbies and pressures by powerful groups.[5] Notwithstanding their
interesting insights, these 'demand centred' explanations are often too
simplistic. They neglect the supply side of the regulatory market,
namely the state's own policy goals and administrative motivations
which could certainly be independent from those of the dominant
classes.[6] More specifically, they neglect the use of regulations and economic policy by governments as instruments for obtaining support and
securing social control.

For these reasons, other groups of analysts of Colombian policy-
making have identified a complex system where strong business
demands for favourable regulation interact, within a more-or-less formal and decentralised setting, with government officials to agree finally
on policies. In this process, supply and demand for regulation often
meet through negotiations and accords. To describe this reality, these
analysts have used a variety of models, incorporating elements such as
corporativism, societal corporativism, elitist pluralism and consociational democracy.[7] They suggest that negotiations and accords
concerning regulations and policies have only been the economic coun-
terpart of business-supported political pacts, among which the National
Front stands out. In addition, most observers indicate that a stable

technocracy was capable of simultaneously establishing a more or less conservative macroeconomic framework.[8]

The influence of agricultural lobby groups on the activities of the Ministry of Agriculture are often given as a typical example of this type of policy-making. This is also the case in the system of consultations between the Ministry of Development and the various industry associations. But perhaps the best examples of this sort of corporatism, because of its impact on regulatory policy making, were the operations of the Monetary Board, and the network of subsidised credit administered and financed by the Central Bank. Although the private sector was not directly represented in the Monetary Board, it was customary, and very much accepted, that sectorial ministries – more often than not coming directly from the main production lobbies – were devoted to capture some rents for the sectors they represented. By the same token, within a more-or-less stable relationship between the Bank's bureaucracy and its clientele, the Central Bank's cheap and directed credit was carefully distributed among a group of privileged customers. This arrangement was supported and organised by the major producer associations and the respective sectorial ministries.

High protection was also institutionalised in the enactment of tailor-made trade and foreign investment policies. Although the main decision-making bodies in these areas – Instituto de Comercio Exterior (INCOMEX) (Foreign Trade Institute) and the National Planning Department – did not formally incorporate private sector representatives into their organisations, their regulatory activities were crafted so as to be highly responsive to business petitions. Thus protection was almost automatically granted to a Colombian firm claiming that a particular good was domestically produced; and subsequently prohibition of foreign investment in competing sectors was easily obtained by local producers.

As a consequence of the previous conditions, especially the lack of clear regulatory institutions and the inordinate emphasis on negotiations, it is no surprise to find that the Colombian state lacked sufficient resources to carry out modern regulation. In particular, it needed educated personnel, economic models and data.

Two reasons explain the shortage of appropriately educated personnel. First, most economists followed a legalistic approach; thus they were prepared to administer the existing complicated regulations already in place, taking little notice of economic implications. Here the most relevant example is the obstructive foreign exchange control system, a command of which was far more important than a knowledge of exchange rate economics. Similar examples could be presented regarding trade policies or monopoly regulation. Second, most of the economists who had studied abroad were specialists in macroeconomics. Because of insufficient demand, applied microeconomists, experts on industrial organisation and public utility regulation, were almost absent from the country. There were exceptions, particularly a growing specialised group of capable people dealing with power sector regulation trained with the support of multilateral entities involved in institution building in the country.

Up to the mid-1980s, no public institution in Colombia actively used economic models to analyse the economic impact of different regulatory policies. The National Planning Department only started to use some economic models in the 1970s and 1980s, mostly in the macroeconomic and trade areas. The technical capacity of the Central Bank was conspicuously low until the 1980s, and the Monetary Board, whose decisions were generally regarded as better prepared, worked with a reduced amount of resources. The rest of the public sector agencies engaged in some form of regulation, had very poor technical capacity – with the exception of the power sector, as already suggested.

Information and data, crucial inputs for regulation, were also scarce. When the country faced a serious macroeconomic crisis around the mid-1980s, multilateral institutions found that Colombia did not have available reliable data on the fiscal situation, foreign debt and important trade matters. The only reliable statistics were those dealing with monetary and monetary-related issues. Information regarding industries was relatively abundant, but entirely provided by firms. The worst situation, which prevails today, was that of the agricultural sector, where no reliable accounting is practised, and where most of the available data is provided by farmers, and negotiated with bureaucrats from the Ministry of Agriculture. In public utilities, only the power sector could provide good information so as to make reasonable regulatory policies.

Naturally, enormous disorganisation together with an ambition to extend itself to virtually all areas of the economy, and failure to attend to its basic duties, greatly weakened the Colombian state. Regarding its regulatory responsibilities, it is worth looking at some of its most outstanding characteristics. The most important markets – capital, labour, and trade in goods and services – were overregulated. Meanwhile, basic regulatory needs were vastly ignored; examples of these were anti-trust actions and regulations over services provided by the state, or by state-fostered monopolies or quasi-monopolies. In addition, the existence of some incipient and weak regulatory institutions, such as the National Tariff Board, setting tariffs and standards for state companies in charge of public utilities, led to confused rules, institutional disorganisation, and, ultimately, to poor services for consumers. Let me look briefly at these characteristics before examining the economic impact of this regulatory system.

As already suggested, for a long time an excessive and confused set of regulations was imposed on markets without a clear, global rationale. Overregulation was mostly a consequence of the agglomeration of many independent decisions, made both in different policy scenarios and at different times, usually with the active intervention of their beneficiaries. Once in force, reversing a regulatory policy was much more difficult than enacting it. Additionally, a significant number of economic groups enjoyed veto-powers, as a result of the above mentioned corporatist policy-making practices. This encouraged the development of a stable and conservative policy regime, where innovations were difficult; the regime was unable to adapt and cope with change rapidly.[9]

These policy-making practices created a fragmented system where compartments, tailor-made market islands, targeted subsidies and privileges were the rule rather than the exception. In capital markets, for example, the foreign exchange control system, while granting monopoly powers over foreign exchange and credit markets to the Central Bank, also gave considerable leeway to the Monetary Board to grant exceptions. In the financial sector, the web of regulations created a complex, specialised banking sector where credit was directed to some groups, and competition was effectively restricted. Moreover, Central Bank mechanisms for directing credit reinforced and, to a large extent, co-ordinated the flow of targeted resources to the various groups involved in concerted policy making. The hostile regime for foreign investment completed the picture of this less than perfect competitive environment.

As for the labour market, complicated legal rules determined by Congress worked against the stability and growth of jobs. Among them, the most remarkable were the costly, retroactive severance payment system and the various laws that granted tenure after ten years of service, especially the one that forced reinstatement of dismissed workers. In the trade sector, the most important instrument of protection was the widespread use of quantitative restrictions (QRs), which were established in a piecemeal fashion, following informal consultations and negotiations between government officials and firms looking for protection. At the beginning of the Gaviria government, 43.3 per cent of the items on the import list – 65 per cent of those in the industrial sector – were subject to *licencia previa* (prior licenses). Indeed in 1990 Colombia had the highest average tariff level in the Andean Pact: 36.8 per cent – 53 per cent for consumer goods; 35 per cent for intermediate goods; and 34 per cent for capital goods. In addition, importing and exporting were plagued by a myriad of procedures and red tape, which imposed a considerable tariff-equivalent disincentive to trade.

In sum, the state, in concert with some regulated agents, promoted monopoly and oligopoly.[10] Its regulatory apparatus was aimed at avoiding competition in various markets, making them less flexible by blocking the entry of new players, and securing rents for tenured participants. This was defended as 'necessary public intervention in the economy', in order to correct certain market failures, improve income distribution, mitigate alleged unfair international competition, and protect infant local industries, among other similar justifications.

In the midst of the confused definition of public and private roles, it is no surprise to find alongside some excessively regulated sectors, certain activities untouched by any regulation whatsoever. In these activities, such as air and maritime transportation, consumers and firms were highly vulnerable to the effects of monopolies and oligopolies, some of which were publicly operated.

One of the most striking examples of the absence of effective regulation was the disregard for anti-trust public activity. While the government was actively involved in promoting market concentration and restricting competition in important markets, it did not pay any attention to existing anti-trust legislation. The Colombian version of anti-trust regulations, Law 155 of 1959 – promoted and pushed through Congress by an isolated liberal Minister of Finance – was never put into practice. Apart from the evident lack of political will, some further reasons explain why in 35 years this law was never implemented.[11] First, within the Colombian tradition of statutory justice, violation of existing regulations must be described in full detail. As these descriptions were either incomplete or non-existent, the law was rendered useless.[12] Second, in order to prosecute unfair practices, the law required detailed proof of both 'cartelisation' (i.e., price fixing agreements) and its damaging effects on the economy – evidence which is difficult to gather (by contrast, US anti-trust law defines some conducts, i.e., price fixing, as illegal *per se*). Third, Law 155 had conceptual limitations: it gave government the capacity to fix some prices in order to defend consumers from monopoly, but it did not rely on expanding competition to reduce market power.

Not only did the government fail to regulate monopolistic or oligopolistic activities, but in some areas it was, itself, engaged in monopolies such as rail transportation, port services, and most social services, such as health and education. Consequently, in these sectors no mechanism protected defenceless consumers from poor services, tariff over-charge, and abuses committed by public enterprises. Moreover, in some instances, a curious form of *de facto* privatisation took place when strong labour unions, facing weak government administrators, held inordinate influence over the direction or management of public monopolies. Needless to say, this situation worsened the already negative impact of public monopolies on consumers and society as a whole. A good illustration of this was the monopolies in charge of rail transportation, ports, some municipal public utilities and, to some extent, public education.

Finally, the lack of regulation also extended to private quasi-monopolies in charge of air and maritime transportation. The entry of competitors to the airline sector was carefully controlled. Most rates were established by the Department for Aeronautics in such a way that competition was severely restricted so as to protect Aerovías Nacionales de Colombia's (AVIANCA) quasi-monopoly. The most egregious restriction occurred in shipping, where the 'flag law' reserved, through the so-called cargo reservation mechanism, 50 per cent of the market share for a domestic shipping line: Flota Mercante Grancolombiana.

Those services provided by public local monopolies – electricity, telecommunications, and water supply and sanitation – were regulated by an incipient and weak institution: the National Tariff Board. Albeit imperfectly, this entity filled a notorious gap within Colombian institutions. Since the mid-1970s there had been an increasing need for some form of regulation regarding rates and consumers' protection. Public protests at high tariffs, suppliers' frequent financial disorders, and pressure from multilateral banks were behind the consolidation of the National Tariff Board in the mid-1980s. This was done under the umbrella of the National Planning Department, in charge of setting tariffs and establishing norms for consumer protection.[13]

In the power sector, the development of a clear regulatory framework was obstructed by the pressure of the largest generators – state entities with strong regional interests. Moreover, the central government, represented by the Ministry of Mines and Energy, and nominally responsible for sectoral planning and regulation, was in a weak position, with no capacity to lead or control the powerful regionally-based state companies. For example, large investment and operational decisions were made through a system of accords and negotiations, on the National Transmission Institute (ISA) Board. These decisions proved to be less than optimal for national interests.[14] While the National Tariff Board was in charge of setting electricity rates, other important areas of regulation were established by ISA's Board. Thus, once more in this area there was no sharp distinction between the regulators and the regulated.[15]

In telecommunications, the Empresa Nacional de Telecomunicaciones (Telecom) held a monopoly as the national and international long-distance carrier. This firm was also a major shareholder in many local carriers. Here, the Minister of Communications had a dual and difficult role: while representing the national interest, he was also Telecom's Board President, in charge of furthering its interests. Telecom was very much involved in regulatory matters because of its legal privileges. In addition, the extremely weak technical capacity at the Ministry forced it to rely on Telecom to carry out its licensing responsibilities. Therefore there were numerous cases of conflict of interest, and complaints of discrimination and unfair practices. Because private carriers were not allowed to function in that market, however, Telecom's clashes were limited to departmental and municipal public enterprises.

A very similar situation prevailed in the energy sector. Here, Ecopetrol, the state monopoly, was simultaneously regulator and competitor in exploration, oil refining and petrol distribution. This was also the case for Carbones de Colombia (Carbocol), which in addition to its coal extracting and exporting activities, also decided on sites and licences for other firms. The Minister of Mines, who presided over the boards of these companies, was forced to play conflicting roles, some of them against competition and innovation. Finally, a side effect of this regulatory setting was the limited involvement of the private sector in this sector. Moreover, fearful private firms had to comply promptly with the whims and desires of bureaucrats.

In water supply and sanitation, the regulatory system was also in great disarray. After the decentralisation reforms of the 1980s, the very inefficient national monopoly (Insfopal) was dismantled, and water supply and sewerage systems were transferred to municipalities. However, regulatory responsibilities remained highly confused: rates were fixed by the National Tariff Board, health norms and water quality standards were set by the Ministry of Health, and technical matters related to equipment and construction standards were established by the

Ministry of Public Works. Needless to say, the private sector was effectively prevented from carrying out any of these public utility functions.

The sectorial and macroeconomic consequences of the described system of regulation was a negative rate of productivity growth together with low and declining economic growth. The extremely complicated and disorganised Colombian regulatory system at the end of the 1980s provided no incentives or signals for a dynamic private economic expansion. Excessive regulation in some sectors, its absolute lack in others, and the prohibition of private activities in essential areas, in the midst of a rent-seeking environment, all intimately meshed together and produced an economy where competition was highly restricted, oligopolistic practices were widespread, innovation was discouraged, and risk-taking investments were not fully rewarded.

In financial and capital markets, for example, the banking sector was very small, and interest rate margins were among the highest in the world. Simultaneously, the expansion and proliferation of cheap Central Bank credit crowded out what in the 1950s and 1960s had been a dynamic stock market: instead of raising funds in the markets, firms opted for lobbying Central Bank officers. A serious side-effect of this multi-purpose Central Bank, engaged in promoting economic development, was its partial disregard for its main goal of reducing Colombia's relatively high inflation rate.

Labour regulations, intended to promote employment and protect job stability, did exactly the opposite: two-thirds of the labour force were compelled to enter the informal sector. Turnover was extremely high: 33 per cent of all legally employed workers lost their jobs every year. In addition, every year about 100,000 workers who were nearing ten years of seniority were fired by employers, thus evading the costly regulations supposedly established to protect workers.

This regulatory system in which the state fostered low competition, was a fertile terrain for monopoly and oligopolistic competition. In fact, oligopolistic practices and market concentration grew in the economy. Almost 70 per cent of Colombian industrial output was produced under oligopolistic structures in 1988.[16] In addition, the situation deteriorated in important areas; for example, while in 1968 49 per cent of intermediate good industries were highly or moderately concentrated, in 1984 that percentage reached 78 per cent. In the capital goods industries, those percentages rose from 24 per cent to 85 per cent.

In the air transportation and shipping sectors, tariffs were much higher than in other similar countries; by the same token, delays, and unreliability of services were high by international standards.[17] Public railways and port monopolies also provided very high cost and deficient services. In addition, they were in the clutches of strong unions, and because of their enormous costs, produced elevated deficits.[18]

Most public utilities, also provided by monopolistic enterprises, were in trouble. While electricity coverage in cities was 95 per cent, in the countryside it was only 41 per cent, and most power enterprises were insolvent, with a seriously limited capacity to undertake required expansion projects. Telephone coverage (eight lines per 100 inhabitants in 1990) was internationally acceptable but its quality, cost and service reliability were all poor. International long-distance rates were between 15 and 50 per cent higher than those in more competitive countries. Water supply and sewerage coverage and quality remained very low in important areas: while it was around 90 per cent in the three main cities, it was below 60 per cent in several intermediate cities, and only 24 per cent in rural areas.

Because of the lack of competition, serious distortions, and inefficient essential services, as illustrated above, productivity and innovation in the country's economy were lagging behind. The contribution of total factor productivity (TFP) to economic growth steadily declined from the mid-1970s to the late 1980s.[19] While it grew steadily from 1950 to 1974, it continually declined thereafter. Moreover, TFP was negative (-0.6 per cent) in the period 1980–86. During the 1980–83 period, both output and productivity had negative annual growth rates, -1.3 per cent and -2.6 per cent, respectively. Later, in the 1984–87 period when industrial output had a healthy growth (7.4 per cent a year), TFP continued to decrease at a rate of -0.5 per cent a year. Thus, industrial growth was merely the result of inefficient accumulation of factors, within a closed and secluded economy. Innovation, technological change and a more efficient use of inputs were not present in the Colombian economy.

The proliferation of regulations and the country's negative productivity growth had a negative impact on economic growth. In the 1970–74 period its annual average was 5.3 per cent; it declined to 4.3 per cent in the 1975–80 period, and to only 3.2 per cent in the 1980s. Given that income *per capita* was only US$1,300, the prospect for the next generation of Colombians was to live in a very poor country: with the 1980s rates of growth, it would take 25 years to reach an income *per capita* of as little as US$3,000.

Colombia's rate of economic growth, although lower than that of the most dynamic countries in South-East Asia, was relatively high compared to many of the Latin American countries. It could be argued that this was because of Colombia's more relaxed adherence to the model of state intervention; an almost generalised disregard for regulations by its economic agents; and the state's lack of will and capacity to enforce its own rules. Several facts support this hypothesis. Real economic life operated beyond the intended regulations, as proved by the widespread tolerance of the foreign exchange black market, the extended informal sectors, the very visible and growing 'free trade markets' and other forms of trading in smuggled goods.

Reforming the Regulatory System

Against this background, the regulatory reforms ought to be understood within the general framework of institutional transformations put forward by the new 1991 Constitution. Previous chapters in this volume have touched upon various aspects of these reforms. For the purpose of this essay, suffice it to reiterate here that one of the aims of these reforms was to reorganise and rationalise the roles of both the state and the private sector in order to make them responsive and accountable to Colombian society.

A fundamental element in this redefinition of roles was the constitutional guarantee of free competition, establishing several limitations over monopoly and other restricting practices. Under the new order, competition was defined as a right of both consumers and entrepreneurs, regardless of their size and importance.[20] As a result of these norms many monopolies, public and quasi-public, and also those market compartments created by regulations, lost their juridical foundations. Thus, after the constitutional reform of 1991 a vigorous process of entry into many previously secluded markets was expected to occur.

The expansion of private activities towards areas previously monopolised by public entities was to be encouraged by two instruments: by privatising existing public enterprises, and, more importantly, by eliminating barriers to market competition. Naturally, the latter required a massive deregulatory effort, in sectors ranging from public utilities to industry and mining.[21] Following free entry, and privatisation of important public enterprises, some complementary institutional reforms regarding regulation were indispensable. Ministries and some public enterprises were forced to separate their roles as regulators from their roles as market players. New regulatory institutions had to be created. In this section, I examine in some detail these aspects of the reform process: the various efforts at deregulating, and the establishment of a new set of regulatory institutions.

As already suggested, in order to create a competitive environment, it was indispensable to launch a general effort to deregulate the Colombian economy. The main areas of deregulation were foreign trade, foreign investment, labour and financial markets, public utilities, and air and shipping activities. Other areas in which private activity was encouraged by the constitution were the provision of social services such as education and health. I will deal with these areas individually.

Foreign trade A timid action to open up foreign trade had been started by the Barco administration in early 1990. During the last months of this government, a gradual five-year liberalisation plan was initiated. Barco's reforms were conceived in three steps: an immediate liberalisation of those goods that did not compete with domestic products, which involved moving some goods from licences to the free-trade list; a two-year programme to replace quantitative restrictions (QR) by tariffs for all other goods; once all quantitative restrictions were replaced by tariffs, a three year period of tariff reduction was to ensue. During the first two years, the government was to auction import licences for those items on the restricted list, in order to determine the tariff-equivalent level of protection. Finally, the programme was to reduce the overall average tariff to levels of 25 per cent.

These trade reforms were not put into practice until August 1990, when a new government took power. Moreover, during the first months of the Gaviria administration, a new more ambitious trade reform programme was established. First, QRs, in the form of import quotas, import licenses, and lists of products of forbidden imports – around which favours and privileges were concerted and distributed – were eliminated. Secondly, due to the pressures of the more conservative members of government, a gradual four year reduction programme was launched and announced, which would have brought down average tariffs to 12 per cent by the end of 1993. Soon this gradualism proved to be impractical because both importers and investors took a 'wait and see' attitude that resulted in a very large current account surplus and in an acute reduction of private investment. At the same time, the Colombian private sector generated a forced surplus, and consequently international reserves accumulated sharply while the monetary base grew rapidly. Finally, forced by the macroeconomic situation, the liberalisation programme was accelerated during the first seven months of 1991. As a result, tariffs were drastically reduced from an average of

38.6 per cent in 1990 to less than 12 per cent in 1991. More importantly, the average effective protection was reduced from 75 per cent in 1989 to 34 per cent in 1991, and 21 per cent in 1992.

Foreign investment Similarly, deregulating by dismantling the very obsolete foreign investment regime took place in a very rapid fashion. In this area, the reforms had three elements. In sharp contrast with the immediate past, all economic sectors were opened to foreign investment, with the exception of security related matters and nuclear waste disposal. All prior administrative decisions on foreign investment were eliminated – a crucial step in creating an environment of competition and transparency in what previously was a very closed and protected environment. Only those foreign investments in public utilities were subject to some prior examination by the central government. Foreign investors were granted the same treatment as domestic ones.[22] Additionally, foreign investors enjoyed full monetary convertibility and free access to foreign exchange for making all kinds of transfers abroad. Moreover, according to international standards, the very definition of foreign investment was made more inclusive in order to incorporate portfolio and various other forms of investments channelled through the stock exchange. By the same token, the 1990-94 reforms allowed Colombian investors to enjoy the freedom of investing abroad without prior approval or control by government. Previously, Colombians had been prevented from investing in other countries, which limited their ability to influence their exports directly.

On the institutional side, this deregulatory reform also included the elimination of the Special Unit for Foreign Investment Control in the National Planning Department, and the Committee for Royalties in charge of overregulating various issues related to intellectual property and technology transfer.

Foreign exchange reform This reform simply eliminated the very complicated foreign exchange regime, by abolishing the Central Bank monopoly, and creating a free foreign exchange market.[23] This had a practical consequence: the legalisation of thousands of saving and deposit accounts held in other countries, as a result of the previous excessively restricted regime. Among the advantages of the new regime were the reduction of transaction costs for firms involved in foreign trade, and the introduction of a number of previously forbidden practices such as hedging, forward and futures markets and other similar operations. Simultaneously, the foreign exchange reform allowed the macro-economic authorities to implement market determined foreign exchange rate policies. As a necessary complement of this reform, the Superintendency of Foreign Exchange Regulations – an entity with the impossible task of enforcing the concocted foreign exchange controls – was eliminated.

Labour market The labour market reform, undertaken by Law 50 of 1990, was one of the cornerstones of the structural reforms of the Gaviria administration.[24] It did away with the very costly retroactive severance system and the onerous regulations hopelessly directed at fostering stability of workers with more than ten years of service. Among the latter, we could mention the elimination of forced reinstatement of dismissed workers, and some pecuniary sanctions for firms. In order to avoid unnecessary costs, the Law established a reasonable system of monetary indemnification for affected workers.

Financial reforms Several reforms were introduced to dismantle the existing regulations, and to develop a more competitive financial environment. Among them, we can mention: the elimination of virtually all forced investments by financial institutions; relaxation of norms that forbade competition among different institutions, especially those which segmented credit and saving markets; maintenance of market determined interest rates; the opening of international competition in the financial markets.[25]

One of the most important reforms, following the transformation of the Central Bank and the elimination of the Monetary Board as the major money and credit authority, was the suppressing of various funds devoted to the financing of subsidised directed-credit. Agricultural credit therefore was no longer to be provided by the Central Bank, but by the Caja Agraria and Financiera Nacional Agropecuaria (FINAGRO), a specialised second-tier institution. By the same token, industrial credit was to be concentrated on the Instituto de Fomento Industrial (IFI), and the commercial financial institutions. A serious effort was made to force these institutions to lend at market interest rates and to stop their risk investments, which only masked some transfers and subsidies for private partners. Finally, along with the elimination of the public monopoly on pension funds, private pension funds were allowed in the market. Similarly, severance payment funds, which receive individual accounts with these resources, started to be created by several private financial firms.

Public utilities The reforms of public utilities were centred around granting free entry to private agents in the provision of all kinds of public services.[26] Moreover, it was established that municipalities must grant permits and facilitate private investments in public utilities. Additionally, the reform created numerous mechanisms for public enterprises to become more competitive and to strengthen their managerial and financial resources. Public utilities were open to foreign investors. After a transition period, rates would have to reflect economic costs.

Plans to reform telecommunications were strongly opposed by the unions: Telecom's workers called a national strike in 1992. The reforms did not necessarily envision the privatisation of Telecom, but rather the encouragement of competition. The reforms finally enacted by the Gaviria administration allowed the entry of private suppliers of value-added systems, cellular services, and set in motion the participation of several private operators of domestic and international long-distance services.[27]

Private operators were also explicitly allowed to operate freely in the generation, transmission and distribution of energy power.[28] Only in those poor areas where, due to the size of the market, no private agents would be interested in providing services, could the regulatory commissions confer exclusive rights to private operators. These operators would be selected by public auction, and supported by public resources. In addition, several measures were taken to dismantle the existing vertical integration in the most important electricity companies. In particular, ISA, a powerful public conglomerate, was to be divided into two firms: the first one, in charge of generation, and the second one, of transmission. Each of these could be totally or partially sold to private investors.

Other sectors Other important areas where deregulation was instituted were: air transportation, where an 'open skies' policy was established, and passenger and cargo tariffs were fully deregulated; in shipping, the cargo reservation policy, by which the government forced traders to use the national flag carrier, was also dismantled; the national monopoly over ports was liquidated and, instead, free competition among independent, privately-run ports established; the state monopoly on railways was also ended; and finally, regarding pension funds, a new social security law allowed workers freely to deposit their savings into private pension funds.

These regulatory reforms were complemented by the creation of new institutions to meet the growing demands for new forms of state intervention. The new model accepted intervention but, unlike the previous regime, it had now a clear pro-competition bias. Market players were assured that the powerful macroeconomic instruments in the hand of the Central Bank were not going to be used to favour only some selected groups. It created mechanisms to avoid unfair competition and curtail abuses of dominant market positions. It attempted to regulate natural monopolies to produce market-like outcomes, in terms of prices and quantities.

In this context, the most important institutional transformations were the establishing of an independent Central Bank; the general overhaul of the Superintendency of Industry and Commerce to make it capable of protecting competition policies; the creation of three new Regulatory Commissions for public utilities, and superintendencies for public services, ports and private security.

An autonomous Central Bank A crucial element in reordering economic policy-making and regulation in Colombia was the complete transformation of the hitherto multipurpose and highly heterodox Central Bank. Freed from its previous microeconomic and sectorial obligations – export promotion and directed credit – the goals of the Central Bank have now been limited to clearly established economy-wide objectives: to reduce inflation and maintain price stability; to administer the country's international reserves; and to be a bank of last resort for the financial institutions.

The reform established that the Bank would have a highly technical orientation and that its activities were to be under political control. The new institution is now led by a full-time, fixed-term, and competent Board of Directors. Furthermore, its recently gained specialisation in macroeconomic and financial issues has forced a progressive upgrading of its technical personnel. Moreover, the Bank's net income now belongs to the national government and is included in the national budget. The Superintendency of Banks is in charge of controlling its financial activities, and the Attorney General oversees its personnel performance.

The new Bank was set up to maintain institutional distance from both the private sector and the government. First, the Bank's Board of Directors is explicitly forbidden to lend, issue guarantees or grant any kind of favours to private entities. Board members are specifically ordered to seek only the national interest. To prevent any conflict of interests, members of the Board have to follow a strict code regarding eventual clashes with their previous jobs, their behaviour while serving the Bank, and even their work after they complete their tenure. Secondly, the reforms established severe limitations on the Bank's financial dealings with the government. Loans for the Treasury – one of the causes of macroeconomic instability in the early 1980s – can now only be approved by a consensus of Board members. Moreover, the government, represented by the Minister of Finance, while maintaining the token distinction of presiding over the Board, has only a limited leverage: it was given just one out of seven votes.

Reform of the Superintendency of Industry and Commerce This reform was intended to strengthen the state's capacity to limit monopolistic activities, and, more importantly, to stimulate free competition. As this was the final aim of the new regime, the state had to have an active role in protecting the less powerful market players and consumers from potential abuses – agents capable of fixing prices and taking advantage of their monopolistic or oligopolistic capacity. Therefore, it was necessary to revise the thirty-five-year-old, never used, anti-trust statute: Law 155/59.

This reform, formalised by the Decree-Law 2153/92, sought therefore to modernise the existing anti-trust regime. Consequently, a list of punishable conducts was carefully outlined – this included price-fixing, restriction on outputs, and geographic distribution of markets; the Superintendency received ample powers to investigate and penalise actions against free competition, on its own initiative or at the request of third parties; the Superintendency was endowed with an array of instruments to achieve its goals.

Public utility regulatory commissions With free entry granted for all public utility markets – where natural or local monopolies are frequent – it was necessary to restructure the existing weak state regulatory capacity. The National Tariff Board was abolished and three modern regulatory commissions were created for telecommunications, water supply and sanitation, and electricity and gas. Their general functions were to foster competition and prevent monopolistic practices. More precisely, these commissions were in charge of setting rate formulae, fees, conditions for auctions, and technical and commercial conditions for competitive market development. While promoting competition, these commissions could establish general rules, investigate complaints against unfair practices, order vertical disintegration and suspension of, for example, output restraints and market segmentation.

The composition of these commissions was to be mixed, involving high government officials together with fixed-term independent experts. The government's initial proposal aimed at establishing fully independent commissions – independent from both the government and the private carriers, akin to the US regulatory commissions. But some ministers and members of Congress insisted on, and eventually propelled the creation of, more public and, thus, less autonomous entities. Some ministries argued, for example, that tariff-setting could have a strong political impact, and hence, responsibility should not be left only in the hands of technical experts, while it was the government that would be blamed for their decisions. Likewise, some members of Congress feared that expert-made regulations would be excessively technocratic, without regional and consumer input. Therefore, Congress compromised by approving the above-mentioned three semi-independent regulatory commissions.

In the power sector, the reform carefully sought to avoid the previous leverage of public enterprises on regulatory matters. With this in mind, the Board of Directors of ISA, the transmission and generation holding, was left without any regulatory powers, especially in the operation of the electric system. Moreover, gas and oil regulation by the Ministry of Mines, which had been under the notorious influence of Ecopetrol and Carbocol, was also eliminated. The Ministry was to be devoted to sectoral planning and policy making, and Ecopetrol and Carbocol to production and commercialisation of oil and coal, respectively.

A crucial element required to foster private participation in providing public services was the enactment of a clear-cut, full-cost, recovery tariff policy. In this regard, the reform established a four-year period to eliminate subsidies to middle-class groups. It further instituted that subsidies to poorer groups were to be paid for mainly by the national budget and, residually, by surcharges on higher status consumers.

Superintendency of Public Services A Superintendency of Public Services was established, as a complement to the Regulatory Commissions. Its main function is to protect consumers, and watch over the financial and administrative affairs of public utilities. This entity is to ensure full compliance with the decisions by the Regulatory Commissions, the ministries, and other relevant authorities. It is also in charge of designing accounting and finance systems for those companies providing public services. When the regulatory commissions find evidence of unfair practices, the Superintendency will intervene imposing penalties, ordering the suspension of those practices, sanctioning managers and, eventually, even taking control of or eliminating particular companies.

Other regulatory institutions The creation of two additional institutions in charge of regulating ports and security services, and the transformation of the Superintendency of Banks, are also worth mentioning. When the public monopoly over ports was abolished, a Superintendency of Ports was created in charge of setting rates, licensing, and securing competition in this area. In addition, a Superintendency of Security was set up, under the institutional umbrella of the Ministry of Defence, in response to the chaotic state of security services – such as protecting buildings, farms, and individuals – provided by many private firms. Its main responsibility is to grant licences and to monitor the activities of private security firms. Finally, the Superintendency of Banks was reformed, giving it power to regulate the newly created pension and severance payment funds, as well as certain foreign exchange denominated financial operations.

Conclusions

The deregulatory efforts and the regulatory agencies described above are relatively new and hardly constitute an established model of regulation. Important institutions, such as the Regulatory Commissions and the Superintendency of Public Services, were, at the time of writing these pages, still waiting to be fully developed. Their consolidation requires an enormous effort in terms of government support, financial commitment, and in the selection of the right personnel. Furthermore, many other aspects of Colombian economic life remained unreformed: numerous licences, registration requirement and other formalities, and municipal 'red tape' remain in place. The recent regulatory regime still looms large in many people's minds; the demand for protection and market segmentation is still alive in certain quarters.

Nevertheless, from the description of this process of regulatory reform in Colombia, two questions naturally surface: what had been achieved by 1995? More significantly, are the reforms going to survive?

While most of the deregulatory reforms have taken hold in Colombian economic life, some of the new institutions, although already designed by the appropriate laws and decrees, have not yet been fully developed. Indeed the deregulatory reforms, which preceded the creation of new regulatory institutions, have become part of Colombian

economic life in a short period. Deregulation of trade, foreign investment, financial and labour markets have been in practice for more than
three years. Its economic impact has been remarkably positive, even in
the short run when many observers – the past government included –
expected some increase in unemployment and economic deceleration,
especially because of trade liberalisation. In fact, in the past few years,
economic growth has been higher than 5 per cent, unemployment has
reached a record low, and private investment, domestic and foreign
alike, has been booming. Though for some sectors transition towards
the new model has not been completely smooth, nor free of some indus-
try-specific adjustment problems, most of the business complaints have
been related to exchange rate appreciation (a continental phenomenon
linked to international capital movements) and unfair practices. Moreover, the deregulatory reforms are widely popular among consumers, as
proven in opinion polls, to the extent that no candidate in the 1994
presidential elections, even those traditionally opposed to these policies, were against them.

Unlike most of the deregulatory efforts, however, the creation of a
new Central Bank has been highly controversial. The Bank has not been
openly attacked for failing to play its previous role of development
agency, perhaps because other institutions are performing those functions: public financial entities provide credit and export subsidies. The
Central Bank has been criticised for the sectorial impact of certain macroeconomic outcomes, especially real exchange rate appreciation.
Some congressmen have joined affected business groups in suggesting
that more government intervention in exchange rate policies is required. However, the perdurability of the Central Bank is guaranteed by
the new Constitution, although some legal limitations may be imposed
on its powers to set exchange rates.

The deregulation of public utilities and the organisation of the new
Regulatory Commissions are relatively recent, and in some instances
are just starting. For example, in telecommunications, private carriers
of long-distance telephone and private television channels will enter the
market only in the next few years. Similarly, the first private power
plants are now being built. Even if the slow pace of private entry to
these markets is taken into consideration, public utility deregulation has
gone much faster than the creation of most new regulatory institutions.
Therefore, the accelerated strengthening and consolidation of the new
Regulatory Commissions remains a major challenge in order to reassure
foreign and domestic investors, avoid abuse of market power, and, most
importantly, maintain a successful privatisation policy.

As is to be expected because of their novelty, the Regulatory Commissions are still weak and require the strong backing of government. Only the Energy Regulatory Commission – which inherited large resources from the now dissolved National Tariff Board – has a strong staff at its disposal. It also enjoys administrative autonomy, financial resources, and the respect of the relevant ministries. In fact, it has already produced important results in terms of gas and electricity regulations and has placed itself in an outstanding position within the energy sector. Unfortunately, this is not the case of all commissions. For instance, one of them, because it was set up only in the last months of the previous government, has not been granted full autonomy and remains subordinate to a Ministry. Furthermore, it can hardly be said that its personnel has expert qualifications.

Finally, along with economic dynamism, rapid growth, privatisation, and the general internationalisation of the Colombian economy, new riches, huge transactions not even dreamed of only a few years back, as well as the highly visible operations of conglomerates have been evident. As expected, this has created insecurity and criticism among traditional groups, and has also given way to debates about the fairness of the new system. Fortunately, the last governments have devoted special attention to social spending, directing more public resources to the poorest sectors of society, and thus trying to extend the benefits of the reforms to all economic groups.

However, all the events related to rapid wealth creation also suggest that breathing life into anti-trust regulation is indispensable. Indeed, strengthening the incipient and weak Superintendency of Industry and Commerce is both an economic and a political need in Colombia. In terms of protecting consumers and controlling abuse of dominant positions in the market, this entity in many respects has yet to be born; it lacks essential resources and qualified personnel.

More general and relevant questions are pertinent. Is this model going to survive and take hold in Colombian life? Or is this effort going to be another transitory attempt at trade-opening and modernisation, such as the doomed initiatives of the 1970s and early 1980s? Or, on the contrary, will these reforms constitute a definite breakaway from the conservative, traditional Colombian style of policy-making? Answers to these questions are certainly difficult, and I can only venture some working hypotheses and general observations.

Given the embryonic stage of the reforms, their survival and implementation needs to be nurtured at least by government's commitment to its fundamental principles. In this regard, besides resisting pressures to reverse the new regulatory regime, it will be indispensable to guarantee sufficient financial resources and select and retain capable personnel in the new institutions. In this context it was encouraging that the Samper government announced its general endorsement of the reforms, albeit with certain reservations in some areas.

Though the reforms themselves have created forces favouring the acceleration of the process, they have also unleashed serious threats to their own survival. On the positive side, they definitely enjoy popularity among consumers and a vast group of producers, who serve as a political shield to discourage conservative attempts at reversing the process. Additionally, many private investors who expect to enter the new markets obviously defend the new regime and press for the full development of these reforms. Likewise, they favour strong regulatory institutions designed to secure competition. On the negative side, however, the reforms have adversely affected several groups which lost their sources of rent, and are now forced to compete, innovate and rapidly change. These groups still demand protection and subsidies and seek a return to the old system.

Due to these conflicting forces, the future of regulatory reform will be determined by political realities. The recent economic history of Colombia shows that the weaker the government, the less likely liberalising reforms are to survive. In the past, policy reversals, especially in trade, accompanied by a proliferation of subsidies and targeted benefits, were associated with political crises that weakened past administrations. On those occasions, policy-makers were forced to gain or regain the support of important business groups by granting them additional, targeted protection. Consequently, the reforms' survival will be greatly enhanced by the stability and strength of future governments.

International developments will play an important role in cementing the reforms. International treaties – such as the Andean Pact, G-3 (Colombia, Mexico, Venezuela), World Trade Organisation (WTO), and eventually the North American Free Trade Agreement (NAFTA) or the Mercado Común Suramericano (MERCOSUR) – establish limitations on important domestic variables, and on protection-oriented regulations. Furthermore, in the long-run, the increasing overlap of bilateral, regional and multilateral treaties leans towards the creation of an international set of regulatory standards in areas such as trade, foreign investment, intellectual property and technology. This will further ensure that the Colombian regulatory reforms will be sustained.

Even in the midst of such uncertainties, I must conclude with some degree of optimism. The set of deregulatory reforms and the creation of new regulatory institutions, at least in their basic and broad elements, have a good chance of surviving. Their wide popularity and their positive impact on the economy are their main assets. One of the challenges of the Colombian agenda is to devise new political and economic institutions capable of reflecting the broad interests of society so that governments can form coalitions and obtain political support without the traditional assignment of targeted rents. Only then will regulation not be just another political tool. Only then will the country enjoy a modern incentive system to support its economic development.

Notes

1. See Montenegro (1994), pp. 153–66.
2. For example, Terpel, a public venture in charge of petrol distribution.
3. See Nichols (1973), and De la Pedraja (1989), especially chs. 2, 8 and 14.
4. According to Hartlyn, '. . . the consociational agreement initially weakened the political parties and marginalised Congress from many key decisions as factionalism increased and immobilism led to the granting of power to the Executive Branch'. See Hartlyn (1985), p. 127.
5. See Stigler (1971). On the 'Capture Model', see Laffont and Tirole (1994) especially Chapter V, Section 11, 'The Regulatory Capture', pp. 475–512. The classical text on the 'rent seeking' approach is Krueger (1974). Similar views have been shared by Colombian analysts following Marxist methodologies.
6. See Skocpol (1994a), particularly the introduction, pp. 3–24.
7. For example, see Bailey (1977); Hartlyn (1985), pp. 111–37; Dix (1980), pp. 303–21.
8. Not surprisingly, this system allowed for many microeconomic distortions. On the Colombian technocracy, see Urrutia (1991), pp. 369–92.
9. The long-enduring stability of Colombian policy-making, derived from its consensual style, has been widely discussed.
10. See Hommes (1995).
11. *Ibid.*
12. See Hommes (1995), and Orozco (1993).
13. The National Tariff Board was created by Decree 3069 of 1986. Initially, however, it did not have the capacity to set tariffs, but only to examine and revise several decisions made by companies. The power of tariff setting was given to the Board by decrees 201/74 and 149/76. These new functions were never fully used within a context of regulation. Not until 1984, when Decree 2545 ordered the unification of electricity rates in the country, did the Board assume an active regulatory role. Within this context, resolution 086 of 1986 set the precedent of establishing a consistent tariff policy for the power sector.
14. For example, the infamous *Acuerdo de Cali,* in which the main generation projects were distributed according to a remarkably anti-technical procedure, gave rise

to a distorted, inefficient power sector in Colombia.

15. See, for example, Comisión Nacional de Energía (1991).
16. See Bonilla and Osorio (1993).
17. The World Bank (1994a).
18. See, for example, Hommes et al. (1994), pp. 202–21.
19. A good summary of these figures can be found in World Bank (1989).
20. See article 333 of the 1991 Constitution.
21. The necessary complement of these instruments was the elimination of price controls in all those sectors where sufficient competition was present. Only in those areas where some natural monopoly existed were regulations on tariffs and prices considered necessary to produce market-like outcomes.
22. One of the few exceptions that remained was a tax on profit remittances that, however, was set to decline steadily during the following years.
23. This reform was ordered by Law 9 of 1990. Later it was developed by Resolution 57/92 of the Monetary Board and Resolution 21/93 of the Banco de la República.
24. For an analysis of this reform, see Posada de la Peña (1995).
25. This goal, however, was temporarily postponed because a massive flow of foreign capital forced the monetary authorities to impose different measures aimed at controlling these flows.
26. The Public Utility reform was enacted by Law 142 of 1994.
27. At the very beginning of the Gaviria government, decrees 1900 and 1901 of 1990 were issued. Later on, Law 142/94 completed the new legal framework granting free competition in the telecommunications sector. Some aspects of the 1992 strike are dealt with in Vargas (1993) – at the time, the Minister of Communication.
28. Both Law 142/94 and the so-called Electric Law established the new competitive framework for the power sector.

CHAPTER 10

EVOLUTION AND RATIONALITY OF BUDGET INSTITUTIONS IN COLOMBIA

Rudolf Hommes*

The independence of central banks has an effect on the macroeconomic results of economies and ultimately on inflation.[1] A similar relationship may exist between budget institutions and the fiscal performance of governments: budget institutions may have a bearing on fiscal results.[2] There is evidence that indicates that budgetary procedures favouring a stronger position of the budget authority *vis-à-vis* other members of government, or giving more power to the executive, lead to greater fiscal discipline.[3] Eichengreen has found that 'a number of measures of balanced-budget restrictions are significantly associated with larger surpluses (smaller deficits)'[4] in the state fiscal accounts in the United States. Poterba observed that rules and political factors, such as the control of one party over the state legislature, are important in explaining differences in fiscal performance between different states in the United States.[5]

The premise is that rules and regulations that give the executive more power *vis-à-vis* parliament will produce smaller deficits. Similarly, when the budget authorities are given institutional tools to deal with intra-government conflicts during the preparation of the budget and to control the appetite of the spending ministers, smaller deficits may ensue. The same applies to strict rules governing the execution of the budget in the sense that when the government is not given much flexibility to change budgetary items or to increase expenditures beyond the original authorisation of Congress, presumably the fiscal results will be more conservative when compared with budget regimes in which governments are allowed to move more freely. Budget transparency will support better results because it fosters accountability; and the universality of the budget – no off-budget items – will produce more fiscal discipline.

In the same line of thought, it is possible that formal fiscal restraints such as balanced-budget rules, when binding, or automatic links with taxation that force Congress to increase taxes when the expected deficit is large, will cause smaller deficits (larger surpluses). Coalition governments are particularly adept at increasing the budget and strong governments are more likely to solve budget deficits than weak or divided governments.[6] Moreover, when the budget is prepared in conjunction with a macroeconomic programme, and the budget size and composition is subordinated to the achievement of macroeconomic goals, the fiscal outcome may be more conservative. Finally, it should be noticed that when budget institutions and controls for the state and local governments are weak, the autonomous spending and indebtedness of lower levels of government may contribute to greater deficit spending.[7]

A research project conducted by the Office of the Chief Economist at the Inter-American Development Bank has found preliminary but compelling evidence that the budgetary institutions in Latin America have a significant bearing on fiscal results. The researchers have developed an index of budget institutional development that measures the strength of budget institutions, following the lines of thought described in the previous paragraphs. Figure 1 presents the relationship between this index and the primary deficit for twenty Latin American countries. These results suggest that strong institutions can have an impact on fiscal performance.

Fig. 1 Budget Balance and Budgetary Independence: Latin America, c. 1980–c.1990

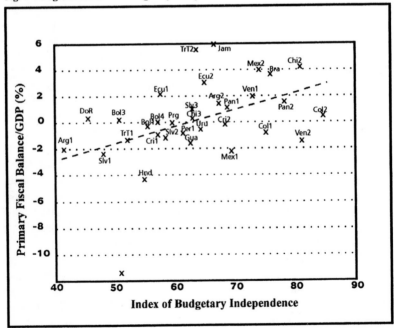

In Colombia, it can be observed that several of these rules and regulations are present and that the system has been gradually developing since the middle of the last century, and very intensely since 1985. Possibly, these institutions and the prudent fiscal policy they foster made it possible for Colombia to exhibit a remarkable record of fiscal stability in the continent (Figure 2) reflected in terms of stable growth and predictable inflation.[8] This chapter looks at the recent reforms of budget institution in Colombia from a historical approach, which should allow us to identify some patterns. In the next section I will look at how these institutions came into effect in the context of the economic history of the country. But before proceeding, let me outline the nature of these Colombian institutions as they presently stand.

Fig. 2 Budget Balance as % of GDP: Latin America, c.1980–c.1990

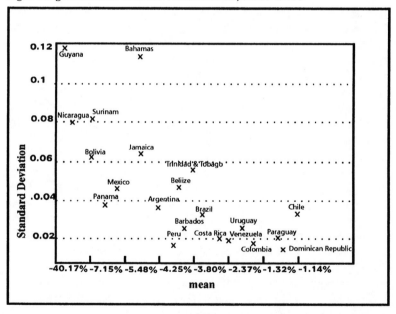

First and foremost, the Central Bank cannot lend to the private sector and can only finance the government when its autonomous Board of Directors votes unanimously in favour. Since 1991, when the new Constitution established the Central Bank as an autonomous institution, there has been no Central Bank financing of the government or the private sector, whereas in the past, the Central Bank was a frequent source of resources. The Minister of Finance is responsible for presenting the budget to Congress, jointly with the President. This gives the Finance Minister more authority than the spending ministers in all matters concerning the size of the budget. The Director of Planning has considerable authority in the distribution and size of its investment component. The law requires that the budget be consistent with a macroeconomic programme approved for the year by the government in co-ordination with the Central Bank. This acts as a formal restraint and may be more effective than fixed balanced-budget rules since budget surpluses and small deficits are not always the best fiscal outcome, nor necessarily desirable under all circumstances.

Relative to Congress, the executive is fairly powerful when it comes to the discussion and the legislative approval of the budget. Congress has been given legal deadlines for approving the budget. If the budget is not voted or not approved, the originally presented budget proposal of the government will automatically become the new budget. Congress is required to vote first, separately, on the size of the budget and then on its composition. It is not allowed to increase expenditures – aggregated or line items – or to reduce revenues without the express authorisation of the Minister of Finance.

A budget can be approved when the revenues and expenditures are not in equilibrium, but when there is a deficit, the government should propose a tax increase to Congress to cover the fiscal gap. If the tax increase is not approved, government can unilaterally cut expenditures to achieve equilibrium. Under normal conditions, except in the case of war or 'socio-economic emergency', the government is not allowed to increase expenditures beyond the budget originally approved by Congress, without going back to parliament for the approval of such increases. When it invokes a state of emergency, this decision will be reviewed by Congress and by the courts to prevent misuse of the emergency powers. There is not a lot of flexibility for changing expenditure items, but the government can reduce the actual expenditures because it has an iron grip on the cash flow –the financial plan. This plan is approved by CONFIS – National Council for Federal Policy – in co-ordination with the Central Bank.

These institutions and procedures provide exceptionally strong budget authority at the Ministry of Finance and at the Direction of Planning, with the power to overrule other cabinet members at different stages of the budgetary process. In comparison with other Latin American budget regimes, Colombia is only surpassed by Chile and by the newly-issued budget procedures of Peru in which the power of the President and of the finance minister is even greater. Let me now examine the historical developments of these institutions in Colombia.

The Evolution of Budget Institutions

The leading role of the Minister of Finance in budgetary affairs dates back to 1847. The then Secretary of Finance, Florentino González, created the Directorate of Taxes in the Ministry of Finance and issued the first set of rules that would regulate the process of budget preparation and approval (Ley 7, June 1847). The Ministry of Finance was made responsible for the presentation of the budget to Congress. The approved budget was to be regarded as a maximum level of expenditures which could not be exceeded. Expenditure items were to be specific and not indefinite, and the debt service had priority over any other expense. This initial regulation was refined in 1851 under the stewardship of Secretary Manuel Murillo Toro (Law 14, June of 1851). During the period 1851–92, the budgeting procedures were contained in the fiscal regulations and although these were subject to numerous reforms, responding to several financial crises, the first modern organisation of the budgeting process did not appear until 1892,[9] in the midst of a crisis provoked by large increases of the monetary base induced by the money financing of the budget.[10] This first 'organic budget law' (Ley 33, October 1892) contained a balanced-budget rule and made the Secretary of the Treasury responsible for suppressing expenditures until they equalled revenues. It also introduced the requirement that all expenditures contained in the budget proposal and in the final budget law approved by Congress must be expressly authorised by a pre-existing law.

Before this law was issued, the new Constitution of 1886 had laid out the general basis for the budget process: (1) no public expenditure could be made without having been approved by Congress or the legislative institutions of the lower levels of government; (2) each ministry could form its own budget proposal and send it to the Ministry of Finance who was responsible for the final project of the national budget and must submit it to the approval of Congress; and (3) Congress must approve the expenditure budget and the means to pay for these expenses. This determined that the Ministry of Finance was the budget authority and that Congress and the legislatures of municipalities and departments were responsible for the approval of the budget. However, the Constitution severely limited the power of the legislature in this process because it established that when Congress did not approve the budget for the year, the previously approved budget could be repeated;

more importantly, it also established that the government could increase the expenditure budget if it judged that additional spending was absolutely necessary ('unavoidable') during the periods when Congress was not in session. To legalise these extraordinary expenditures, all that was necessary was that the Council of Ministers authorise the additional expenditures, and that the Council of State approve this act. When it reconvened, Congress was called to rubber-stamp these decisions.

Many of the reforms of the nineteenth century and some of those enacted during the early twentieth century were not implemented as a response to an imminent crisis or as a result of one. They were introduced by reformist officials. González and Murillo Toro, for example, viewed the budget reform as part of a wider set of economic reforms, seeking to induce dynamism into the export sector of the economy. The 1886 budget legislature was part of a political counter-reform – the 'regeneration' of 1886 – which devolved power to the central government. The counter-reformers had the intention of promoting morality and social discipline and pursuing a greater role for the state.[11] The fiscal, monetary and financial reforms were geared to increase central government control and the efficiency of spending; and to rationalise the use of the very exiguous fiscal resources. In one instance – the 1892 reforms – budgeting regulations were prompted more by the proximity of crisis and as a reaction to the inflationary pressures created by the monetary policy of the government than by a reformist zeal. Most other nineteenth-century budgetary reforms were motivated by the severe scarcity of resources and the need to administer what little there was in an efficient manner. The reformers were mainly motivated by good management principles.

As part of the efforts geared to stabilise the economy in the years following the civil 'war of the thousand days', the budget process was reformed again in 1912 (Ley 110, November 1912). This law gave the Minister of Finance agenda-setting power in the Council of Ministers for discussions of the budget law proposal and of extraordinary expenditures; and for the first time it required that Congress meet strict deadlines for the approval of the budget, thereby increasing the power of the executive *vis-à-vis* the legislature. Another law of the period (Ley 3, July 1916) gave priority to expenditures using earmarked revenues, initiating a budgetary practice that reduces flexibility and tends to increase the size of the deficits. This practice of earmarking became pervasive in the budgetary procedures in Colombia until it was eliminated by the new Constitution of 1991, with the exception of already existing social expenditure commitments. Another law (Ley 7, August

1916) tightened the deadlines to be met by Congress for budget approval even more and introduced the notion that budgetary equilibrium consists of expenditures equalling revenues plus new debt, thereby neutralising the effect that the existing balanced-budget provision could have had as a source of budgetary restraint. This law, however, limited the capacity of Congress to increase expenditures by requiring that any new expenditure must be financed by a new revenue or by other expenditure cuts.

It was not until 1923 that a modern procedural rule was approved for the budgetary processes (Ley 34, July 1923). This law is the origin of the budgetary practices that are still in operation in Colombia. The motivation behind this law was the need to obtain foreign credit. In 1923, Colombia was one of the most backward countries in the continent. Infrastructure ranged from deficient to non-existent. The total length of the railroad network was only 1,481 km., one of the least developed in the region. This prompted the government of Pedro Nel Ospina (1922–26) to seek foreign loans to finance public investment, thereby increasing the leverage of the US indemnity for the takeover of Panama, and taking advantage of the Wall Street boom of the early 1920s. Foreign bankers pressed for reforms such as the creation of a Central Bank, adherence to the gold standard and adoption of 'modern' budget procedures. To accomplish this, the Colombian government engaged the consulting services of a mission led by Princeton economics professor Edwin W. Kemmerer – 'the Money Doctor of the Andes'. The reforms were thus imposed from the outside and were motivated by the scarcity of resources and the desire to obtain foreign financing. [12]

The Kemmerer mission drafted the new law ruling the formation of the budget and its execution and control. After it was approved by Congress, it set most of the basic principles for the management of the budget in Colombia until the present day. This new law established that Congress could not unilaterally increase the size of the budget and that any new expenditure to be included in the budget required the previous approval of the executive. This was an important step to strengthen the executive in the budget negotiations. Furthermore, the new law clearly established that loans could not be assimilated to revenues and required that current expenditures should be less than total government revenues, imposing a soft restraint rule that would foster public savings. It also defined precisely what extraordinary – 'unavoidable'– expenditures were, limiting the capacity of the executive to increase the budget through the Council of State loophole without congressional approval. Finally, it enabled the government to cut expenditures already approved by law when the current expenditures exceeded total revenues.

Kemmerer was recalled in 1931 to lead another mission to advise the government on financial and monetary affairs, when Colombia was suffering from the effects of the 1929 Wall Street crash and the world recession. Coffee prices had fallen dramatically and the country was having difficulties servicing the foreign loans obtained by the central government and the local governments during the boom years. As a result of this mission, a new organic budget law was drafted that refined the rules created by the previous mission (Ley 64, May 1931). This law limited even more the capacity of Congress to increase expenditures and the size of the budget and strengthened the authority of the Minister of Finance, requiring that any new expenditure must have the previous approval of this official before it could be included in the budget. This law also eliminated the reserve of budget residuals at the end of each year except for items related to debt service, for current expenditures already approved and sanctioned by the Ministry of Finance that had not been paid at the end of the fiscal year and for ongoing contracts, provided that these same amounts would be included in the budget of the following year. Unfortunately, these last provisions were considered too restrictive and were reformed by a questionable administrative act of the Contraloría General de la República.[13]

The procedures contained in this law continued virtually intact until 1950, when they were reformed by a 'state of siege' decree (Decreto 164, January 1950). This decree was part of a number of measures taken to control the upsurge of inflation that had remained unchecked during the 1946–50 period and that reached its peak (20.5 per cent) in 1950.[14] In this decree, a Directorate of the Budget was created within the Ministry of Finance, responsible for the preparation of the budget proposal and for the stewardship of its execution and internal control. This definitely established the predominance of the Ministry of Finance over all other ministries in matters related to the budgetary process, giving the ministry, through the Directorate of the Budget, ample powers to cut the budget during the execution process and to monitor the effectiveness of expenditures throughout the government. This decree also eliminated the earmarking of resources to specific expenditures.

During the years of the Colombian National Front (1958–74), Congress did not intervene directly in the setting of new budgetary procedures, but it gave the government blanket authorisations to reform procedures and institutions. As a result government was given the upper hand, but these authorisations were not always used in a way that would promote smaller deficits. For example, in 1963 (Ley 21, August 1963), a Monetary Board was created, independent of the Central Bank, that would become the monetary, credit and exchange authority of the country until the new Constitution of 1991. The members of this board were the Minister of Finance, the Director of Planning and two spending ministers – Agriculture and Industry – in addition to the Governor of the Central Bank, the Superintendent of Banks, the Director of the Institute of International Trade (INCOMEX), and two technical advisers who would set the agenda and participate in the discussions but could not vote.

The composition of this board and the financing practices that were introduced in the same law (the use of bank reserves to finance government expenditures and the establishment of a monetary budget to finance the government and private sector activity) were the seeds of a long-lived inflationary bias during the period 1963 to 1991.[15] This formally introduced the practice of quasi-fiscal financing for the private sector that survived until 1991. The budget was left for the executive and the politicians to divide, and the quasi-fiscal expenditure for the private sector through subsidies and bail-outs. The law also gave the government authorisation to reform the rules for the budgetary process (Decreto 1675, June 1964). This decree introduced the concept that the budget should reflect the targets and objectives of the development plan and of the government investment plans. This created a link between the short-term and the long-term management of the economy, and provided the basis for a future co-ordination between the macroeconomic policy and the budgetary process. It introduced the Department of Planning as a new budget authority, in charge of the investment budget, but still subordinated to the Ministry of Finance in the final decisions of budget preparation and execution. The decree restated that earmarking was not permitted and reinforced the power of the Director of the Budget. It also increased the power of the executive *vis-à-vis* the legislature, because it determined that when the budget is not approved by Congress, the previous year's budget would apply plus all the additions decreed by the government during congressional recesses. However, this new regime consecrated the 'budget reserves' consisting of keeping alive expenditure authorisations from the previous year, overlapping the new authorisations for the current year. This created a backlog of authorisations that pressed for greater expenditures and blurred the transparency of the budgetary process and its macroeconomic consequences.

Using a blanket authorisation of Congress, the government enacted a new budgetary regime in 1973 (Decreto 294, February 1973). This regime integrated the budgets of independent public institutions into the national budget, limiting the off-budget component of the public sector expenditures. It gave a co-ordinating role to CONPES (Council of Economic and Social Policy) that would eventually evolve into the formulation of a macroeconomic programme that would become a source of restraint for the government budget. It gave the Department of Planning a new role in the allocation of resources for investment, but subject to the resource limitations imposed by the Ministry of Finance. This role of the Planning Department continues today and creates a dichotomy of functions that fosters tensions between Finance and Planning that are healthy in terms of development but may also exert pressure for greater budgets – the Planning Department, although co-responsible for the macroeconomic performance of the economy, is always pressing for greater investment expenditures. This, in a well managed economy, would result in greater public savings, a higher level of public investment and faster growth. But, when politics intervene, it results in greater budgets and presumably higher inflation – through monetary financing – depending on the strength of the Ministry of Finance and the support it receives from the President.

Independently of the formal power granted to the Finance Ministry and the budgetary authorities, the President plays a key role in fiscal restraint because all these authorities are appointed officials who can be dismissed and replaced without hesitation in the event of a disagreement between the President and his Minister.

In 1981, the government regulated the budget process of lower levels of government along similar lines to those existing for the central government and its institutions (Decreto 2407, September 1981). It should be noticed that the authorisations for public indebtedness of all levels of government were always centralised in the Ministry of Finance, until 1994 when the new law of public contracting gave more flexibility to departments and municipalities despite the opposition of the Ministry of Finance.

After a severe economic and financial crisis at the beginning of the 1980s, the government convened a group of economists and other experts in 1985 to evaluate the fiscal and budgetary problems of the public sector, under the co-ordination of Luis Fernando Alarcón, then Director of the Budget, who would later become Minister of Finance. This group, and the adjustment initiated by Finance Minister Roberto Junguito in 1984, signalled the beginning of a process of institution building that is still under way and that has deeply reformed budgetary customs in Colombia.

Starting in the last years of the Betancur administration and during the Barco and Gaviria administrations, the government sharpened its technical skills for budget management and public sector macroeconomic and financial programming and co-ordination. For the first time, during those years, the government was capable of routinely producing evaluations of macroeconomic consistency, to follow up the fiscal and macroeconomic variables and to programme coherently the fiscal, monetary, foreign exchange and credit policies. These skills were a by-product of the fiscal crisis of 1982–89. The repeated visits of the IMF monitoring missions under Article IV of the Fund agreement made it necessary for the government to train and maintain technical staff capable of producing and understanding the data required by the IMF missions on a regular basis, using the format and methodology of the Fund. Initially, only the Central Bank had the technology, but after several missions these technical skills were diffused to Finance and Planning.

It was in this environment of higher programming skills that a thorough reform of the budget regime was enacted (Ley 38, April 1989, Decreto 3077, December 1989, Decreto 411, April 1989 and Decreto 2162, September 1989). The government was given more power to limit the budget of the legislature and the judiciary, it was also given authority to set financial targets for the other public companies (the so-called 'paraestatales') and to follow up on their financial performance. This extended the control of the fiscal authorities to the whole non-financial public sector.

The new law formally introduced an instrument of macroeconomic co-ordination of the budget – the financial plan – which covered the programming of effective operations for the whole of the public sector and called for consistency with an annual macroeconomic programme. It required that this financial plan be compatible with an annual cash budget and with the targets of the monetary and exchange policies. In these new regulations, the budget was also an element of co-ordination with the medium- and long-range planning of the government. These are all legal requirements, but the end result of economic importance is that programming and budgeting have been integrated into the macroeconomic management as essential functions that have to be co-ordinated into an overall policy with those of other institutions. Curiously, in the past, budgeting had been a purely bureaucratic or accounting activity that formally complied with the legal provisions of the budget law and supervised the compliance of other public institutions with it. This is no longer so. The institutions have changed to become active participants of policy and decision-making. However, they are still very poorly equipped to deal with the problems of efficiency of public expenditures. In addition, budgeting still is not considered an activity for economists but rather something akin to accounting.

An important feature of the new regime, and a break with the tradition of concentrating the budget authority in the Ministry of Finance, was the establishment of the Council for Fiscal Policy (CONFIS) which was responsible for submitting the financial plan of the public sector to CONPES for approval – the formal procedure that guaranteed macroeconomic co-ordination – and to approve the annual effective operations and budget execution programmes, key fine-tuning mechanisms that had previously been under the domain of the Director of the Budget. This was a step backwards for the authority of the Ministry of Finance because attributions that previously had been exclusively the prerogative of the ministry, such as programming the cash flow, budget execution, follow-up of the financial and budgetary performance, and monitoring the budget execution of the public sector, were now given to the Council which had two spending ministers in its midst. Why was this done? Probably what happened was that politicians and other public officials had suffered from the excessive rigour of the Finance Ministry's rule during the adjustment period of 1984–86. Public sector salaries had been slashed in real terms during those years and public investment had suffered. These changes were part of a reaction within government and in Congress against the concentration of fiscal power in one place.

To increase the effectiveness of public spending, this law required that all investment projects had to be evaluated and incorporated in a 'project bank' as a necessary condition for their inclusion in the investment plan. This is a very important new feature because all other procedures and institutions are geared to control the quantity of fiscal expenditures and this is the first attempt to address the problem of quality of public investment in a technical context. Cost-effectiveness is a concept alien to fiscal and budgetary management in Colombia, as in most of Latin America. In Colombia, the absence of quality controls and the consequent lack of economic effectiveness of public investment are vividly highlighted by the fact that cuts in public investment during the adjustment periods do not appear to have significant effects over economic growth (see the section on Rationality of Fiscal Procedures and Institutions).

The government was also authorised to reduce expenditures when revenues are expected to fall below the amount approved in the budget. For the executive this is a useful tool that allows flexibility in the case of negative revenue shocks. The law also restructured the Directorate of the Treasury and limited the congressional authorisation to utilise Central Bank financing to the level of eight per cent of the current revenues of the government in the previous year. Although this limitation is still very lax considering that the average Colombian deficit is of the same order of magnitude, it represented a step in the right direction. Additionally, the new regime subjected all public indebtedness to the previous authorisation of the central government. This is particularly important to avoid excessive municipal indebtedness and the indebtedness of parastatals.

A major change in the budgetary process was introduced by the new Constitution of 1991. First of all, the Central Bank was granted autonomy. It was to be ruled by a seven-member Board of Directors – five autonomous members, the Governor of the Bank and the Minister of Finance. The Governor is elected by the Board. The Finance Minister has no veto power except when the budget of the Bank is approved, and the President of Colombia can only appoint two members during his term. The Bank is the independent authority in monetary, credit and exchange matters. The government is responsible for providing the Bank with sufficient resources to intervene independently in the financial markets with its open market operations and to monitor the exchange rate. The Bank is responsible for bringing down inflation every year. The Constitution also prohibited Central Bank credit for the public sector, except to provide liquidity to the financial sector and when the Bank is a bank of last reserve.

Additionally, the Constitution established the all-inclusiveness – universality – of the budget, prohibiting off-budget expenditures and subjecting all taxes and contributions to congressional approval. The new Constitution added to the transparency of the process by requiring that the budget submitted to Congress and the budget law that it would eventually approve should include all the expenditures and revenues. It did not foresee a balanced budget but called on government to obtain the additional revenues required in a separate project to balance the budget. If this is not achieved, the Constitution entitled the government to cut expenditures until the budget is balanced. This way, the government is fully responsible for the fiscal outcome, and the approval issued by Congress can only be regarded as a maximum authorisation. This enables the government to conduct a coherent fiscal policy that is consistent with macroeconomic objectives.

The new Constitution increased the power of the executive by establishing a deadline for the approval of the budget by Congress and allowing the government to adopt its own budget proposal in the event that Congress does not approve the budget law by the time of this deadline. It also stated that Congress could not increase expenditures or add expenditure items, nor cut existing revenues without the express authorisation of the Minister of Finance. Additionally it suppressed the figure of parliamentary grants – *auxilios parlamentarios* – that had been created by Abdón Espinosa, Minister of Finance in the Carlos Lleras administration. Through this figure, all Congressmen obtained budgetary resources for their political non-profit foundations, presumably for good deeds and public works of local importance. However, these funds increasingly had been used to finance their political campaigns and to foster a corrupt patronage system that gave excessive political advantages to the incumbents. Originally, the idea had been that Congressmen would become interested only in the amount allotted for these grants and that this would give the government a free hand during the approval of the rest of the budget once the size of the grants was settled. This proved to be correct, but the cost was that the budget approval process was contaminated by personal interest and that Congress abdicated one of its main responsibilities in a democracy – the discussion and approval of the budget – in exchange for these grants.

However, outlawing the congressional grants did not calm the appetite for 'pork-barrel' funds of politicians and the willingness of executive officials to accommodate them. As it stands, the budget approval process is an open season for 'pork'. Politicians seek regional projects and find ways to divert resources to political targets. As a result, there are economists in Colombia who think that the formal prohibitions to allot small grants to congressmen will render larger deficits in the future and that giving up that mechanism to satisfy the clientelistic drive of Congress will be costly in terms of governance and fiscal stability. In fact, the system that operated before 1981 had a well-defined division of labour and of resources. Urrutia claims that industrialists, politicians and labour unions were quite distinct from each other and that they had separate realms for exerting influence. According to him, the budget did not favour the private sector but rather, it was spent in a fairly progressive way in programmes that had some distributive consequences.[16] The portion of the budget taken by politicians for their own clientelistic programmes was small, and the private sector carved up the quasi-fiscal deficit of the Central Bank through its directed credit programmes, but not the budget. With the creation of an autonomous Central Bank that cannot lend to the private sector, pressures are mounting to obtain subsidies from the budget. Similarly, politicians are demanding 'pork' now that they do not have access to grants. Altogether, the system is progressing to a more participatory democracy, but it may become more costly until new rules are developed to deal with the new mounting pressures for greater expenditure.

Another important contribution of the new constitution was the deletion of the procedures for increasing the budget during legislative recesses which, in fact, gave the government and the Council of State legislative powers that did not contribute to fiscal restraint or to the independence of the judiciary. It also eliminated all earmarking, except pre-existing earmarking for social expenditures, but required that the social expenditure would have priority over any other expenditure (previously, this priority was given to debt service) and that the social investment budget should always be a non-decreasing proportion of the total budget. These two rules should contribute to increase the budget size over time. So far, their effect has been negligible because of the creativeness of the staff of the Budget Director, but eventually they will become effective pressures on expenditure. Regarding the distribution of social expenditures, it called for rules of distribution that would take into consideration the relative needs and levels of destitution, and also the fiscal performance and administrative effectiveness of the regions.

The Constitution took a very important step towards the financial decentralisation of government and, consequently, of the budget. It required that every year an increasing proportion of the budget would be allocated to finance the supply of services that would be the responsibility of departmental and municipal governments. Furthermore, it also ruled that the municipal governments should obtain a proportion of the current revenues of the government to finance social investment at the local level. This proportion was determined to be 14 per cent in 1993 and to increase to 22 per cent of current revenues in 2002.

The law established that the proportion of the current revenues of the central government to be shared by lower level governments should increase from 34 per cent in 1993 to 42 per cent by the year 2002. The services that should be taken over by the lower levels of government are essentially education, basic health, water and sewage, police, local public works, environmental protection and recreation.

If local governments seriously take over these responsibilities and use the transferred resources to pay for them, the effect on the budget should be negligible. But it has been observed that the central government and the politicians do not want to surrender these functions, because the whole structure of political clientelism controlled from the top was built on them. The basis for the old-order governance mechanisms was the provision of these functions by the central government. This way, congressmen influenced the allocation of services, and government rewarded or punished local governments by channelling more or fewer services to them. As a consequence, the central government is re-assuming the financing of some of these services in a way that smacks of recentralisation and also creates an undue pressure on the budget because most expenditures have to be financed twice: once through revenue-sharing and then, a second time, through *ad hoc* transfers to departments and municipalities to obtain political support.[17] Furthermore, the decentralisation process may have adverse fiscal consequences because in the early stages of the transition from centralised to decentralised forms of government, it is unlikely that strong budget institutions develop at the local level *pari passu* with decentralisation.

At the end of 1994, Congress passed a law that set the new rules for the budget process under the Constitution of 1991. This law contains several innovative features that must be singled out: it introduces as basic principles of the budgetary process both the macroeconomic consistency of the budget and the need for the process to be self-regulating in the sense that when revenues increase above normal levels, due to a positive revenue shock such as a temporary boom, the excess revenues should not be immediately incorporated as current revenues but, rather, saved and gradually absorbed in later years. This gives government the possibility to save the proceeds of the new increase in oil production and to distribute this portion of current revenues to lower-level governments only when the revenues are gradually incorporated in the budgets of future years. In the first semester of 1995, another law was approved that makes this saving in an oil stabilisation fund mandatory for revenues from the new oil fields.

The new budget law of 1994 also gave CONFIS back to the Ministry of Finance, restoring the budgetary authority of this institution. It created the formal link between the budget process and the monetary, credit and exchange policies by requiring that the Central Bank advise Congress on the macroeconomic effects of the budget proposed by the government, that the budget be consistent with the macroeconomic programme approved by CONPES for the year, and that the government and the Central Bank co-ordinate the contents of the financial plan to which the budget must be subordinated.

It also authorised the government to delete all budget items that have not been spent at the end of each year (they have to be incorporated in the new budget if the government and Congress so decide) and to create a stabilisation fund – the Fund of Surplus Resources – when revenues are earned that could cause a macroeconomic disequilibrium.

The law created a new budget approval feature: the budget commission must first approve the rise of the budget and then vote on its contents. It was hoped that this procedure would help control the appetite of Congress during the budget discussion by settling the size rapidly at the beginning of the process of approval. However, it does not appear to be an effective rule because when the size is being decided, the members of the budget commission are already making sure that their projects and those of their colleagues obtain financing.

The law gave new powers to the Ministry of Finance authorising it to cut expenditures when revenues fall, when Congress does not approve an increase in taxes that would balance the budget, or when 'macroeconomic coherence' calls for such cuts. This, coupled with the definition of the budget approved by Congress as a maximum, gives the government a variety of tools to exercise budgetary restraint. This is a far cry from the situation described by Eduardo Wiesner who, as outgoing Minister of Finance in 1982, publicly doubted that any government would have the political backing to detain the process of fiscal deterioration that had reached a critical level under his stewardship.[18] There are signs, however, that prevent us from taking an overly optimistic approach. The absence of grants to quench the thirst of politicians, the detachment of politicians from the monetary base and the democratic reforms that prevent the executive from approving budget additions without congressional approval, will require additional skills, both political and managerial, from the Ministry of Finance. It is also possible that new rules and regulations – additional institutions – will be necessary.

However, a lot of progress can be shown after a ten-year period of institution building that started in the second semester of 1984, and culminated with this budget law at the end of 1994. The budgetary procedures that have developed in Colombia have empowered the executive to exert greater control over fiscal outcomes. Consequently, government can be held totally accountable for the fiscal results. Centring the responsibility on the government and moving it away from Congress, where it could be diluted, does not ensure good fiscal management, but does increase the probability of careful fiscal administration.

The Rationality of Fiscal Procedures and Institutions

The evolution of the budget institutions suggests that the Colombian polity has traditionally supported orthodox financial policies and has empowered the government to perform accordingly. Easterly observes that 'in Colombia the management of fiscal deficits and their financing has been generally sound. Episodes of loose fiscal policy have been minor in comparison with other Latin American countries. The near-crisis of the early 1980s was addressed in a timely way through a sharp fiscal adjustment.'[19]

Where does the political backing come from? Why is there political support for lower deficits in a country beset by unsatisfied basic needs and deficient infrastructure? Why is it that Colombian ministers of finance are expected to be ruthless in their pursuit of lower deficits and are publicly condemned when they fail to be so or even when they find the means to augment public expenditures without increasing the deficits? In trying to answer these questions, the starting point, and perhaps one of the most crucial elements, is to look at the extent to which fiscal deficits are good indicators of macroeconomic health; how do they affect macroeconomic performance in Colombia?

The first factor to consider is the relationship between deficits and inflation. In Colombia public expenditures or deficits do not exhibit by themselves a demonstrable statistical relationship with inflation. Figure 3 shows the behaviour of inflation and the primary deficit of the central government between 1950 and 1992; Figure 4 shows that of inflation and the non-financial public sector deficit from 1960 to 1992. No clear relationship between the public deficits and inflation can be discerned.[20] This is confirmed by other studies that have recently been published and does not appear to be a typical Colombian trait but rather a fairly general finding.[21] 'Inflation and deficits show no simple correlation. But there is a long-running association between inflation and one means of deficit financing – money creation.'[22] There is also evidence that the volatility of public deficits shows an association with the volatility of inflation, when the deficits are large in comparison to the size of the domestic financial markets.[23]

The money financing of deficits can be linked to higher inflation rates.[24] When the public sector deficit – or the private deficit – is financed through money creation, it contributes to increase inflation. Figure 5 traces the relationship between Central Bank financing and public sector deficits since 1950, indicating that the Central Bank financing of the deficit had been substantial before 1984,[25] except during

Fig. 3 Annual Inflation (%) and the Primary Deficit (% GDP), 1950–92

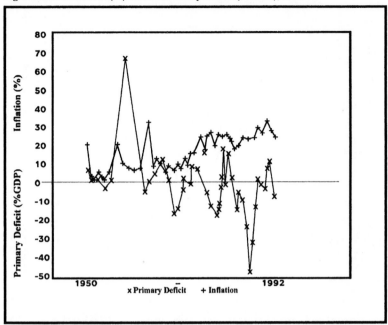

Fig. 4 Annual Inflation (%) and the Public Sector Deficit, 1960–92

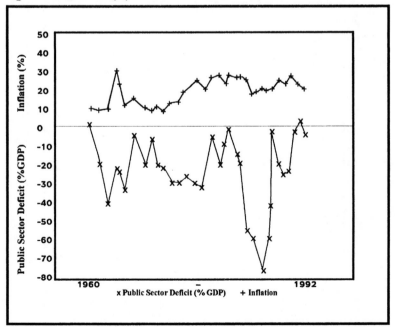

Fig. 5 Central Bank Financing and Public Sector Deficit, 1950–92

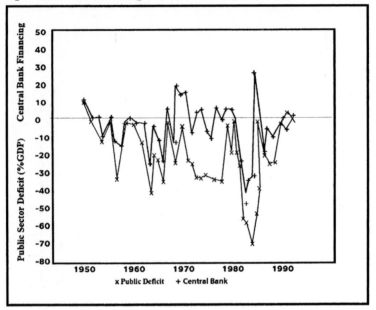

x Public Deficit   + Central Bank

Fig. 6 Public Sector Deficit, Domestic and Foreign Borrowing, 1970–92 (%GDP)

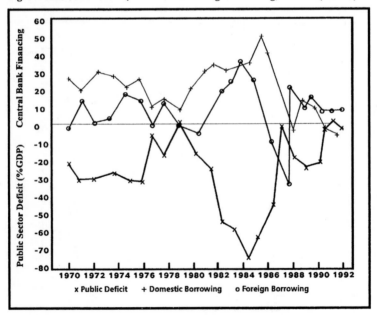

x Public Deficit   + Domestic Borrowing   o Foreign Borrowing

the Lleras Restrepo (1966–70) and López Michelsen (1974–78) administrations. After 1984, this source of financing was sharply reduced and the practice was virtually abolished in 1991 with the new Constitution, eliminating a source of inflationary pressure. However, it was not entirely removed, because the Central Bank continued to use seignorage as a financing source for its own activities of money-market and exchange rate intervention.

There is public awareness in Colombia that when deficits grow beyond a relatively small threshold, the sources of financing required – Central Bank finance, external and domestic credit – generate other side effects that have negative macroeconomic consequences. As shown in Figure 6, when the deficit grows above normal historical levels its domestic financing becomes unusually large. Attempts to finance the public deficit with domestic credit induce sharp increases in the domestic interest rate. There is also a private sector fear that public expenditure will inhibit private investment because the country has lived more frequently under conditions of credit rationing that cause public spending to displace private investment than under conditions of capital abundance. 'Public capital has had a negative effect on private investment (. . .) and the contribution of public investment to growth is highly uncertain.'[26] In other words, delaying or halting public investment has not had demonstrably negative consequences on growth. This is probably caused by the ineffectiveness of public spending; at any rate it has made the trade-off between adjustment and growth less relevant in the past history of Colombia.

There is a strong relationship between the size of the deficit, the flows of external credit (Figure 6) and the trade balance. These two factors – fiscal deficit and foreign financing – contribute to the trade deficit in the same direction: an increase in the public sector surplus contributes to higher trade surpluses and a decrease in the foreign financing of the deficit has a similar effect.[27] Moreover, an increase in the trade surplus contributes to the depreciation of the real exchange rate (RER), whereas a decrease acts in favour of an appreciation. In this manner, greater fiscal deficits will indirectly cause an appreciation of the currency. Government spending in Colombia, on the other hand, has shown a positive relationship with the real exchange rate in the past – greater government spending as a percentage of GDP is associated with depreciation of the exchange rate.[28]

In view of the behaviour of domestic interest rates, considering the foreign financial constraint, and the low impact of public spending on growth, permanently seeking fiscal balance has been a rational approach. The government has responded to political pressures to increase expenditures by seeking to maintain the deficit at comparatively low levels, pushing up revenues each time that expenditures grow. When this rule is frequently adhered to, as has been the case of Colombia, the process becomes almost self-regulating.

This also acts as a powerful deterrent against deficit creation when the Central Bank is independent and if the availability of foreign credit is constrained from abroad. The government cannot overly depend on domestic credit, given the very strong relationship between public sector deficits and domestic interest and the negative consequences of high interest rates on stability and growth. Private opinion-makers react negatively to increases in the real domestic interest rate because they cause a drop in the ratio of private investment to GDP and ultimately affect growth.[29] The relationship between the real exchange rate and the public deficit is another powerful deterrent against deficit creation in Colombia, because of the existence of a very strong exporter lobby and due to the traditional overwhelming influence of the coffee producers and other exporters who are forever seeking higher domestic prices for their products and abhor the real appreciation of the currency.

Accordingly, in balancing the short-term political objectives with the long-run demands of economic management, the advantages of a conservative financial policy are clear to anyone willing to do the analysis because large deficits affect negatively all the variables that are the key elements of macroeconomic stability and economic progress – growth, private sector investment, inflation, real exchange rates and the trade balance. What still remains unclear is why the government has sought a policy that is sound and very rational in the long run without yielding to the short-term attractiveness of deficit spending. To answer this it is necessary to delve into political economy. The preference shown for budget institutions and for economic rationality in the long run has to be a reflection of who really holds power in Colombia.

One aspect that must be understood is that the constituency of finance ministers in Colombia is not the political parties, nor the public at large, but the relatively powerful and very vocal business associations. Another aspect that must be highlighted is that, traditionally, the most powerful pressure group in Colombia has been the Federation of Coffee Growers, a combined business conglomerate and lobby that had virtual monopoly of foreign exchange during many years and represented the interests of the principal producers of exported goods of the country. The other business associations consist either of exporters or of producers of export substitutes. There is no strong organisation of consumers, and fortunately for Colombia, there is no powerful importer lobby,[30] nor a well organised populist party. The left has been a confused focus of opposition to the traditional parties and has never had significant popular backing or influence over public opinion.

In economic matters, the opinion makers are predominantly the economic pressure groups, independent think tanks like Fedesarrollo and individual economists. There is also a small economic technocracy that can apply peer-group pressure on the government. Given this mix of public opinion sources, there must be and there is a definite bias in favour of policies that do not cause large deficits. There also is strong public opinion pressure to avoid policies that may cause the real exchange rate to appreciate. This was not always so, but since 1967 it has been the rule. Furthermore, the private sector nearly always favours lower interest rates; and given the scarcity of foreign financing, there must be a strong preference for smaller public sector deficits and for positive trade balances.

Since those groups that would pressure for more populist policies do not have permanent political and public opinion representation, the policy mix that is rewarded in Colombia is macroeconomic prudence. Politically it has made sense for governments to have given so much weight to the creation and maintenance of strong budget institutions that prevent expenditure excesses by Congress and control executive indebtedness because the principal constituencies of economic policy gain from stable and prudent fiscal policies. The new constitutional charter of an independent Central Bank puts an end to its previous excesses as a source of finance and has the same political constituency of strong fiscal institutions.

This political organisation may be criticised for being unduly oligarchical in nature or for not letting other mechanisms of democratic participation flourish, but in purely fiscal terms it has been a blessing. It has facilitated Colombia's slow but steady transition from being one of the poorest countries in the continent to the middle-income status it has enjoyed since the 1970s.

It is particularly interesting how the government and business organisations have worked together to imprint a real exchange rate objective on fiscal policy. For example, in the past, the adjustment to positive shocks in international coffee prices has been achieved more through fiscal means than through changes in the real exchange rate. Similarly, when coffee prices fall, domestic prices of coffee are sustained using fiscal resources of the National Coffee Fund. This helps explain why for long periods the real exchange rate has moved independently from international coffee prices.[31] Producers of export goods other than coffee, and of import substitution goods, have been shielded from the full appreciating effects of the international booms on the real exchange rate, and have been able to grow and develop with relative independence from the variations in prices of the main export commodity. In the long run, this has made the country more resilient *vis-à-vis* external shocks through export diversification.

With all its merits, the government-business consensus that ruled in Colombia during the 1967–91 period also had some drawbacks, mostly in terms of inflation and growth. This is closely related to fiscal policy and merits some analysis: although Colombia has had a stable fiscal policy, it has not been overly restrictive. As a rule, the government has chosen to generate moderate and stable deficits, producing surpluses only when required by extremely favourable external conditions; and even in these circumstances, the surpluses have also been moderate. The rate of inflation has also been stable but quite high. These policy results seem to reflect a national preference for the middle ground. A favourite Colombian aphorism says: 'don't place the candle so far from the saint that it cannot be seen; nor so close that it will burn it'. In economic policy, this has been the rule.

From the late sixties to the early nineties, Colombia had a nominal exchange rate policy that attempted to favour exporters through a crawling-peg mechanism; the nominal exchange rate was confined to a path determined by expected domestic and foreign inflations. The rates of inflation were carefully monitored and forecast on a monthly basis and the rate of devaluation was determined by this expectation. Forecasts and macroeconomic programming were based on a stable inflation assumption.

Additionally, the Central Bank financed the private sector through development credit schemes or by granting direct credit to firms in sectors that were depressed or in distress. These activities were wholly or partly financed through monetary expansion. The money base was collected and distributed by a Monetary Board that treated it as a budget to be allocated and disbursed; the growth of the base and the money supply were carefully programmed so that the nominal exchange rate and the credit to the private sector and to government could be accommodated. The implicit programming rule was that M1 would grow at the same rate as the expected growth of nominal GDP, assuming stable inflation. The nominal exchange rate devaluation would be programmed by targeting a stable real exchange rate. This made inflation and devaluation easily predictable and it became a self-fulfilling rule. The accommodation with higher inflation was started in the early seventies and continued until 1991. The Pastrana government had narrowly won the presidential election of 1970 and sought to gain public support through expanded public expenditures and higher quasi-fiscal credit subsidies. With time, the government and the public came to a tacit agreement. If inflation was to be kept to around 24 per cent per year in a band that would not exceed 30 per cent, the public would not seek to reduce their monetary assets. The government also tolerated the indexation of nominal contracts and eventually accepted a form of indexation of wages, by yearly adjusting the minimum wage to the past inflation.[32]

Given these monetary management customs and in view of the strong pressure to keep the exchange rate from appreciating, it is small wonder that Colombia has one of the most remarkable records – stable moderate inflation. Even in a closed economy, keeping money and the exchange rate under control is an improbable mission, but it explains why fiscal restraint is essential: there are just not enough degrees of freedom when most other variables are already predetermined. Still, the government obtained the financing it required for a number of projects it favoured and for its statist development programmes, including its export-promotion strategy, at the cost of higher inflation.

Jorge García García has expressed how this policy mix succeeded in keeping a consensus alive 'mostly on false premises' with some costs but yielding very stable macroeconomic results:

[Nominal] devaluation did not prevent a real appreciation of the peso . . . ; nor did it favour exporters or protect those sectors that compete with imports. However, it produced an illusion that something had been done in favour of domestic producers. It also contributed to keeping inflation high. The public believed that establishing real targets motivated more exports and never questioned whether a relationship existed or not between trade liberalisation and export promotion; and the country maintained (for many years) a very restrictive foreign trade regime. Colombia had a stable economy but a repressed economy.[33]

Colombia has shown remarkable stability in terms of inflation and public deficits, unparalleled in the continent and with few rivals abroad. A similar record may be claimed in terms of economic growth. As we have seen, budget institutions have played a role in this picture of stability and moderate growth. Still, a question remains: how important have institutional and legal changes been for the fiscal performance? A simple test was therefore devised comparing the size of primary deficits as a proportion of GDP for the three years immediately preceding every major twentieth-century budget reform from 1931 to 1989 with the size of those in the three years immediately following the year of the reform. This yielded two samples of fifteen observations. The average primary deficit of the years preceding the reforms was on average 1.35 percent of GDP larger than those for the years following the reforms.[34]

A casual observation of Figure 3 shows that the deficits are becoming smaller, but that there is a cyclical pattern. Governments allow the situation to deteriorate, then they correct it. This may be concluded also from the before and after reform comparison. It appears that periodic reforms are required to build up a morale for deficit slashing, and that this zeal will disappear with time, making it necessary for another set of reforms to arouse the orthodox spirit once again. In conclusion, it appears that institutions really matter, but also that governments and public opinion must keep on working at it because the effectiveness of the rules appears to wane with time.

Conclusions

The development of budget institutions in Colombia has spanned a period that started a few decades after independence and is still continuing. It has been a gradual development and, except for the decentralisation of government induced by the new Constitution of 1991, which opened a parallel path for local government institutional development now in its infancy, the process has pointed almost continuously in one direction. The thrust of the institution-building inertia has been to give the central government the power autonomously to determine the outcome of fiscal policy in a democratic setting. The Constitution of 1991 gave new democratic meaning to the budget approval process, and it gave Congress more power than it had had in budgetary matters. Nevertheless, at the present time the Colombian government has the institutions and mechanisms that ensure that it controls the fiscal outcome.

These are mainly derived from the legal rules and institutions that govern the budget formation, approval and execution process in which the government has been given the upper hand. The principal feature of this legal framework is the independence of the Central Bank because this assures that government cannot appropriate an inflation tax to finance deficits or to subsidise the private sector. Then, there is the required consistency of the budget and its distribution with a macroeconomic programme, in the design of which the Central Bank has played a key role in co-ordination with government. This provides the fiscal restraint that is often sought when 'balanced-budget rules' are imposed without the hindrances derived from those rules. Additionally, if the President is fiscally responsible, the Ministry of Finance in Colombia has greater power than the spending ministries in the budget formation process. The Ministry can impose its authority in the final count when the budget is taken to Congress for approval.

Perhaps the most interesting aspect of the process is that there are sound economic reasons behind the political backing that orthodox fiscal policy has received in Colombia. The maintenance of a small public sector deficit has helped Colombia to maintain a stable and competitive real exchange rate, it has helped to avoid large swings in the current account balance and to maintain it within sustainable levels, and it has been a key factor to avoid substantial increases in foreign indebtedness, which would have brought down the trade balance and added to the appreciation of the currency. Furthermore, the political economy of fiscal management in Colombia can be enriched when it is taken into consideration that public investment is not a complement of private investment, but rather an undesirable substitute; and that in Colombia growth does not suffer considerably when the government has to reduce its investment to accommodate fiscal adjustment programmes. This is particularly critical because it may be an indication that despite all the procedures that act in favour of reduced deficits, there are no institutions that would control the quality and effectiveness of public spending.

The analysis of the political economy of fiscal and macroeconomic policy since 1967 yields several interesting conclusions. First, it provides a political framework to explain why Colombians prefer to control public expenditure rather than to let it run out of control. A careful management of public deficits yields a more stable macroeconomic performance, which tends to benefit the private sector and receives its support. Since there are no active competing constituencies with opposing objectives, this policy has been more easily maintained than in countries where populism was organised as a political party or where political factions had stronger claims on the budget. Inflation was kept at its moderately high levels during many years, without any serious attempts to reduce it on a permanent basis, because there was a monetary financing of the – mostly – moderate deficits; and the private sector tolerated the predictable level of moderately high inflation in exchange for cheaper credit and a stable real exchange rate. The policies were successful to the extent that they yielded stability and moderate growth. Time will tell if economic management in the more open economy that was started in 1991 will be able to yield better results. So far, it is already noticeable that in an open economy the government has to apply even tighter fiscal restraint if it is to continue providing price and real exchange rate stability.

Notes

*   The author was a consultant for the Office of the Chief Economist of the Inter-American Bank at the time of writing this paper. This chapter is part of a research project concerning the effect of budget institutions on the fiscal performance of Latin American countries conducted for this office by Alberto Alesina, Ricardo Hausmann, Ernesto Stein and the author.
1.   Alesina (1988), pp.13–52.
2.   A very good review of the literature on the subject and of the prevailing hypothesis may be found in Alesina and Perotti (1994a).
3.   Von Hagen (1991), pp. 99–110.
4.   Eichengreen (1991), p. 31.
5.   Poterba (1994), pp. 799–821.
6.   These characteristics of the budget procedures and institutions are discussed in greater detail in Alesina and Perotti (1994a), pp. 18–34, where several empirical studies are reviewed.
7.   Hommes (1995b).
8.   Hommes (1995c and 1995d).
9.   López (1992), pp. 113–5.
10.   Meisel Roca and López (1990), pp. 71–3.
11.   Bushnell (1993), pp. 141–2
12.   López (1990), pp. 239–49. Also see Eichengreen (1989).
13.   This piece of information was contributed by Alfonso Palacio Rudas, who was linked to the Contraloría when this happened. Curiously, history repeats itself because the politicians are pressuring the government to repeal the 1994 provision that gradually eliminates the reserve of unspent items contained in the new budget organic law.
14.   Meisel Roca and López (1990), p. 421.
15.   Urrutia (1994), pp. 45–7.
16.   Urrutia (1991).
17.   The relationship between governance and recentralisation and the political setting in which *ad hoc* transfers to lower-level governments affect the final budget performance may be seen in Hommes (1995b), p. 28.
18.   Wiesner (1982).
19.   Easterly (1994), p.262.
20.   The correlation for the period 1970–92 between the primary deficit of the government and the annual rate of inflation is 0.28 ($t=1.31$ with 21 degrees of freedom – d.f.).

21. Easterly (1994), pp. 254–5.
22. The World Bank (1993).
23. Ongoing research conducted by the Office of the Chief Economist at the Inter-American Development Bank indicates that the effects of fiscal deficits on inflation are not first- but second-moment effects: The volatility of inflation shows a significant relationship with the volatility of fiscal deficits relative to the size of the financial markets.
24. Easterly (1994), p. 253.
25. The correlation between the public sector deficit and Central Bank credit to the government for the 1950–90 period is 0.77 (t=7.49 with 39 d.f).
26. Easterley (1994), p. 262.
27. *Ibid.*, pp. 257–9.
28. The correlation between the RER and the trade balance for the period 1975–92 is 0.8 (t=5.33 and 16 d.f.). The correlation between the RER and government expenditures in period t-1 for the same year is 0.64 (t=3.36 and 16 d.f.). The correlation between trade balance and the public sector deficit for the period 1970–92 is 0.81 (t=6.44 with 21 d.f.).
29. Easterly (1994), p. 251.
30. Urrutia (1991).
31. Cárdenas (1994), pp. 351–80.
32. Carrasquilla (1994).
33. García García (1994).
34. Reforms took place in 1931, 1950, 1963, 1973 and 1980. The average primary deficit for the 15 years preceding the reforms was 1.11% of GDP and the average primary surplus of the 18 years following the reforms was 0.24% of GDP. The difference of 1.35% of GDP is significant (t=3.61, p=0.0005).

BIBLIOGRAPHY

Abel, C. *Política, iglesia y partidos en Colombia* (Bogotá, 1987).

Afanador, J. P. *Democracia en Sanjil o Cartas del ciudadano José Pascual Afanador Dirigidas a los señores de la Nobleza Sanjileña, sobre la naturaleza y efectos de un Programa* (Socorro, 1851, republ. Bucaramanga, 1990).

Alesina, A. 'Macroeconomics and Politics', *NBER Macroeconomics Annual* 3, (1988).

Alesina, A. and Roberto Perotti 'Budget Deficits and Institutions', 1st. draft, mimeo (November, 1994a).

'The Political Economy of Growth: What do we Know?', Departamento Nacional de Planeación, Seminario Latinoamericano sobre Crecimiento Económico (Bogotá, 28 June, 1994b).

Anderson, B. *Imagined Communities: Reflections on the Origins and Spread of Nationalism* (London, 1993).

Arnove, R. 'Políticas educativas durante el Frente Nacional', *Revista Colombiana de Educación*, no. 1 (1978).

Bailey, J. J. 'Pluralist and Corporatist Dimensions of Interest Representation in Colombia', in J. M. Malloy (ed.), *Authoritarianism and Corporatism in Latin America* (Pittsburgh, 1977).

Barkin, J. S. and B. Cronin 'The State and Nation: Changing Norms and the Rules of Sovereignty in International Relations', *International Organisation*, vol. 48, no. 1 (winter 1994).

Barona B. G. *La maldición de Midas en una región del mundo colonial. Popayán 1730–1830* (Cali, 1995).

Beetham, D. *The Legitimation of Power* (Basingstoke, 1991).

Bejarano, A. M. 'Recuperar el estado para fortalecer la democracia', *Análisis Político*, vol. 22 (May-August, 1994).

Betancourt, D. and M. L. García, *Contrabandistas, marimberos y mafiosos. Historia social de la mafia colombiana 1965–92* (Bogotá, 1994).

Betancur, B. *El homo sapiens se extravió en América Latina* (Bogotá, 1990).

Bobbio, N. *El futuro de la democracia* (Madrid, 1985).

Estado, Gobierno y Sociedad. Por una teoría general de la política (Mexico, D.F., 1989).

Bolívar, S. *Obras Completas*, 2 vols. (Havana, 1947).

Bonilla, G. and H. Osorio 'Estructura de Mercado y Prácticas Comerciales en los Sectores Industrial, Minero-Energético y de Servicios Públicos en Colombia', *Revista de Planeación y Desarrollo*, vol. XXIV, no. 2 (1993).

Bonilla Pardo, G. and A. Valencia Villa *Justicia para la justicia: violencia contra jueces y abogados en Colombia, 1979–1991* (Bogotá, 1992).

Bramley, G. 'The Impact of Land Use Planning and Tax Subsidies on the Supply and Price of Housing in Britain', *Urban Studies*, vol. 30 (1993).

Bravo Lira, B. et al. *Fuentes ideológicas de Codificación Latinoamericana* (Buenos Aires, 1992).

Brubaker, G. A. 'Santa Fe de Bogotá: A Study of Municipal Development in Eighteenth-Century Spanish America', unpubl. PhD thesis (University of Texas at Austin, 1960).

Brungardt, M. P. 'Tithe Production and Pattern of Economic Change in Central Colombia, 1764–1833', unpubl. PhD thesis (University of Texas at Austin, 1974).

'The Economy of Colombia in the Late Colonial and Early National Periods', in J. Fisher, A. Kuethe and A. McFarlane (eds.), *Reform and Insurrection in Bourbon Nueva Granada and Peru* (Baton Rouge, 1990).

Bushnell, D. *The Making of Modern Colombia: A Nation in Spite of Itself* (Berkeley, 1993).

Bushnell, D. and N. Macauley *The Emergence of Latin America in the Nineteenth Century* (New York and Oxford, 1988).

Caballero, C. and M. Rodríguez Gómez 'Crecimiento económico y cambio estructural', in J. Ramírez (ed.), *Una aproximación al futuro: Colombia, siglo XXI* (Bogotá, 1991).

Calderón, C. 'La tasa de cambio real: mitos y realidades', mimeo (Washington, D.C., 1994).

Camacho Roldán, S. *Memorias*, Tomo I (Bogotá, 1923).

Cárdenas, M. 'Stabilisation and Redistribution of Coffee Revenues: A Political Economy Model of Commodity Marketing Boards', *Journal of Political Economy*, no. 44 (1994).

and M. Urrutia 'Macroeconomic Instability and Social Progress', in Rudiger Dornbusch and Sebastian Edwards (eds.), *Reform, Recovery, and Growth: Latin America and the Middle East* (Chicago, 1995).

Caro, M. A. *Escritos sobre cuestiones económicas* (Bogotá, 1943).

Escritos políticos, vol. 3 (Bogotá, 1991).

Carrasquilla, A. 'Desarrollo reciente de las políticas monetaria y cambiaria en Colombia', *Borradores Semanales de Economía, Banco de la República* (Bogotá, 1994).

Castro, J. 'El Inscredial: un Incora urbano', *Revista Camacol*, no. 39 (1989).

Cataño, G. 'Luis E. Nieto Arteta: del derecho penal al derecho civil', *Ideas y Valores*, nos. 85–6 (Bogotá, Aug. 1991).

Cepeda Ulloa, F. (ed.), *La corrupción administrativa en Colombia. Diagnóstico y recomendaciones para combatirla* (Bogotá, 1994a).

Ley Estatutaria: Instituciones y mecanismos de participación ciudadana (Bogotá, 1994b).

Dirección política de la reforma económica en Colombia (Bogotá, 1994c).

Cepeda, M. J. *Introducción a la Constitución de 1991* (Bogotá, 1993).

Chubb, J. *Patronage, Power and Poverty in Southern Italy* (Cambridge, 1982).

Clapham, C. (ed.) *Private Patronage and Public Power* (London, 1982).

Cobban, A. *National Self-Determination* (Oxford, 1945).

Collier, D. *Squatters and Oligarchs* (Baltimore, 1976).

Colmenares, G. *Partidos Políticos y Clases Sociales* (Bogotá, 1968).

'Popayán: continuidad y discontinuidades regionales en la época de la Independencia', in R. Liehr (ed.), *América Latina en la época de Simón Bolívar. La formación de las economías nacionales y los intereses económicos europeos, 1800–1850* (Berlin, 1989).

Comisión Nacional de Energía *Evaluación del Sector Eléctrico Colombiano, 1970–1990* (Bogotá,1991).

Corbo, V. and L. Hernández *Macroeconomic Adjustment to Capital Inflows: Latin American Style versus East Asian Style* (Washington, 1994).

Coulomb, R. and C. Sánchez *¿Todos propietarios? Vivienda de alquiler y sectores populares en la Ciudad de México* (Mexico, 1991).

Cubillos, J. S. 'El fenómeno del clientelismo en educación', unpubl. MSc diss. (Universidad de los Andes, Bogotá, 1982).

Dawson, F. G. *The First Latin American Debt Crisis. The City of London and the 1822–25 Loan Bubble* (New Haven and London, 1990).

De la Pedraja, R. *Energy Politics in Colombia* (Boulder, 1989).

De Soto, H. *The Other Path* (First publ. in Spanish 1986; London, 1989).

Deas, M. 'Algunas notas sobre caciquismo en Colombia', *Revista de Occidente*, no. 127 (1973).

'La presencia de la política nacional en la vida provinciana, pueblerina y rural de Colombia en el primer siglo de la república', in M. Palacios (comp.), *La unidad nacional en América Latina. Del regionalismo a la nacionalidad* (Mexico, D.F., 1983).

'Venezuela, Colombia and Ecuador: The First Half-Century of Independence', in L. Bethell (ed.), *The Cambridge History of Latin America*, vol. 3 (New York, 1985).

Del poder y la gramática y otros ensayos sobre historia, política y literatura colombianas (Bogotá, 1993).

and F. Gaitán *Dos ensayos especulativos sobre la violencia en Colombia* (Bogotá, 1995).

and C. Ossa (eds.) *El gobierno Barco* (Bogotá, 1994).

Delpar, H. *Red Against Blue: The Liberal Party in Colombian Politics* (Tuscaloosa, 1981).

DNP (Departamento Nacional de Planeación) *Las cuatro estrategias* (Bogotá, 1972).

Cambio con equidad (Bogotá, 1983).

'Programa de vivienda social', *Revista Camacol*, no. 45 (1990).

La Revolución Pacífica (Bogotá, 1991).

'Avances del programa de vivienda social', *Revista Camacol*, no. 50 (1992a).

'Apertura regional y descentralización', *Revista Camacol*, no. 51 (1992b).

La revolución pacífica: evolución del programa de vivienda, mimeo (Bogotá, 1993).

'Política de vivienda social urbana, Consejo Nacional de Política Económica y Social' (CONPES), doc. 2729 (Bogotá, 1994a).

'La Revolución Pacífica: programa de vivienda', *Revista Camacol*, no. 58 (1994b).

El Salto Social: Plan Nacional de Desarrollo: ley de inversiones 1994–1998 (Bogotá, 1995).

Dix, R. H. 'Consociational Democracy', *Comparative Politics* (April 1980).

Duarte, J. 'Corrupción en la educación pública e inequidad en Colombia: algunas observaciones', in F. Cepeda Ulloa (ed.), *La corrupción administrativa en Colombia. Diagnóstico y recomendaciones para combatirla* (Bogotá, 1994), pp. 81–95.

'The Politics of the Administration of Public Teachers in Two Colombian Regions', unpubl. DPhil diss. (Oxford University, 1995).

Dugas, J. (ed.) *La Constitución de 1991: ¿Un pacto político viable?* (Bogotá, 1993).

'The Economic Imperative of Decentralisation in Colombia,' paper presented at the Latin American Studies Association, 10–12 March 1994 (Atlanta, Georgia, 1994).

et al. (eds.) *Los caminos de la descentralización. Diversidad y retos de la transformación municipal* (Bogotá, 1992).

and R. Sánchez and E. Ungar 'La Asamblea Nacional Constituyente: ¿Expresión de una voluntad general?', in R. Sánchez (ed.), *Los nuevos retos electorales* (Bogotá, 1991).

Easterly, W. 'Colombia: Avoiding Crises through Fiscal Policy', in Aparicio, M. and W. Easterly et al. (eds.), *Crecimiento económico. Teoría, instituciones y experiencia internacional* (Bogotá, 1994).

Echegaray, A. 'Los fundamentos de una política habitacional social y económicamente eficiente', *Revista Camacol*, no. 50 (1992).

Edwards, S. *Crisis and Reform in Latin America. From Despair to Hope* (Oxford, 1995).

Eichengreen, B. 'House Calls of the Money Doctor: The Kemmerer Missions to Latin America, 1917–1931' (1989).

Should the Maastrich Treaty be Saved? (Princeton, 1991).

Eisenstadt, S. N. and L. Roginer *Patrons, Clients and Friends (Interpersonal Relations and the Structure of Trust in Society)* (Cambridge, 1984).

Escorcia, J. 'Desarrollo político, social y económico, 1800–1854', in *Sociedad y Economía en el Valle del Cauca* (Bogotá, 1983).

Esguerra Fajardo, A. *Latinoamérica de nuevo* (Bogotá, 1995).

Fedesarrollo, 'Perspectivas y retos macroeconómicos, 1994–1998', mimeo (Bogotá, 1994).

'Prospectiva: perspectivas económicas de corto y mediano plazo' (Bogotá, Jan. 1995).

Fei, F. and Chang Chih-i *Earthbound China* (London, 1948).

Flood, J. and J. Yates 'Housing Subsidies and Income Distribution', *Urban Studies*, no. 4 (1989).

Forero, C. 'Participación participativa: una primera evaluación', *Revista Foro*, no. 26 (1995).

Fresneda, O and J. Duarte 'Elementos para la historia de la educación en Colombia: alfabetización y educación primaria', unpubl. diss. (Universidad Nacional, Bogotá, 1984).

Gaitán, P. and C. Moreno *Poder local: Realidad y utopia de la descentralizaciónen Colombia* (Bogotá, 1992).

García García, J. 'Crecimiento, estabilización y ajuste en Colombia: lecciones del período 1966–1992', in Aparicio, M. and W. Easterly (eds.), *Crecimiento Económico. Teoría, instituciones y experiencia internacional* (Bogotá, 1994).

García Mejía, A. 'The Transformation of the Indian Communities of the Bogotá Sabana during the Nineteenth-Century Colombian Republic', unpubl. PhD thesis (New School for Social Research, New York, 1989).

Garrido, M. 'La política local en la Nueva Granada, 1750–1810', *Anuario Colombiano de Historia Social y de la Cultura*, no. 15 (1987).

Representaciones y reclamos. Variaciones sobre la política en el Nuevo Reino de Granada, 1770–1815 (Bogotá, 1994).

Geertz, C. *The Interpretation of Cultures* (New York, 1973).

Gellner, E. *Nations and Nationalism* (Oxford, 1983).

Gilbert, A. G. 'The Provision of Public Services and the Debt Crisis in Latin America: the Case of Bogotá', *Economic Geography*, no. 66 (1990).

In Search of a Home (London, 1993).

The Latin American City (Latin America Bureau, 1994: forthcoming in Spanish, Siglo XXI, Mexico City).

and J. Gugler *Cities, Poverty and Development: Urbanisation in the Third World* (Oxford, 1992).

and A. Varley *Landlord and Tenant: Housing the Poor in Urban Mexico* (London, 1991).

and P. M. Ward *Housing, the State and the Poor: Policy and Practice in Three Latin American Cities* (Cambridge, 1985). Publ. in Spanish as *Asentamientos populares versus el poder del estado* (Mexico, 1987).

Gilmore, R. *El federalismo en Colombia, 1810–1855* (Bogotá, 1995).

Giraldo, F. 'Colombia: estudio de pobreza. El gasto público social en vivienda de interés social' (CENAC, 1993).

'La vivienda de interés social: poco subsidio y nada de equidad', *Revista Camacol*, no. 58 (1994).

and J. C. Cortés Cely 'Los ciclos de la edificación en Colombia, 1950–1993: otra mirada', *Revista Camacol*, no. 60 (1994).

González, B. 'José María Espinosa: Abanderado del arte y de la patria', *Catálogo de una exposición* (National Museum of Colombia, Bogotá, 1994).

González, F. *Caudillismo y regionalismo en el Siglo XIX Latinoamericano* (Bogotá, 1982).

Guerra, F.-X. *Modernidad e independencias* (Madrid, 1992)

'La desintegración de la Monarquía hispánica: Revolución de Independencia', in A. Annino, L. Castro Leiva and F.-X. Guerra (eds.), *De los imperios a las naciones: Iberoamérica* (Zaragoza, 1995).

Gutiérrez Cuevas, C. 'ICT: 50 años cumpliendo con Colombia', *Revista Camacol*, no. 39 (1989).

Hall, J. A. and G. J. Ikenberry *The State* (Milton Keynes, 1989).

Halperin Donghi, T. 'Argentina: Agrarian Liberalism in a Country Born Liberal', in J. Love and N. Jacobsen (eds.), *Guiding the Invisible Hand. Economic Liberalism and the State in Latin America* (New York, 1988), pp. 35–62.

Hansen, E. and J. Williams 'Economic Issues and the Progressive Housing Model', in C. V. Patton (ed.), *Spontaneous Shelter: International Perspectives and Prospects* (Philadelphia, 1988), pp. 303–25.

'Urban electoral behaviour in Colombia', in H. Dietz and G. Shidlo (eds.), *Urban Elections in Democratic Latin America* (forthcoming).

Hanson, E. M. 'Administrative Development in the Colombian Ministry of Education: a Case Analysis of the 1970s', *Comparative Education Review*, vol. 27, no. 1 (1983).

'Decentralisation and Regionalisation in Educational Administration: Comparisons of Venezuela, Colombia and Spain', *Comparative Education*, vol. 25, no. 1 (1989).

Hardoy, J. E. and D. Satterthwaite *Squatter Citizen: Life in the Urban Third World* (London, 1989).

Harris, N. (ed.) *Cities in the 1990s: The Challenge for Developing Countries*, (London, 1992).

Hartlyn, J. 'Producer Associations, the Political Regime and Policy Process in Contemporary Colombia', *Latin American Research Review*, vol. 20, (1985).

The Politics of Coalition Rule in Colombia (New York, 1988).

Held, D. *Models of Democracy* (Stanford, 1987).

Prospects for Democracy (Cambridge, 1993).

Helg, A. 'La educación primaria y secundaria durante el primer gobierno de Alfonso López Pumarejo', *Revista Colombiana de Educación*, no. 6 (1980).

La educación en Colombia, 1918–57. Una historia social, económica y política (Bogotá, 1987).

Helguera, J. L. 'The Problem of Liberalism versus Conservatism, 1849–85', in F. Pike (ed.), *Latin American History. Select Problems* (New York, 1969).

Helm, D. (ed.) *The Economic Borders of the State* (Oxford, 1992).

Herbert, A. and E. Kempson *Water Debt and Disconnection* (London, 1995).

Hobsbawm, E. J. *Nations and Nationalism Since 1780* (Cambridge, 1990).

Hommes, R. 'Regulation, Deregulation and Modernization in Colombia', (Washington, DC, mimeo, 1995a).

'Conflicts and Dilemmas of Decentralization', paper presented at the Annual World Bank Development Seminar (Washington, DC, 1 & 2 May, 1995b).

in Guillermo Calvo et al. *Debt, Stabilization and Development; Essays in Memory of Carlos Díaz Alejandro* (Oxford and Cambridge, 1995c).

'Colombia: An Underestimated Success?', paper presented in Zurich in Seminar on Latin America sponsored by FUNDES (24 May 1995d).

and Montenegro, A. and P. Roda (eds.) *Una apertura hacia el futuro: balance económico 1990–94* (Bogotá, 1994).

Hoskin, G. 'The Impact of the National Front on Congressional Behavior: The Attempted Restoration of *el país político*', in R. Hellman, A. Berry and M. Solaún (eds.), *Patterns of Compromise: Coalition Government in Colombia* (New Brunswick, 1980).

'The Consequences of Constitutional Reform on the Colombian Party System', paper presented at Latin American Studies Association, 10–12 March (Atlanta, Georgia, 1994).

'Urban Electoral Behavior in Colombia', in H. Dietz and G. Shidlo (eds.), *Urban Elections in Democratic Latin America* (forthcoming).

Hoskin, G. et al., *El Congreso Colombiano, Tomo II* (Bogotá, 1974).

Huntington, S. P 'Political Modernisation: America vs. Europe', *World Politics*, vol. XVIII, no. 3 (1966).

Iglesias, E. V. *Reflections on Economic Development: Toward a New Latin American Consensus* (Washington, DC, 1992).

INURBE (Instituto Nacional de Vivienda de Interés Social y Reforma Urbana) 'Informe sobre el subsidio familiar de vivienda durante el período comprendido entre los años 1991 y 1994 dirigido a la honorable junta directiva del INURBE' (Bogotá, 16 June 1995).

Jaramillo Uribe, J. 'El proceso de la educación del Virreinato a la época contemporánea', in Colcultura, *Manual de Historia de Colombia* (Bogotá, 1984).

Jaramillo, S. 'La política de vivienda en Colombia ¿hacia una redefinición de sus objetivos?', *Desarrollo y Sociedad Cuaderno*, no. 4 (1982).

Kalmanovitz, S. 'Las teorías económicas contemporáneas en Colombia', in J. A. Ocampo (ed.), *Gran Enciclopedia de Colombia. Economía*, vol. 8 (Bogotá, 1994).

Katz, R. S. and P. Mair 'Changing Models of Party Organisation and Party Democracy', *Party Politics*, vol. 1, no. 1 (1995).

Knight, A. 'State and Civil Society in Mexico since the Revolution', *Texas Papers on Mexico*, nos. 90–91 (Austin, 1993).

Kommers, D. *The Constitutional Jurisprudence of the Federal Republic of Germany* (London, 1989).

König, H. J. *En el camino hacia la nación. Nacionalismo en el proceso de formación del estado y la nación de la Nueva Granada, 1750–1856* (Bogotá, 1994).

Krasner, S. D. 'Sovereignty: an Institutional Perspective', *Comparative Political Studies*, no. 2 (Apr. 1988).

Kresge, S. and L. Wenar (eds.) *Hayek on Hayek. An Autobiographical Dialogue* (London, 1994).

Kriegel, B. *The State and the Rule of Law* (Princeton, 1995).

Krueger, A. O. 'The Political Economy of the Rent Seeking Society', *American Economic Review*, no. 69 (1974), pp. 3291–303.

Kusnetzoff, F. 'The State and Housing in Chile – Regime Types and Policy Choices', in G. Shidlo (ed.), *Housing Policy in Developing Countries* (London, 1990).

Labrouse, A. *La droga, el dinero y las armas* (Mexico, 1993).

Laffont, J. and J. Tirole *A Theory of Incentives in Procurement and Regulation* (Cambridge, Mass., 1994).

LaPalombara, J. *Democracy Italian Style* (New Haven and London, 1987).

Latorre, M. *Elecciones y Partidos Políticos en Colombia* (Bogotá, 1974).

Laun, J. I. 'El estado y la vivienda en Colombia: análisis de urbanizaciones del Instituto de Crédito Territorial en Bogotá', in C. Castillo (ed.), *Vida urbana y urbanismo* (Bogotá, 1976).

Lawson, K. and P. Merkl (eds.) *When Parties Fail* (Princeton, 1988).

Leal Buitrago, F. *Estado y política en Colombia* (Bogotá, 1984).

—— and A. Dávila *Clientelismo: El sistema político y su expresión regional* (Bogotá, 1990; 2nd edn. 1991).

—— (ed.) *En busca de la estabilidad perdida* (Bogotá, 1995).

—— and L. Zamosc *Al filo del caos. Crisis política en la Colombia de los años 80* (Bogotá, 1990).

Lebot, I. 'Elementos para la historia de la educación en Colombia en el siglo XX', *Boletín Mensual de Estadística*, no. 249 (1972).

Lemer, A. C. 'The Role of Rental Housing in Developing Countries: A Need for Balance', *World Bank Report*, no. UDD-104 (1987).

Linn, J. F. *Cities in the Developing World: Policies for their Equitable and Efficient Growth* (Oxford, 1983).

Lipset, S. M. and S. Rokkan 'Cleavage Structures, Party Systems, and Voter Alignment: An Introduction,' in Lipset S. M. and S. Rokkan, *Party Systems and Voter Alignments* (New York, 1967).

Londoño, J. L. 'Income Distribution During the Structural Transformation: Colombia 1938–1988', unpubl. PhD diss. (Harvard University, 1990).

López, A. 'Realizaciones, limitaciones y tensiones internas de la Misión Kemmerer en Colombia', in *El Banco de la República: Antecedentes, evolución y estructura* (Bogotá, 1990).

López, L. F. *Historia de la Hacienda y el Tesoro en Colombia* (Bogotá, 1992).

López Michelsen, A. *El estado fuerte* (Bogotá, 1968).

Lora, E. and L. Helmsdorff *El futuro de la reforma pensional* (Bogotá, 1994).

Losada, R. *Clientelismo y elecciones* (Bogotá, 1984).

Loy, J. M. 'La educación primaria durante el federalismo: la reforma escolar de 1870', *Revista Colombiana de Educación*, no. 3 (1979).

'Los Ignorantistas y las Escuelas: La oposición a la reforma durante la federación colombiana', *Revista Colombiana de Educación*, no. 9 (1982).

Lynch, J. *The Spanish American Revolutions, 1808–1826* (New York, 1986).

Macpherson, C. B. *The Life and Times of Liberal Democracy* (Oxford, 1977).

Marichal, C. *A Century of Debt Crisis in Latin America* (Princeton, 1989).

Martínez, N. H. 'Productividad social de la nueva política de gasto social. Anotaciones y recomendaciones', mimeo (Bogotá, 1996).

McFarlane, A. *Colombia Before Independence. Economy, Society and Politics under Bourbon Reform* (Cambridge, 1993).

McPherson, J. M. *Battle Cry of Freedom. The American Civil War* (Oxford, 1988).

Matthey, K. (ed.) *Beyond Self-Help Housing* (London, 1990).

Melo, J. O. (ed.) *Colombia hoy* (Bogotá, 1995).

Means, R. C. *Underdevelopment and the Development of Law. Corporations and Corporation Law in Nineteenth-Century Colombia* (Chapel Hill, 1980).

Megbolugbe, I. F. and P. D. Linneman 'Home Ownership', *Urban Studies*, no. 30 (1993).

Meisel Roca, A. and A. López 'Papel moneda, tasas de interés y revaluación durante la regeneración', in *El Banco de la República: antecedentes, evolución y estructura* (Bogotá, 1990).

Memoria del Secretario de Instrucción Pública Dirigida al Presidente de Colombia, 1881 (Bogotá, 1881).

Ministerio de Desarrollo Económico 'Ciudades: ciudadanas y ciudadanos: la política urbana del Salto Social', mimeo (Bogotá, 1995).

Ministerio de Educación Nacional *Proyecto de Ley por la cual se dicta el Estatuto General de la Educación* (Bogotá, 1971).

Molano, A. *Selva adentro. Una historia oral de la civilización del Guaviare* (Bogotá, 1992).

Molina, G. *Las ideas Liberales en Colombia*, tomo I (Bogotá, 1970).

Molina, H. 'Bogotá: Competition and Substitution Between Urban Land Markets', in P. Baross, and J. van der Linden (eds.), *The Transformation of Land Supply Systems in Third World Cities* (Avebury, 1990).

et al. 'El gasto público en educación y distribución de subsidios en Colombia (Informe Final)', mimeo, Fedesarrollo (Bogotá, 1993).

Montenegro, A. 'El Sector Privado y la Reforma del Estado', *Planeación y Desarrollo*, vol. XXV (1994).

'Justicia y desarrollo económico', *Planeación y Desarrollo*, vol. XXV (Jul. 1994a).

and C. E. Posada 'Criminalidad en Colombia', mimeo (Bogotá, 1994b).

Montes Hernández, J. 'La responsabilidad contractual de la administración y de los funcionarios públicos', *Temas. La Revista de la Contraloría*, no. 4 (Barranquilla, 1994).

Mörner, M. *Estado, razas y cambio social en la Hispanoamérica colonial* (México, 1974).

Murillo, G. and E. Ungar 'Políticas de vivienda popular en Colombia a partir de la década del setenta', *Desarrollo y Sociedad Cuaderno*, no. 4 (1982).

Naim, M. *Paper Tigers and Minotaurs. The Politics of Venezuela's Economic Reforms* (Washington, 1993).

'Latin American Post-Adjustment Blues', *Foreign Policy* (autumn, 1993a).

Neuman, S. *Modern Political Parties* (Chicago, 1956),

Nichols, T. E. *Tres Puertos de Colombia* (Bogotá, 1973).

Ochoa, F. J. 'Política de tarifas de energía eléctrica adoptada por el gobierno de Colombia', *Revista ANDI* 93 (1989).

Orjuela, L. J. 'La descentralización en Colombia: paradigma para la eficiencia y la legitimidad del estado', in J. Dugas et al., *Los caminos de la descentralización: diversidad y retos de la transformación municipal* (Bogotá, 1992).

Orozco, C. 'Marco legal para la promoción de la competencia en el derecho comparado y en Colombia', *Planeación y Desarrollo*, vol. XXIV, no. 2 (1993).

Ortiz, C. 'The Impact of Current Global Housing Strategies on the Development of the Housing Sector in Colombia', *DPU Working Paper*, no. 71 (London, 1995).

Ortiz Sarmiento, C. M. 'Historiografía de la violencia', in Universidad Nacional, *La historia al final del milenio. Ensayos de historiografía colombiana y latinoamericana* (Bogotá, 1994).

Pacheco, E. 'ICT: hay que actuar para salvarlo', *Revista Camacol*, no. 39 (1989).

Pacheco, M. *La fiesta liberal en Cali* (Cali,1992).

Palacios, M. 'La fragmentación regional de las clases dominantes en Colombia: una perspectiva histórica', *Revista Mexicana de Sociología*, vol. XLII, no. 4 (Oct.–Dec., 1980).

'Modernidad, modernizaciones y ciencias sociales', *Análisis Político*, no. 23 (Sep–Dec., 1994).

Panebianco, A. *Political Parties: Organisation and Power* (New York, 1988)

Pateman, C. *The Problem of Political Obligation* (Cambridge, 1985).

Peñaranda, R. 'Surveying the Literature on the Violence', in C. Bergquist et al., *Violence in Colombia. The Contemporaruy Crisis in Historical Perspective* (Wilmington, 1992).

Pennington, K. 'Bartolomé de las Casas and the Tradition of Medieval Law', *Church History*, vol. 39 (1970).

Persaud, T. 'Housing Delivery System and the Urban Poor: a Comparison among Six Latin American Countries', *World Bank, Latin America and the Caribbean Technical Department Regional Studies Program Report*, no. 23 (1992).

Phelan, J. L. *The People and the King* (Wisconsin, 1978).

Pierson, C. *The Modern State* (London and New York, 1996).

Pinzón, P. *Pueblos, Regiones, y Partidos* (Bogotá, 1989).

Pizarro Leongómez, E. 'Elecciones, partidos y nuevo marco institucional: ¿En qué estamos?, *Análisis Político*, vol. 22 (May–August, 1994).

Plank, D. N. 'Public Purpose and Private Interest in Brazilian Education', *New Education*, vol. 12, no. 2 (1990).

'The Politics of Basic Education Reform in Brazil', *Comparative Education Review*, vol. 34, no. 4 (1990b).

Pombo, M. A. and J.J. Guerra, *Constituciones de Colombia. Recopiladas y precedida de una breve reseña histórica*, 4 vols. (Bogotá, 1951).

Poggi, G. *The State. Its Nature, Development, and Prospects* (Cambridge, 1990).

Posada-Carbó, E. *The Colombian Caribbean. A Regional History, 1870–1950* (Oxford, 1996).

Posada de la Peña, F. *Libertad para trabajar. La ley 50 de 1990 y la política laboral. Filosofía, historia y comentarios* (Bogotá, 1995).

Poterba, J. 'State Responses to Fiscal Crisis: the Effects of Budgetary Institutions and Politics', *Journal of Political Economy*, vol. 102, no. 4 (1994).

Presidencia de la República, *El Plan Social: Bases para el Plan de Desarrollo, 1994–1998* (Bogotá, 1994).

Reichel-Dolmatoff, G. 'Casta, clase y aculturación en una población de Colombia', Offprint of *Estudios Antropológicos* published in homage to Dr. Manuel Gamio (Mexico, DF, 1956).

Restrepo, J. M. *Historia de la Revolución de la República de Colombia en la América Meridional*, tomo I (Bogotá, 1942).

Richards, B. 'A Home of One's Own: Housing Policy Under Neoliberalism in Chile', unpubl. PhD diss. (University of London, 1994).

Robledo, J. *El drama de la vivienda en Colombia y la política del 'sí se puede'* (Bogotá, 1985).

Rodríguez Piñeres, E. *El Olimpo Radical* (Bogotá, 1965).

Romero Aguirre, A. *Un radical en el Congreso* (Bogotá, 1949).

Rubio, M. 'Crimen y crecimiento en Colombia', mimeo (Bogotá, 1994).

'Crimen y crecimiento en Colombia', *Coyuntura Económica* (March, 1995).

Russell, R. 'Critical Bibliography on La Violencia in Colombia', *Latin American Research Review*, vol. 8, no. 1 (1973).

Safford, F. 'Social Aspects of Politics: New Granada, 1825–1850', *Journal of Social History*, vol. 5 (1972).

The Ideal of the Practical. Colombia's Struggle to Form a Technical Elite, (London, 1976).

Aspectos sociales en la política de la Nueva Granada (Medellín, 1977).

'Race, Integration and Progress: Elite Attitudes and the Indian in Colombia', *Hispanic American Historical Review*, vol. 71, no 1 (1991).

Salazar J. A. *No nacimos pa' semilla* (Bogotá, 1990).

274   Bibliography

Mujeres de fuego (Medellín, 1993).

and A. M. Jaramillo *Medellín: Las subculturas del narcotráfico* (Bogotá, 1992).

Salazar, S. E. 'Vivienda social', *Revista Camacol*, no. 61 (1994).

Sánchez, G. 'La Violencia in Colombia: New Research, New Questions', *Hispanic American Historical Review*, vol. 65, no. 4 (1985).

Santamaría, R. and G. Silva *Proceso Político en Colombia* (Bogotá, 1984).

Sarmiento et al. *Análisis del sector educativo con énfasis en sus aspectos administrativos y financieros* (Bogotá, 1987).

Serrano, M. and V. Bulmer-Thomas (eds.) *Rebuilding the State: Mexico After Salinas* (London, 1995).

Seton-Watson, G. H. N. *Nations and States* (London, 1977).

Scully, T. *Rethinking the Center: Party Politics in Nineteenth- and Twentieth-Century Chile* (Stanford, 1992).

Sharp, W. F. *Slavery on the Spanish Frontier. The Colombian Chocó, 1680–1810* (Oklahoma, 1976).

Shidlo, G. (ed.) *Housing Policy in Developing Countries* (London, 1990).

Shugart, M. 'Economic adjustment and political institutions: foreign vs. domestic constituents in Colombia', unpubl. paper (University of California, San Diego, 1992).

Shugart, M. and J. Carey *Presidents and Assemblies: Constitutional Design and Electoral Dynamics* (New York, 1992).

Skinner, R. J., Taylor, J. L. and E. A. Wegelin (eds.) *Shelter Upgrading for the Urban Poor: Evaluation of Third World Experience* (Manila, 1987).

Skocpol, T. *Social Revolutions and the Modern World* (Cambridge, 1994a).

et al. (eds.) *Bringing the State Back In* (Cambridge, 1994).

Smith, A. *Theories of Nationalism*, 2nd edn. (London and New York, 1983).

Stigler, G. J. 'The Theory of Economic Regulation', *Bell Journal of Economic and Management Science*, vol. 2, no. 1 (1971).

Stoller, R. 'Liberalism and Conflict in Socorro, Colombia, 1830–1870', unpubl. PhD diss. (Duke University, 1991).

Thorp, R. *Economic Management and Economic Development in Peru and Colombia* (Basingstoke, 1991).

Tirado Mejía, A. 'El estado y la política en Colombia,' *Manual de Historia de Colombia,* tomo II (Bogotá, 1979).

Tovar Zambrano, B. *La intervención económica del estado en Colombia, 1914–1936* (Bogotá, 1984).

UNCHS (United Nations Centre for Human Settlements (Habitat)), *Strategies for Low-Income Shelter and Services Development: The Rental-Housing Option* (Nairobi, 1989).

Ungar, E. (ed.) *Gobernabilidad en Colombia. Retos y desafíos* (Bogotá, 1993).

Urrutia, M. 'The Changing Nature of Economic Planning in Colombia', in M. Urrutia and S. Yukawa (eds.), *Development Planning in Mixed Economics* (Tokyo, 1988).

'On the Absence of Economic Populism in Colombia', in R. Dornbusch and S. Edwards (eds.), *The Macroeconomics of Populism in Latin America* (Chicago and London, 1991).

'Autonomía del Banco de la República', in O. L. Acosta, and I. Fainboim (eds.), *Las reformas económicas del gobierno del Presidente Gaviria: Una visión desde adentro* (Bogotá, 1994).

'Colombia', in John Williamson (ed.), *The Political Economy of Policy Reform* (Washington, DC, 1994b).

'La planeación y los órganos de decisión económica', in J. A. Ocampo (ed.), *Gran Enciclopedia de Colombia. Economía*, vol. 8 (Bogotá, 1994c).

Urueña, J. 'La idea de heterogeneidad racial en el pensamiento político colombiano: una mirada histórica', *Análisis Político*, no. 22 (May–Aug. 1994).

USAID Office of Housing and Urban Programs: Bureau for Private Enterprise *Annual Report 1991* (Washington, 1992).

Valença, M. M. 'The Inevitable Crisis of the Brazilian Housing Finance System', *Urban Studies*, no. 29 (1992).

Valencia Llano, A. *Estado soberano del Cauca. Federalismo y regeneración* (Bogotá, 1988).

Valenzuela, A. *Political Brokerage in Chile: Local Government in a Centralised Polity* (Durham, NC, 1977).

Vargas, J. H. *Memoria de Hacienda* (Bogotá, 1938).

Vargas, M. *Las memorias del revolcón. La historia íntima del polémico gobierno de César Gaviria, revelada por uno de sus protagonistas* (Bogotá, 1993).

Vargas Velásquez, A. 'Violencia en la vida cotidiana', in F. E. González et al., *Violencia en la región andina: el caso Colombia* (Bogotá, 1993).

Velásquez, F. E. 'La planeación en Colombia: ¿Es el tiempo de la gente?', *Revista Foro*, no. 26 (1995).

Vélez, C. M. 'El cambio institucional. Reto de las administraciones locales', *Debates de Coyuntura Económica*, no. 33 (Sept. 1994).

Vittorio, C. and L. Hernández 'Macroeconomic Adjustment and Capital Inflows: Latin American Style versus East Asian Style' (Washington DC, 1994).

Von Hagen, J. 'A Note on the Empirical Effectiveness of Formal Fiscal Restraints', *Journal of Public Economics*, no. 44 (1991).

Von Humboldt, W. *The Limits of State Action* (Indianapolis, 1993).

Ward, P. M. (ed.) *Self-Help Housing: A Critique* (London, 1982).

Weber, E. *Peasants into Frenchmen* (London, 1987).

Weber, M. *Economía y Sociedad,* tomo II (Mexico, 1964).

White, H. *The Content of the Form. Narrative Discourse and Historical Representation* (Baltimore, 1987).

Wiesner, E. 'El orígen político del desequilibrio fiscal', unpubl. paper, Department of Economics, Universidad de los Andes (Bogotá, 23 June 1982).

World Bank *Shelter* (Washington, DC, 1980).

Latin America and the Caribbean Regional Office, 'Colombia: Country Economic Memorandum: Productivity Growth and Sustained Economic Development', rep. no. 7629-CO (1989).

World Development Report, 1990 (Oxford, 1990).

Urban Policy and Economic Development: An Agenda for the 1990s (Washington, DC, 1991).

Poverty Reduction Handbook (Washington, DC, 1992).

Housing: Enabling Markets to Work, policy paper (Washington, DC, 1993).

Policy View from the Policy Research Department, *Outreach No. 10* (May 1993).

Poverty in Colombia (Washington, DC, 1994).

'Colombia Private Sector Assessment', rep. no. 13113-CO (1994a).

'Colombia: Poverty Assessment Report', rep. no. 12673-CO (Washington, DC, April, 1994b).

Yepes, G. 'La situación de la EAAB desde una perspectiva internacional', *Revista Camacol,* no. 55 (1993), pp. 76–82.

INDEX